Painting the Town Red

By the same author

LSE: A Question of Degree
Lessons of the General Strike, 1926
Budapest for Children
Blue Guide Hungary (editions 1–3)
Blue Guide Budapest (editions 1–2)
Budapest 1956—Locations of Drama
Budapest: A Cultural and Literary History
Inside Hungary From Outside
Every Statue Tells a Story—Public Monuments in Budapest
Hungary 1930 and the Forgotten History of a Mass Protest

Painting the Town Red

Politics and the Arts During the 1919 Hungarian Soviet Republic

Bob Dent

PLUTO PRESS

First published 2018 by Pluto Press
345 Archway Road, London N6 5AA

www.plutobooks.com

British Library Cataloguing in Publication Data
A catalogue record for this book is available from the British Library

ISBN 978 0 7453 3777 7 Hardback
ISBN 978 0 7453 3776 0 Paperback
ISBN 978 1 7868 0272 9 PDF eBook
ISBN 978 1 7868 0274 3 Kindle eBook
ISBN 978 1 7868 0273 6 EPUB eBook

This book is printed on paper suitable for recycling and made from fully managed and sustained forest sources. Logging, pulping and manufacturing processes are expected to conform to the environmental standards of the country of origin.

Typeset by Stanford DTP Services, Northampton, England

Simultaneously printed in the United Kingdom and United States of America

For Kati and Anna, with love

Contents

Author's Preface viii
Acknowledgements xi
A Note on Terminology xii

Introduction 1
1. The Political and Historical Context 5
2. Budapest Turns Red 19
3. Poster Power 42
4. Art for the People 56
5. Cultural Polemics 69
6. The Silent Screen Talks Politics 81
7. Opening up the Auditoriums 96
8. Music for All 113
9. The Pen goes to Battle 127
10. Why? 148
11. What Went Wrong? 171

Postscript: What Happened to Them? 198
Sources Used and Useful Sources 216
Index 226

Author's Preface

The Hungarian Soviet Republic of 1919 has received relatively little attention outside Hungary—despite its dramatic nature, comparable in some ways to what happened in Russia in 1917–18 and beyond. The reasons are arguably twofold. So much was happening elsewhere in the aftermath of the First World War, that Hungary's short-lived 'Bolshevik experiment' of 1919—which lasted for a mere 133 days—has been overlooked. Perhaps the language difficulty has also been a factor. How many non-Hungarian historians have been familiar with Hungarian to make research a practical possibility?

When Hungary's 1919 revolutionary period is mentioned, almost invariably the focus has been on the international situation and the country's unstable position. Hungary was on the losing side of the First World War and in 1919 was subject to pressure—including military pressure, particularly from Romanian as well as Czechoslovak forces—which threatened the country's territorial integrity. (The threat became a reality and would be set in stone by the 1920 Treaty of Trianon, one of the treaties of the post-1918 Versailles peace process.)

If the domestic politics of the Hungarian Soviet Republic are touched on by non-Hungarian writers, normally highlighted, sometimes to the exclusion of all else are the dictatorial nature and use of terror of the regime under its communist leader Béla Kun. Only rarely is reference made, usually in passing, to broader domestic issues, including the interaction between politics and the arts in 1919, and to the role that many prominent personalities of Hungarian cultural life—painters, sculptors, writers, musicians, film-makers, actors and others—played during the Soviet Republic, at least in its early period.

This book aims to redress that imbalance by describing and examining that interaction with a view to casting some light on how it came about that many noted cultural figures wholeheartedly supported what were presented as, and perceived to be, revolutionary developments of an extreme nature. The intention is neither to justify nor to condemn the Soviet Republic, but to survey and understand one of its hitherto neglected aspects.

Within Hungary, itself the 'memory' of 1919, has involved both condemnation and justification, ranging from extremely negative to very positive interpretations. The ultra-conservative regime of Miklós Horthy, which followed the Soviet Republic and lasted for over 20 years, understandably wanted to erase all positive memory of what had happened. From its perspective, that was fuelled by the fact that a large number of the Soviet Republic's leading figures were Jewish or of Jewish descent. Indeed, that enabled many people after 1919 to conflate Bolshevism and Jewishness, conveniently mixing anti-Communism and anti-Semitism, even though the majority of Hungarian Jews cannot be said to have been out and out supporters of the Soviet Republic, nor did the new commissars act in the name of Jews as such. However, that didn't stop the conservative nationalists. From their point of view the experience of the Commune, as it was often called, helped to 'justify' the widespread atrocities which followed in the wake of its downfall. It perhaps also partly explains Hungary's *Numerus Clausus* of 1920, one of the first anti-Jewish laws of twentieth-century Europe.

After 1919, Hungarian Communists also had problems with the Commune in terms of proclaiming its glories, while explaining (away) its utter defeat. It wasn't just, as is often stressed, that Béla Kun and his comrades had not followed Lenin's example of distributing the land to the peasants, thus losing their sympathy (in this sense they were more 'radical' than Lenin, preferring, at least in theory, collectivisation). More important as time passed, certainly from a psychological point of view, was the fact that the majority of the communist people's commissars of 1919, who, in various stages, had emigrated to Moscow, fell victim to the Stalinist purges of the late 1930s. When the Hungarian Communists came back into power soon after the Second World War, how could they extol the achievements of 1919 when many of its leaders, including Kun, had lost their lives under Stalin, who continued to rule in Moscow until his death in 1953?

In contrast, in the decades following the 1956 Uprising, a central element of which involved breaking with the Stalinist model, there was a significant shift in the amount of attention paid in Hungary to the 1919 events. Beginning with the 40th anniversary in 1959, there was an explosion of publication, particularly in specialist journals, about what had happened in 1919. Thereafter, each round-figure anniversary would see the appearance of new books and studies about the period.

After the political changes of 1989–90 there was another shift. Recent times have seen a downturn of interest in the Soviet Republic, and what happened during the period is now commonly regarded as constituting one of the most negative episodes of the country's twentieth-century history.

Among the foreigners who very early on reported about 1919, British journalist H. N. Brailsford was an early enthusiast, as were the American reporters Alice Riggs Hunt and Crystal Eastman. All three wrote quite positively about their experiences in the Budapest of 1919. Such enthusiasm could perhaps be explained by the 'politically friendly outsider' factor, famously exemplified by the Americans John Reed and Louise Bryant, and reflected in the former's dramatic eyewitness account of the Russian Revolution, *Ten Days That Shook The World*, and in the evocative 1981 film *Reds*. Indeed, like John Reed in Russia, Crystal Eastman was an activist as well as a reporter. At one point she prepared a message of greetings for a meeting of the Budapest Workers' and Soldiers' Council.[1]

At the same time, a positive reflection of the Hungarian events by a then youthful insider has been left by Arthur Koestler, who was a 13-year-old Budapest schoolboy in 1919. In his autobiographical volume, *Arrow in the Blue*, Koestler emphasises his upbeat impressions of the time. He was stirred by the music in public places, whether it was Chopin's *Funeral March* being played during communist burial ceremonies, or the then ever-present *La Marseillais* and *The Internationale*. He was struck by the new teachers who appeared in his school, dealing with subjects which were novel for him, ranging from the life of farm workers to economics and constitutional government. On May Day 1919 a schoolmate of his gave a speech praising Danton and Saint Just, prominent figures of the French Revolution. He was also impressed after attending a workers' class his cousin Margit had given at a factory in Újpest, on the north side of Budapest. It seemed to him, on reflection years later, that something exciting was happening and that the world was gloriously being turned upside down.

How far can we trust this cheerful recollection of a teenager's experience? In his monumental and scholarly biography of Arthur Koestler, David Ceserani shows that Koestler wrote and re-wrote his autobiographical essays and works with a view to the time when he wrote them and with an eye as to which audiences he believed he was writing for. *Arrow in the Blue* appeared not in the early 1930s, when Koestler was an ardent communist, but 20 years later, when he was well into his anti-communist and Cold Warrior phase, and so it is of some interest to note his summary of the Hungarian Commune.

While remarking that the 1919 communism of Hungary 'would in due course have degenerated in a totalitarian police state, forcibly following the example of its Russian model', believing that 'no Communist Party in Europe has been able to hold out against the corruption imposed on it from Moscow', Koestler admits that this later 'knowledge' does 'not invalidate the hopeful and exuberant mood of the early days of the Revolution in Hungary ...'[2]

1. Lukács (1987), p. 618.
2. Koestler (1952), p. 66.

Acknowledgements

I am particularly grateful for all the encouragement, suggestions, information and research material I have received from Alex Bandy, former head of the Budapest bureau of Associated Press and author of *Chocolate and Chess*, a fascinating study of the strange case of Imre Lakatos, who became a well-respected philosopher of science and mathematics at the London School of Economics. It provides at the same time a wonderful insight into the politics of Hungary in the decade following 1945.

I am thankful for the existence of the following libraries and grateful to their staff members, who have always been very helpful whenever I have turned to them for assistance: The Municipal Szabó Ervin Library in Budapest, the library and archives of the Institute of Political History in Budapest, the library of the Central European University in Budapest, the British Library in London and the library of the London School of Economics.

I also thank the following individuals for their valuable help, which has included observations, comments, suggestions and/or the provision of research material: Pál Bozsik, Tamás Dezső, Marty Goodman, Emőke Gréczi, Miklós M. Nagy, Jason Rodrigues, Eszter Szablyár, Eszter Timár, Judy Tither, David Walters, Nigel Willmott and James Yeoman.

Very special thanks are due to Katalin Rácz, who critically read the entire manuscript and offered much help, particularly with translations.

Needless to say, responsibility for any errors in this book lies entirely with the author.

A Note on Terminology

For the sake of variety, in this book the terms **Soviet Republic, Council Republic** and **Republic of Councils** are used interchangeably in relation to the period from 21 March 1919 to 1 August 1919 in Hungary. 'Council Republic' is a literal translation of the Hungarian word normally used (*Tanácsköztársaság*). The use of 'Soviet' (meaning 'council' in Russian) reflects the affinity the Hungarian leaders had for their Bolshevik counterparts. In both Hungary and Russia the new regimes claimed to be representing the proletariat and that their power was based on the councils, or soviets, of workers' and soldiers' deputies. Another term which sometimes appeared about the same period in Hungary is '**Commune**', echoing the Paris Commune of 1871. Interestingly, the word was used by people of quite divergent political views. For simplicity's sake and unless otherwise indicated, when used in this book 'in 1919' is often short for 'during the 1919 Hungarian Soviet Republic'.

What was, in effect, the government of the Council Republic was known as the **Revolutionary Governing Council**. Its members—a coalition of Communist Party and Social Democratic Party leaders—were known as **People's Commissars**, echoing the Bolshevik practice. In effect, they were like ministers, and their ministries were called **People's Commissariats**.

As this book is primarily about the arts, the most frequently referred to commissariat is the **People's Commissariat for Public Education**, which is the literal translation of its title in Hungarian. However, the commissariat dealt not only with education, but cultural matters in general. Hence, for the sake of clarity, in this book the term People's Commissariat (or Commissar) for Education and Culture is often used. In addition, sometimes the simple formula 'cultural commissariat' is employed. When the Soviet Republic was established, the Social Democrat Zsigmond Kunfi was appointed People's Commissar for Education and Culture. György Lukács, a Communist Party member, became deputy commissar. After a few weeks, however, the term 'deputy' (in this and other commissariats) was dropped.

Directory was the name given to a variety of bodies usually operating under the auspices of the People's Commissariats. Thus there was a Music Directory, a Writers' Directory, a Directory for the Arts, and so on, indeed for all sorts of activities. There was even a Directory for Matters Concerning Physical Education. The name echoes the term *Directoire* from the era of the French Revolution. The Council Republic, in its vocabulary and iconography, often reflected the experience of not only the Russian Revolution but also the French Revolution.

Chrysanthemum Revolution is a term used for the period of upheaval in Hungary beginning in late October 1918 when, at the end of the First World War as the Habsburg Empire—and with it the Austro-Hungarian Dual Monarchy—collapsed, Hungary became independent. The term derives from the white chrysanthemums which rebellious soldiers and others donned at the time. The traditional Hungarian Marxist term for the upheaval was 'Bourgeois Democratic Revolution', which reflected the attempt to equate the events and their outcome with the Bolshevik's perception of the February 1917 events during the Russian Revolution. The events are sometimes simply called the 'October Revolution'.

The term **Károlyi regime** is used in relation to the period from Hungary's 1918 Chrysanthemum Revolution at the end of the First World War to the declaration of the Hungarian Soviet Republic on 21 March 1919. The left-liberal politician Mihály Károlyi was the Hungarian prime minister in the early part of this period, and from 11 January 1919 up to the declaration of the Soviet Republic, the country's president.

Introduction

On 21 March 1919 a coalition of Communist Party and Social Democratic Party leaders assumed power in Hungary, formed a Revolutionary Governing Council of People's Commissars and proclaimed the Hungarian Soviet Republic.[1]

The opening chapter of this book sets the scene with an overview of the historical and political context in which the Soviet Republic was born. It briefly describes what happened in Hungary from the end of the First World War and the collapse of the Austro-Hungarian Dual Monarchy—the period of the so-called Chrysanthemum Revolution—to the formation of the Council Republic in March 1919.

The second chapter goes directly to 1 May 1919 and what happened in Budapest during the May Day celebrations. The Revolutionary Governing Council, which had only been in power a little over one month, commissioned artists to literally paint the town red for the celebrations on what was billed as the country's 'first free May Day'. There were red flags, red draperies, red posters and red slogans everywhere.

It wasn't only artists who participated. As will be seen, members of the different arts professions were all involved. This was a great showcase for the regime to display its support from the arts world, and it turned into a spectacular jamboree, with massed ranks of marchers and musicians parading through the decorated streets of the Hungarian capital.

The next chapter takes a specific look at the poster art of 1919. It was often the modernist and avant-garde artists who were at the forefront of the battle of ideas in that they were co-opted to visually publicise and dramatise the new order and its proclamations. Revolutionary placards were everywhere and a genuinely outstanding poster art developed. Images of red proletarians under slogans such as 'Proletarians of the World Unite!' and 'Forward Red Soldiers!' were plastered around the city. Mihály Biró's by then already classic red proletarian figure, wielding a hammer, originally a Social Democratic Party icon, was reproduced countless times during the 1919 events.

Public art and art for the public were taken seriously by Hungary's commissars in 1919 and by the various artistic 'directories' set up to manage

1. For the terminology used in this book, see 'A Note on Terminology', which precedes this introduction.

and promote culture for the masses, as well as to ensure the livelihood of the artists themselves, who now had become state employees, freeing them, it was believed, from the vicissitudes of capitalist art market relations. At the same time, efforts were made to spread art education to a wider public. The fourth chapter takes a look at some of those efforts by focussing on two of the free schools for artists which functioned in 1919, headed by the artists Károly Kerstock and Béla Uitz, the latter's school perhaps appropriately being called The Proletarian Fine Arts Apprentice Workshop. The chapter also describes what could be called the 'exhibition of the century', a massive display of Hungarian and other works of art, which had been 'socialised', namely taken from private owners and put into public ownership.

The cultural policies of the Soviet Republic were fashioned in an essentially spontaneous manner and were articulated by the two leading commissars in the People's Commissariat of Education and Culture, the Social Democrat Zsigmond Kunfi and the Communist György Lukács, particularly the latter, who wrote many proclamations and made many speeches during the events. Lukács's views about politics and the arts were relatively liberal in that in principle he opposed the imposition of a Party line, but there was always a hint at judging matters in terms of broad political perspectives as interpreted by the Party (or by Lukács himself), which didn't suit everyone, including some supporters of the regime, such as Lajos Kassák, a prominent figure in Hungary's radical arts scene. Chapter 5 takes a look at some of the polemics which raged between Kassák with his journal *MA* (Today) and Lukács, in which the political leader Béla Kun also intervened.

The following three chapters deal, in turn, with professionals involved in cinema, theatre and music, and their activities during the period of the Soviet Republic.

Film production and film distribution were nationalised, but that did not mean an end to finance. On the contrary, film was subsidised to a great extent. Film culture, despite being in its youthful stage, was perceived as being of supreme importance. The first issue of the magazine *Vörös Film* (Red Film), published on 12 April 1919, spoke of getting rid of old-style films, full of false capitalist ideology, and producing instead films appropriate to the current revolutionary times. Yet interestingly, its long list of envisaged new films was dominated by proposed cinema versions of Hungarian and foreign literary works, many from established authors. It may come as a surprise to many that Alexander Korda was involved with film-making in Hungary in 1919, and that early in the life of the Commune a short propaganda film was made by Mihály Kertész, who would later, as Michael Curtiz, become renowned as the director of the cinema classic *Casablanca*.

The chapter on cinema concludes with an overview of the documentary cinema newsreels produced during the Council Republic.

The world of theatre in 1919 was no less affected than the world of art and cinema. All theatres were nationalised, making actors state employees. A 'Decree on Theatres', issued on 24 March, just three days after the Council Republic was formed, declared: 'From now on, the theatre belongs to the people! Art will not any more be the privilege of the leisurely rich. Culture is the rightful due of the working people.'[2]

Cheap tickets were available through the trade unions and the theatres were crowded, whatever the performance. There was a genuine desire to open up the auditoriums to a wide audience. Even though the idea was to encourage theatrical innovation, old plays with emphasis on what was perceived as progressive were the order of the day.

The music scene of 1919 is of particular interest in terms of modern-day perceptions of the personalities involved. Both Zoltán Kodály and Béla Bartók participated in the activities of the Music Directory in 1919.

Many special concerts for workers were organised and they were well attended. The streets were full of music, especially on May Day and during recruiting campaigns for the Red Army. The British journalist H. N. Brailsford, in Budapest in 1919, was particularly enamoured of the public music festivals he encountered. 'One had the irresistible feeling,' he wrote, 'in these bright days of spring, as the music of these festivals floated on the lilac-scented air over the Danube, that youth and art, and talent and creative impulse were with this spirited movement.'[3]

The role of writers in 1919 is the subject of Chapter 9. Writers were divided concerning the degree and consistency of support they afforded the Soviet Republic, though many of them rallied to its defence, writing short stories, commentaries and reports for newspapers. Even more participated in the new institutions established for their profession, though arguably they felt obliged to do so, in order to be able to receive some income. As regards what could be published, the official line, on the surface at least, was one of tolerance, although couched within a certain ambiguity.

Chapters 10 and 11 address, in turn, two key questions: why did so many leading figures in the arts world actively support the Hungarian Soviet Republic of 1919 and what happened to their enthusiasm, namely what went wrong as the weeks went by? The answers to both these questions involve a variety of factors and these are explored in these two chapters.

The Postscript, 'What Happened to Them', takes a brief look at the post-1919 fates of a selection of people who feature in this book. As will be

2. Fekete & Karádi (1981), p. 93.
3. Brailsford (1919), p. 13.

seen, what happened to different people varied. With the fall of the Soviet Republic most of the leading politicians and many people in the arts world left Hungary. Some would never return to their homeland. Others found their way back at some point.

The book concludes with a detailed listing of the sources used, which are mainly in Hungarian. English translations of Hungarian titles are included, as are short descriptions of many of the works cited.

1
The Political and Historical Context

In September 1918, towards the end of the First World War, the powerful politician Count István Tisza, who had been Hungary's prime minister (for the second time) from June 1913 to May 1917, travelled to Bosnia. During the course of a dinner in Sarajevo, some of those present expressed the wish for political independence on the part of the Austro-Hungarian Dual-Monarchy's South Slavs. Tisza, who was not known for being sympathetic to Hungary's ethnic minorities, interjected saying: 'Do you think I've come here to listen to such stupidity? Take note—the Monarchy is living and is going to continue to live!'[1] By the end of the following month, neither the Monarchy nor Tisza would be living, the former having disintegrated, the latter having been assassinated.[2]

This opening chapter provides an overview of what happened in Hungary from the end of the First World War and the collapse of the Dual Monarchy to the formation of the Soviet Republic in March 1919.[3]

The manifesto of 16 October 1918, which transformed the Austrian part of the Austro-Hungarian Dual Monarchy into a federal state, led to Tisza and others renouncing dualism, and coming out in favour of Hungary having an independent army and foreign service, with the link to Austria being maintained only via the person of the emperor-king. For Tisza '... this renunciation of dualism was the abandonment of a lifelong conviction, which had previously guided all his thoughts and actions'.[4] Equally dramatic

1. Borsányi (1988), pp. 43–4.
2. Tisza was killed on 31 October 1918 by soldiers who broke into his villa on the edge of Budapest's City Park. István Tisza was widely held responsible for Hungary's entry into the war and thus for the resulting deaths, injuries and privations. Furthermore, many people were strongly critical of Tisza as a social reactionary, an inflexible opponent of land ownership reform and even modest proposals to extend the suffrage.
3. To do it full justice, the period, although covering only about five months, would require a separate book. The information in this brief, essentially chronological account of the main political developments of this complex period is primarily derived from Vincze et. al. (1979), Borsányi (1988), Siklós (1988), Vermes (1971), Pastor (1976) and Romsics (1999b). Details about developments in the cultural sphere during the same period, some of which arguably had a 'carry-over' effect in the subsequent Council Republic period, are included in Chapter 10.
4. Vermes (1971), p. 31.

was Tisza's admission in Parliament on 18 October that Hungary had lost the war. The day before, his political opponent Count Mihály Károlyi, who had opposed the war for some time, had said the same thing.

The radical liberal politician Károlyi had been born into of one of Hungary's wealthiest landowning families. Although a fine horseman and reckless gambler in the tradition of his background, he was also an avid reader and somewhat 'odd' in that he refused to beat servants, or slaughter birds, foxes or stags. He entered parliament in 1910 as an MP for the opposition Party of Independence. Initially a supporter of the war, he changed and became the war's most outspoken critic in parliament. Too radical for his own party, he formed a new one in 1916 with the name United Party of Independence and of 1848, generally known as the Károlyi Party. As will be seen Mihály Károlyi, would play a major role during the events of 1918-19.

In Hungary, the war had resulted in major social, economic and political problems, which involved far more than the personal fate of István Tisza.[5] Hungary's military casualties included over half a million dead, nearly 1.5 million wounded and over 800,000 taken as prisoners of war. There were shortages of labour, due to the call-up, leading to a decline in productivity and rationing of food items. By 1918 the wheat harvest had dropped to half the pre-war level. Industrial production was subordinated to the war effort with many key factories being placed under military control and their output being directed to serving the army. There was massive inflation and a drastic reduction in real wages. Increasing numbers of war widows, orphans and disabled ex-servicemen found themselves in desperately poor circumstances. Meanwhile, a thriving black market with astronomical prices benefitted only a minority.

During the course of the war, public opinion dramatically shifted from initial patriotic fervour to disillusionment and bitterness. Desertion from the ranks and refusal to obey orders affected the army. Membership of the Social Democratic trade unions increased and strikes became increasingly common. There were demonstrations by an influx of ex-servicemen, particularly the tens of thousands of former prisoners of war held in Russia who had returned from captivity. Affected by the social tensions, leaders of Hungary's ethnic minorities—which together constituted about half the population prior to the war—began to voice increasingly strong demands.

In September 1918 the trial began of student members of the Galileo Circle, a radical, anti-war group of mainly young intellectuals. Held under

5. The summary which immediately follows is based on Romsics (1999b), pp. 85–6.

arrest since the previous January, one of their leaders was the 21-year-old, romantic revolutionary Ilona Duczynska, who had met Russian emigré radicals when she was in Switzerland. There was a wave of public sympathy for her and her fellow accused. Student demonstrations became widespread and continued into October. The imprisoned young radicals would be released at the end of that month.

On 30 September Ervin Szabó died. Szabó was a scholarly and innovative librarian. From 1904 he worked as founder and director of the Budapest Municipal Library, which today is named after him. At the same time, he was also noted as one of Hungary's most prominent radical, left-wing thinkers. Interestingly, he was attracted more to anarcho-syndicalist concepts than to the orthodox Marxism of Hungary's solidly trade union based Social Democratic Party (SDP), though he had been an active member of the party from the turn of the century. Significantly, his influence spread beyond the SDP, and even beyond the labour movement.

On 2 October, the funeral ceremony for Ervin Szabó, who had opposed the war throughout, drew a large crowd to Budapest's Farkasrét cemetery, which included, alongside many workers, even the mayor of Budapest, István Bárczy, and his deputy, Ferenc Harrer, who gave one of the speeches, as did the radical intellectual Oszkár Jászi. Simultaneously, workers in a number of large Budapest factories stopped work for ten minutes as a sign of their respect for the deceased.

Lajos Kassák would remember Szabó as someone who had few friends, but who was respected even by his enemies as a scholarly thinker and a steadfast fighter. The crowd attending the funeral, says Kassák, was massively infiltrated by police and detectives. 'Could the authorities have feared that this now cold corpse would rise up and step out of the coffin? His body had died for eternity, but his spirit, which had taken possession of us, could not be driven out of us by either policemen or detectives.'[6]

Three weeks later, during the night of 23–4 October a meeting took place at the mansion of Count Mihály Károlyi in central Budapest (today the building houses the Petőfi Literary Museum). Those present included representatives of Károlyi's own party, which was relatively small, the similarly small Radical Party of middle-class intellectuals, headed among others by Oszkár Jászi, and the much larger Social Democratic Party. The decision was made to form a National Council, a kind of embryo authority, or government in the waiting. The following day the SDP executive approved the decision, students from the University of Technology demonstrated for

6. Kassák (1983), pp. 414–15. For biographical details of Kassák, see the opening paragraphs of Chapter 5.

a democratic Hungary and journalists began to subvert the censorship by not submitting their copy in advance for authorisation.

The Hungarian National Council was officially established on 25 October. A twelve-point list of demands was approved and published the following day. Actually touching on more than twelve issues, the demands included: resignation of the government; dissolution of the Lower House; universal suffrage with secret ballot; land and social welfare reforms; self-determination with a federation of equal peoples; territorial integrity based on common economic and geographical bonds; independence for Hungary; withdrawal of military units from Hungary; repudiation of the German alliance; invalidation of the treaties of Brest and Bucharest; an immediate cessation of hostilities; the delegation of democratic politicians to the peace conference; the forging of political and economic links with neighbouring states; a general amnesty for political prisoners; freedom of association and assembly; and the abolition of censorship.[7]

It seemed like a policy manifesto for a new government and in effect that is what it was, particularly since the members of the National Council believed they constituted the only legitimate political authority in Hungary and even appealed publicly for recognition as such. It turned out to be a shrewd move, at least on the domestic front, given that in the immediate aftermath many individuals and organisations declared their allegiance to the National Council. However, foreign powers, in particular the victorious Entente states, were reluctant to give positive, enthusiastic recognition to any emerging force in Hungary and lift the wartime blockade, and that would prove to be a serious problem.

The day the National Council was officially set up, also saw the formation of a Soldiers' Council. It involved numerous reserve officers who had returned from Russia. On the Italian front mutinies took place. In addition, 3000 students gathered at the University of Technology, proclaimed their acceptance of the National Council's twelve points and then marched to the Castle District to present their demands to the authorities. They

7. This list is based on that given in Siklós (1988), p. 39. The Treaty of Brest (or Brest-Litovsk) was signed on 3 March 1918 between the new Bolshevik government in Soviet Russia and the Central Powers. It ended Russia's participation in the First World War, though it imposed harsh conditions on the country. The (initially secret) Treaty of Bucharest was signed in August 1916, between Romania and the Entente states. Romania agreed to join the war on the side of the Entente on the basis of certain conditions, notably the promise of territorial gains, particularly in parts of what was then Hungary. The encroachment of Romanian forces into Hungarian territory over many months following the end of the world war would prove to be a major headache for Hungary.

were joined by several hundred soldiers. Clashes with mounted police led to many injuries. In the evening there was a demonstration in front of parliament and another outside the headquarters of the Károlyi Party in Gizella Square (today Vörösmarty Square) in central Pest. Participants called for an independent Hungary and a republic.

On 27 October the National Council organised a massive demonstration in front of parliament. The speakers, who included representatives of the Social Democratic and Radical Party leaderships, articulated the demands of the Council. The crowd called for peace and the establishment of a republic.

The following day witnessed one of the major clashes of the October events, the so-called Battle of the Chain Bridge. The Károlyi Party had called for a mass meeting in front of its headquarters. The idea was to present the next steps of the National Council. During the event, part of the crowd hived off and started marching to Castle Hill to demand from Archduke Joseph, the king's representative in Budapest, that Mihály Károlyi be appointed prime minister. As the crowd reached the Chain Bridge linking Pest and Buda, police attacked the demonstrators. Four were killed and dozens were injured.[8]

How many people in Budapest involved in all the excitement would have noticed that two days previously a Slovak National Council had been formed in Túróczszentmárton (today Martin in Slovakia) and that on the day of the Battle of the Chain Bridge the Czech National Council had declared the independence of Czechoslovakia. Then on 29 October in Zagreb, Croatian independence was proclaimed, along with the intention of establishing a Serbo-Croat-Slovene state formation. These moves had direct implications for the fate of large numbers of Hungary's Slovak and South Slav minorities. There would be worse to come for the politicians in Budapest to digest.

In Budapest on 29 October there was still plenty of excitement. A half-hour strike took place in response to the previous day's Chain Bridge clashes. Some workers' groups seized weapons and even the Budapest police now declared allegiance to the Hungarian National Council. A revolutionary process appeared to be underway, particularly as demonstrators in the streets included large numbers of soldiers who had sided with the National Council. The rebellious soldiers wore white chrysanthemums in their caps and buttonholes. The flower was widespread in Hungary at this time of year, since traditionally they would be taken to cemeteries and laid on graves at the time of All Saints' Day and All Souls' Day. It became

8. The figure of four deaths is given by both Vincze (1979, p. 479) and Borsányi (1988, p. 77), though Romsics (1999b) puts the number of those killed on the spot as three.

the symbol of the rebellion and thus the designation Chrysanthemum Revolution was born.

Also on 29 October, the executive committee of the National Council was formed, comprising Mihály Károlyi, as president, plus representatives of his party, as well as those of the Social Democratic and Radical parties. In addition, there were a number of others, such as Lajos Hatvany, representing the press, and the feminist Róza Bédy-Schwimmer.[9] The evening saw further demonstrations by students and soldiers in different parts of the capital. Crowds congregated in front of the Astoria Hotel in central Pest, where the National Council had installed itself. Overnight, railway stations, the telephone exchange and food stores were occupied. The atmosphere on the streets was electric.

According to one witness, the Astoria was like a 'besieged castle', though the crowd around it were actually celebrating. Messengers rushed in and out of the building. Faces of well-known politicians appeared. Journalists clutching notebooks and military officers without insignia on their uniforms came out through the door. Vehicles stationed in front of the building were packed with armed people. From time to time, someone would appear on the balcony and address the crowd.[10]

On 30 October, the Slovak National Council, again meeting in Túróczszentmárton, declared secession from Hungary and accession to the Czechoslovak Republic. In Budapest, members of the soldiers' council toured the barracks agitating for allegiance to the Hungarian National Council. A meeting of workers called by the SDP accepted the idea of forming a workers' council. Then a gathering of Budapest police authority representatives declared its refusal to participate in politically motivated acts against the press or to prevent peaceful demonstrations. In the evening another large crowd assembled outside the Astoria Hotel. The city-centre streets were thronged with crowds of soldiers and workers demanding revolution and a republic. At the Eastern Railway Station weapons seized from a train scheduled to leave for the front were distributed among the crowd. The National Council managed to have railway traffic heading

9. Rózsika Schwimmer, as she is often called, was born in Budapest in 1877. At the age of 20 she became an activist on behalf of the National Association of Female Civil Servants, eventually becoming its president. In 1903 she helped establish the Hungarian Association of Working Women and later became a founder of Hungary's Feminist Association, for many years editing its paper, A nő (Woman). Having become involved in the international women's and peace movements, during the First World War Schwimmer worked in London for the International Women's Suffrage Alliance and was a militant anti-war campaigner. Always a radical for her time in personal behaviour, smoking cigarettes and drinking wine, she had a vibrant personality and was an impressive public speaker with a sense of humour.

10. Kassák (1983), p. 433.

for Budapest stopped, thus preventing the arrival of troops sent to quell the rebellion. During the night, the telegraph office, main post office, rail stations, the bridges and other strategic points were occupied by armed soldiers and workers.

The following morning (31 October) more barracks were occupied, political prisoners were freed and even the Budapest Municipal Council declared allegiance to the National Council. At 7 a.m., having been called by Archduke Joseph, Mihály Károlyi went to the Castle, where he was asked to form a government. At an afternoon session the executive committee of the National Council established a government comprising members of the political parties represented in the Council. In the evening they adopted a programme calling for immediate peace, democratic freedoms, protection for workers and radical agrarian reform. Under the effects of events in the capital, demonstrations and meetings took place in provincial centres, where local organisations of the National Council were established. The revolution, it seemed, had succeeded!

Indeed on 1 November the National Council and the Social Democrats declared the revolution had been completed and called for an end to strikes, a resumption of production and general calm. However, factory meetings and demonstrations continued, with demands for a republic to be declared. Meanwhile, in Sarajevo the Bosnian National Council declared it was assuming power locally.

The Budapest Workers' Council held its founding meeting on 2 November. The majority comprised leading members of the Social Democratic Party and its affiliated trade unions. Around this time, too, individual factories across the capital set up their own workers' councils. On the following day in Padua, an armistice signifying the end of the war was signed by representatives of the Monarchy and the Entente. One clause of the agreement stated that Hungary was obliged to withdraw from Croatia.

On 4 November in faraway Moscow, a meeting of prisoners of war comprising members of Hungary's different ethnic groups established what would become the Communist Party of Hungary. A temporary central committee was elected and a decision was made that communists should return to Hungary as quickly as possible.[11] In Budapest there were

---

11. The person who emerged as the leader of the communists was Béla Kun. Born in 1886 in Transylvania, Kun became an active Social Democrat at an early age. He worked as a journalist and later as an official of a workers' insurance organisation. During the First World War he was recruited to the army, but in 1916 fell into Russian captivity. In Russia he was strongly influenced by the Bolsheviks and became a communist. He wrote articles and also took part in certain actions during 1917–18. He was a personal acquaintance of Lenin.

tensions between the new government and the Soldiers' Council, but the next day saw an agreement whereby it was recognised that executive power would be the prerogative of the government, while the two important councils of soldiers and of workers would have overseeing and propaganda functions.

Czechoslovak forces moved into parts of western Slovakia on 6 November as a Hungarian delegation including Károlyi and Jászi travelled to Belgrade to conduct further negotiations about the armistice conditions with General Franchet d'Espèry, representing the Entente. Over the next week or so Serbian troops moved into Voivodina, an area with a large Hungarian population, and Czechoslovak forces continued their encroachment of Slovakia.

On 13 November a Hungarian delegation headed by Oszkár Jászi, the new government's minister with responsibility for ethnic minority affairs, was in Arad (then in Hungary, today in Romania) to negotiate with leaders of the Romanian National Council, which was demanding sovereignty over areas in Hungary mainly populated by ethnic Romanians. The Hungarians offered autonomy within Hungary, along the lines of Jászi's pet idea for an 'eastern Switzerland' type of federation. The Romanians held out for full sovereignty and independence, and the talks stalled. Matters were moving swiftly in other areas, too. At the time the Hungarian delegation was engaged in the talks at Arad, King Charles IV had resigned from the Austrian throne and from claims to state authority over Hungary. At the same time, Romanian troops were entering Transylvania.

Back in Belgrade, an agreement was signed with Franchet d'Espèry on 13 November. The 18-point agreement harshly compelled Hungary to withdraw its troops from Transylvania and other areas, and stipulated that it should have a standing army of no more than six infantry and two cavalry divisions. Furthermore, it had to ensure the unhindered movement of Entente forces anywhere in the country. The Hungarians hoped the measures were only temporary. As if taking the agreement as a signal, Serb, Czech and Romanian troops continued their advances. On 14 November in Prague, the Republic of Czechoslovakia was officially proclaimed, with Tomáš Masaryk as president.

All troubles were temporarily forgotten on 16 November, at least in Budapest, as a meeting of the National Council in the parliament building formally declared independence and the establishment of what was officially called the People's Republic of Hungary. The existing two houses of parliament were dissolved and the now greatly enlarged National Council assumed the role of an interim national assembly. People's Law No. 1 conferred supreme state power on the government headed by Károlyi.

Filling the square in front of the building, a massive crowd welcomed the news with joyful enthusiasm.

In addition to the unfriendly attitude of the Entente powers, the dissatisfaction of the country's minorities and the hostile activities of neighbouring states, the new government also had to face major economic and social problems on the domestic front. The war had left the economy in a disastrous state. Production was disrupted, shortages were rife and were not eased by the fact that the wartime economic blockade imposed by the Entente remained in place.[12] The villages lacked kerosene, salt and tobacco, while the towns were short of coal and wood. In Budapest gas and electricity consumption had to be restricted, and shops and businesses were forced to close early. Inflation was rampant. The number of unemployed workers shot up to several hundred thousand as an influx began of Hungarian refugees from occupied territories. The volume of desperate people was greatly increased by the return of thousands of former prisoners of war held in Russia and the masses of soldiers returning from the front, many of them suffering from injuries and wounds.[13] The war wounded, the widows and the orphans all presented huge social problems, for the solution of which the government lacked resources. The same could be said about the many people living in miserable conditions, without food or proper clothing, some without a roof over their head.

One of the most pressing and at the same time contentious issues involved the need for land reform. Big landowners opposed immediate, wide-ranging appropriation of estates, while the Social Democrats agitated for socialisation in the form of cooperatives. They opposed the breaking up

---

12. The Entente lacked sympathy for Hungary as a defeated nation, but there were also conflicts about certain individuals, such as Rózsika Schwimmer, who was appointed by Mihály Károlyi in November 1918 to be Hungary's ambassador to Switzerland, thus becoming the first female ambassador in the history of the modern world. The status of the world's first woman ambassador is often attributed to Alexandra Kollontai, a representative in Norway of the Soviet government, but only from 1923, so arguably the designation rightly belongs to Schwimmer. According to Peter Pastor's 1976 work, her appointment created a fury. France's foreign minister apparently called the move 'a perfidious act' (p. 70). The Swiss government declared Schwimmer an undesirable alien, refusing to recognise her credentials. It seems the head of the US Legation in Switzerland disliked Schwimmer, though in contrast with the others, who appeared to object to a woman taking up the post, his distaste seems to have been more on the grounds that she was Jewish (p. 76). Her appointment was even ridiculed by an editorial in the *New York Times* (p. 77). Whether despised as a woman, a Jew or a radical—or maybe all three—the result was that Schwimmer was 'frozen out' and Károlyi was obliged to recall her on 18 January, two months after her appointment.

13. According to Vincze et al. (1979, p. 488), in the period 10–30 November more than one million soldiers returned from the front.

of estates and distribution of land to the rural poor on ideological grounds, believing that would encourage the development of a new conservative layer in the countryside. In contrast, the other parties in the government generally favoured land distribution. After fierce debate this latter policy was adopted and a framework law was eventually passed in mid February 1919. However, time ran out before the proposals could be put into effect.

On an apparently more positive note, moves were made to extend the suffrage quite dramatically. The issue was close to the heart of the Social Democratic Party, which had been advocating and demonstrating for universal suffrage for many years. But the other parties in power also supported extending the right to vote. Yet it wasn't until early March 1919 that a law was ratified about elections to a constituent assembly based on a new suffrage. This would have enfranchised literate men of 21 and over, plus women of 24 and over, but only if they had been Hungarian citizens for at least six years. Even with these restrictions, the change would have increased the electorate to around nine million, or 50 per cent of Hungary's pre-1918 population, putting the country on the level of the top-ranking Scandinavian countries in terms of the breadth of the suffrage.[14] New parliamentary elections were scheduled for April 1919, but by that time the Soviet Republic had been established and notions of 'bourgeois parliamentary democracy' were quickly abandoned in favour of elections to soviets (although the new regime was also, in principle, supportive of women's political emancipation).

Attempts were made to introduce other, social policy measures. Unemployment benefit was introduced. The employment of children under 14 was outlawed and there were plans to introduce an eight-hour working day, along with an extended social insurance scheme. Former front-line soldiers were allocated a small lump-sum payment. Yet given the constraints of the economic situation and once again the time limit, such reforms did not have any substantial impact.

On the domestic political front, 24 November saw a development which would have a major impact in the following months—the Communist Party of Hungary[15] was officially formed in Budapest, Béla Kun and others having arrived from Russia a week before. The new party comprised former prisoners of war who had been radicalised in Russia, left wing and dissident Social Democrats and a small group called the Revolutionary Socialists.

Within a couple of weeks the party started to issue its own newspaper, *Vörös Újság* (Red Gazette). The 'line' promulgated was for the overthrow

---

14. Romsics (1999b), p. 95.
15. Strictly speaking (reflecting the internationalist ideology of the time), the Party of Communists in Hungary—a Kommunisták Magyarországi Pártja.

of capitalism and the introduction of a Bolshevik-style socialist system. The party's seductive, internationalist utopian vision and agitprop political demands were welcomed by society's downtrodden, the unemployed and war invalids, as well as some romantically inclined young intellectuals. As the weeks went by, the party certainly made inroads. According to historian Ignác Romsics: 'By March 1919 its membership in Budapest was some 10,000-15,000, with another 20,000-25,000 outside the capital, though its alluring slogans were capable of mobilising many times more than those numbers suggest.'[16]

On 25 November there was another blow on the international front when the Serbian National Council declared that the counties in southern Hungary occupied by their forces would now be considered part of Serbia. But there were also developments within the country which were potentially worrying for the government and potentially threatening whatever results the Chrysanthemum Revolution had been able to achieve. At the end of November a far-right organisation of army officers called the Hungarian Association of National Defence was formed in Budapest. Other groups with a similar, anti-liberal, anti-socialist political orientation were established, such as the Association of Awakening Hungarians. In the future they and others would organise anti-government meetings and demonstrations.

Then on 1 December there was a major political bombshell. At a meeting in Gyulafehévár (today Alba Iulia in Romania), representatives of Hungary's large ethnic Romanian population in the form of the Romanian National Assembly declared for union with the Kingdom of Romania. The next day Romanian troops crossed the demarcation line agreed in the Belgrade armistice and began to occupy territories which Romania had been secretly awarded by the 1916 Treaty of Bucharest. By Christmas Eve 1918, Romanian forces had already reached the major Transylvanian city of Kolozsvár (Cluj-Napoca, Romania). Within a week Czech forces had entered Kassa (today Košice in eastern Slovakia), and even French troops had entered Szeged, a major town in southern Hungary. Three days into the New Year, the Budapest Workers' Council decided to issue an appeal to the international proletariat to oppose the machinations of the Entente against Hungary.

By the end of the first week of January, there was a government crisis. Both international and domestic tensions had led to criticism of Károlyi, even among members of his own party. At the same time, many Social Democrats joined the Communists in their criticism of the sluggish pace

16. Romsics (1999b), p. 98.

of social transformation. The result was a reshuffle. The National Council appointed Károlyi as provisional president of the republic. He held onto his portfolio for foreign affairs, but his position as prime minister was taken over by Dénes Berinkay, who had been the Minister of Justice. Some in the SDP and the Workers' Council argued for a new government comprising only Social Democrats, but in the end a coalition was maintained, with the number of SDP ministers doubling from two to four.

This didn't put an end to the widespread discontent. In Budapest there was a large demonstration of the unemployed on 23 January, followed by another four days later, and then a third on 4 February. During February the government decided to take measures against its critics. Searches of the headquarters of a number of right-wing groups were initiated, as well as searches of the editorial offices of *Vörös Újság*.

On 20 February a meeting of the unemployed at the Vigadó, a large hall in central Budapest, was followed by a march to the *Vörös Újság* offices, where Béla Kun and others addressed the crowd. There was condemnation of *Népszava* (People's Voice), the Social Democrat's newspaper, for criticising aspects of the unemployed movement.[17] Thereafter the crowd moved on to the editorial offices of *Népszava* to demonstrate their disapproval, at the same time protesting against the police who had been sent to protect the building. During the fighting and chaos that ensued some people were killed and many injured.[18] In the evening the government decided to have the communist leaders arrested and overnight Béla Kun and others were taken into custody. The party headquarters and the *Vörös Újság* offices were closed, and by the end of the month dozens of communists had been arrested.

Two days after the clashes in front of the *Népszava* offices, the SDP organised what has been called the largest demonstration of the post-war, pre-Council Republic period.[19] In essence it was an anti-communist protest, although there were calls for steps also to be taken against 'rightist counter-revolutionaries'. There were similar demonstrations in a number of provincial towns. However, the mood was undermined by a journalist's

17. Vincze (1979), p. 514. Borsányi (1988, p. 190) says that criticism of the SDP was voiced, but there was no direct call for an attack on the *Népszava* offices.
18. As often happens during and in the wake of chaotic events, the reports and the figures can vary. Vincze (1979, p. 515) says that shots were fired from a nearby building into the crowd and the police, resulting in four deaths and several injuries. Vermes (1971, p. 53) makes no mention of any shooting, but says six policemen were killed and several others wounded. Borsányi (1988, p. 191) refers to shots being fired and says that both sides had weapons. He gives a total of eight deaths—three policemen, two guards, one worker (probably demonstrating) and two passers-by.
19. Borsányi (1988), p. 192. Borsányi puts the number of demonstrators at 200,000, though other sources only give half that number.

eyewitness report appearing that day in *Az Est* (Evening News), which described how, following his arrest and while still in custody, Béla Kun had been very badly beaten. The news generated a wave of public sympathy for the arrested communists, thus somewhat countering the intentions of the organisers and the hopes of the government. The shock reaction also resulted in the imprisoned communists being granted preferential treatment within the confines of their prison. The communists still at large quickly organised an alternative central committee and soon had *Vörös Újság* appearing again. Not surprisingly, they made the most of the 'martyrdom' of their imprisoned colleagues.

On 23 February, following enactment of the Land Reform Bill, president Mihály Károlyi, in what was a symbolic gesture but also a practical move, personally divided up his own land holdings at Kápolna to the east of Budapest. Lack of time, plus opposition from both right and left, meant that the intentions of the bill were never realised across the country.

Three days later in distant Paris, a decision was made at the Peace Conference, calling for Hungary to withdraw its eastern troops even more, allowing Romanian forces to advance to a line roughly equivalent to today's Hungarian-Romanian border, and for a further, large area to the west of that, including towns such as Debrecen and Békéscsaba, to become a neutral zone. That decision was personally delivered to Károlyi by French Lieutenant-Colonel Fernand Vix, the Entente's senior representative in Budapest—but only three weeks later, on 20 March. The content of what notoriously became known as the Vix note and the short time allocated for its implementation—just 18 hours, making it an ultimatum—was too much for Károlyi to swallow. His reluctance to comply, leading to formal rejection of the note the next day, would in effect signal the end of the regime of which he was president.

Meanwhile, the Communist Party had been recovering from the blow inflicted on it in February. On 9 March the party held a huge rally in Budapest's City Park, where the government was criticised, the accusations against the communists in connection with the events of 20 February were denied, and the release of the imprisoned party leaders demanded. Two days later, with a view to furthering cooperation with those Social Democrats who were more sympathetic towards the communists, Béla Kun issued a statement setting out conditions for unifying the two workers' parties. He proposed, *inter alia*, that the SDP break with the bourgeois parties and, together with the Communist Party, establish a Soviet Republic, that a workers' militia be formed, that land and factories be nationalised and that the connection between the churches and schools be severed. Talks between certain SDP figures and the imprisoned communists took place inside the prison, but initially they produced no concrete result.

Nevertheless, the left-wing leaders of the SDP were gaining ground during the first half of March. Their programme was published in *Népszava* on 19 March. It called for a workers' government, nationalisation of big industry, mines and transport, as well as the creation of agricultural cooperatives instead of land distribution.[20] There was clearly a basis in that for broad-ranging agreement with the communists.

In addition to a series of workers' mass meetings in Budapest and elsewhere, thousands of unemployed demonstrated on 19 March in front of the Ministry of Public Welfare. Their demands included work, welfare and the nationalisation of land and industrial enterprises. Adding to the tension were disturbances in the countryside. Already in February, large estates had been expropriated and collectives formed in Somogy county, to the south of Lake Balaton. A socialist directorate took over the county administration. In March similar events, though on a smaller scale, took place in other provincial towns and villages. However, many peasants had an ambiguous attitude to such developments. While perhaps welcoming the losses suffered by landowners, collectivisation did not satisfy their hunger for land.[21]

With his refusal to accept the conditions of the Vix note, Károlyi planned to appeal for national resistance, while seeking help from Soviet Russia. He hoped to induce the Social Democrats to establish a government, with himself remaining as president. The Social Democrats, not wishing to form a government on their own, without Károlyi's knowledge entered into negotiations on 21 March with Béla Kun and other communist leaders still held in prison. There they agreed on a fusion of their two parties and a joint takeover of power. Some moderate Social Democratic leaders opposed the plan, but the majority were in agreement.[22]

Support for the new situation created by the two parties was offered later in the day by both the Soldiers' Council and the Budapest Workers' Council. Armed workers and soldiers began to occupy banks, warehouses and other public buildings. In the late evening, prominent members of the SDP and the Communist Party, whose leaders had now been freed from prison, met and formed a new government, which they christened the Revolutionary Governing Council.[23]

Thus was born the 1919 Hungarian Soviet Republic.

---

20. Hajdu (1979), p. 11.
21. Vermes (1971), p. 53.
22. Romsics, (1999b), p. 99.
23. Vincze et al. (1979), pp. 528–9.

2
Budapest Turns Red

It was a real First of May.
The entire city was out in the streets.
Everyone, as I remember,
got his lost hopes back on loan for that day.

– Gyula Háy[1]

'Throughout the entire life of this city, as it has observed its reflection in the passing waters of the Danube during the centuries of its rich and varied history, there was never such a mighty day as witnessed yesterday on 1 May …'

With these words *Az Est* (Evening News) began its coverage of the 1919 May Day events in Budapest.[2] The report continued in an even more enthusiastic tone.

'The most beautiful aspect, however, was *the liberated human being* [emphasis in the original—B. D.] individually and as part of the mass, because the self-consciousness of people freed from their chains shone in every eye, resounded in the anthem of *The Internationale* and echoed in the footsteps of millions.'

Millions? The paper itself reported that half a million had participated (other sources said 600,000). Nevertheless, ignoring the hyperbole, the opening lines were surely justified—Budapest had never seen anything like it, and arguably has never seen anything similar since.

By 1 May 1919, the Hungarian Soviet Republic had been in existence for less than six weeks, but here was an opportunity to make a really impressive political display. The whole city was taken over (commandeered would not be an inappropriate word) to celebrate May Day, the international day

1. Hay (1974), p. 71.
2. *Az Est*, 3 May 1919, p. 2. Reports of the May Day events in this and other newspapers appeared on 3 May since the papers were not published the day before, presumably because 1 May was a non-working day for journalists, editors and print workers, and so a 2 May edition was not prepared.

of labour. People across the arts world—painters, sculptors, actors, film-makers, musicians and writers—were all involved in the celebration in some way or other.

Buildings were festooned with red drapery, red flags flew everywhere, political statues and monuments symbolising the past were covered with specially designed structures allegedly representing the future, temporary statues and busts of politically acceptable heroes were placed in the major public spaces of the city. Exhorting slogans and posters were everywhere, work stopped for the day as people gathered at various points and marched through the city, political speeches were delivered, bands played, there was entertainment for old and young alike, and everywhere there was red, red and more red.[3]

Two-thirds of the front page of the May Day edition of *Népszava* (People's Voice) was taken up by 'Vörös Május' (Red May), a resounding poem penned by Zseni Várnai, a 29-year-old poet with a track record

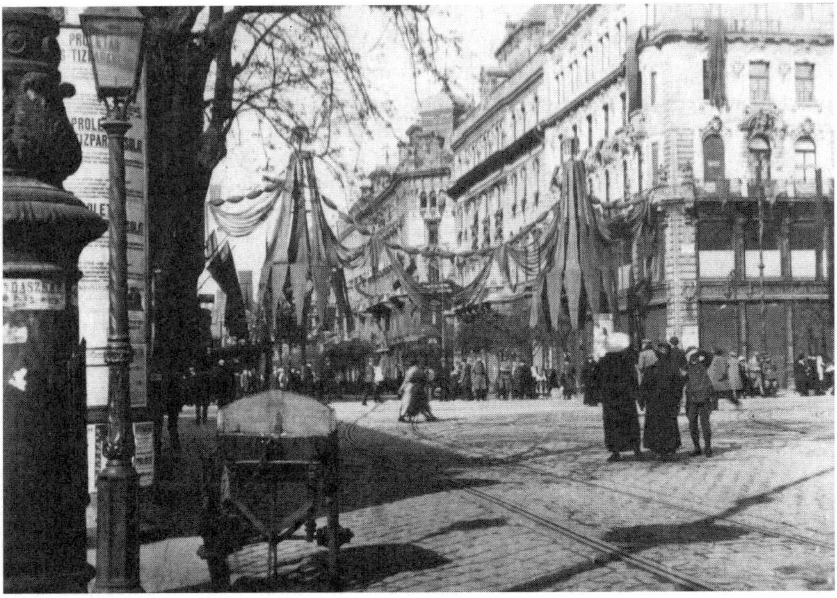

Figure 2.1 All the major streets and buildings were decorated for May Day with flags and banners.

Photo: FORTEPAN/Frigyes Schoch

3. The details in this chapter about the 1919 May Day events in Budapest and how the city was decorated are based on a comparison and cross-checking of reports in contemporary newspapers, the evidence provided by archive photographs and newsreel footage, participants' memoirs and certain more recent studies, for example by Boldizsár Vörös (see bibliography).

of poignant verses published in the labour movement press.[4] Several thunderous verses all ended with 'The Great May has Arrived!' leading to a final crescendo in the last stanza, which read:

A world upheaval brought it, a world upheaval is driving it,
From the red East to the pale West.
There's no stopping it, and woe to the forces
Who build barricades to stop the conflagration.
It will parch them dry –
The Great Red May!

On 1 May 1919 the main body of marchers in the city converged in central Pest on the east side of the Danube and proceeded along Andrássy Avenue, a major urban thoroughfare of Budapest. Having walked its length, they passed by the Millennium Monument in the square, which is today called Heroes' Square, and then into the City Park beyond.

'Occupying' Andrássy Avenue in this manner in 1919 was a symbolic snub to the bourgeois character of Budapest, since the avenue represented in its most concrete form the wealth which the city had accumulated in the decades prior to the First World War.

The social divisions of Hungary were symbolised by the architecture of Andrássy Avenue. The villas at its top end had been built as exclusive residences for the wealthy. The apartment blocks in the first section were constructed to house both rich and poor, but there was clear segregation and differentiation in that the rich owners usually occupied large, lavish, multi-room, first-floor apartments overlooking the avenue, reached by elegant stairways, while poorer occupants were relegated to the sides or rear of the inner courtyards, and often had to make do with just a single room, sharing a toilet and other facilities, and were obliged to use a simple rear staircase.

Most workers lived in the outer areas, in the great factory districts encircling the city, but on 1 May 1919 workers flocked from the outskirts and took over its central areas, most notably Andrassy Avenue.

The city centre was prepared to greet them. By the start of Andrássy Avenue a huge, red triumphal arch had been erected. On one side was

4. *Népszava* had been for many years the newspaper of Hungary's Social Democratic Party. With the formation of the Council Republic and the merging of the Social Democratic Party and the Communist Party, whose paper was the much shorter-lived *Vörös Újság* (Red Gazette), it was agreed that *Népszava* would be the daily morning paper of the united party and that *Vörös Újság* would be its mouthpiece in the afternoon. The two papers often reported the news in the same way, but they weren't always singing, so to say, from the same proof sheet.

a bust of Karl Liebknecht, the German socialist who, along with Rosa Luxemburg, had been murdered three and a half months previously following the ill-fated Spartacist uprising in Berlin. There were several busts of Liebknecht placed in prominent positions throughout Budapest for the 1 May 1919 events, but the records seem to give little indication of any similarly prominent homage being paid to Rosa Luxemburg, which is interesting in that arguably she would become a more important figure in the memory of European left-wing movements. However, Luxemburg had been a long-standing opponent of Lenin's ideas about organisational centralism and had criticised the authoritarian practices of the Bolsheviks during the Russian Revolution, so this might explain her 'absence' on a day which was very much 'pro-Lenin' and 'pro-Bolshevik'.[5]

Above the bust of Karl Liebknecht there was a slogan proclaiming: 'The Red Soldier fights not against his proletarian brothers, but against international capital!' On the other side, above a bust of Karl Marx's colleague Freidrich Engels, there was another slogan: 'Destroy capital, so that on its ruins we can build the world society of international communism!'

As the marchers entered Andrássy Avenue they were greeted by a military band. Another band was playing on the balcony of the Opera House in the first part of the avenue and archive film indicates that there was yet more music in front of the Abbazia Coffee House at the Oktogon junction.

Some of the musicians participating in the May Day events had been up for a long time. In its report of the day's activities, *Vörös Újság* claims that things had got going at 5.15 in the morning, when eight military bands and 200 theatre musicians went through the city playing *The Internationale* and *La Marseillaise*. Did people mind being woken up so early in this manner? Not according to *Vörös Újság*.[6]

'The windows of the workers aroused early for the great day opened and the first cheerful, happy faces appeared in the fresh dawn of May.'

From 7 a.m., the paper says, groups started forming at 28 designated meeting points across the city. An hour later music was being played by St Stephen's Basilica in Pest and the Matthias Church on Castle Hill in Buda. By 8.30 a number of bands with wind instruments were parading through the streets. Gypsy bands and workers' ensembles played at the spots where people were congregating. *Vörös Újság* says a gypsy band played *The Internationale* outside the Rókus Hospital by Rákóczi Road and claims there was a warm reception: 'The windows open and the hospital patients, their eyes shining and waiving kerchiefs, listened to the anthem of the new world.'

5. See Luxemburg's *Organisational Questions of Russian Democracy* (1904) and her *The Russian Revolution*, written in prison during the First World War.
6. *Vörös Újság*, 3 May 1919, pp. 3 ff.

There had been an attempt to get young people involved, too. An announcement in *Pesti Napló* (Pest Diary) on 22 April had called for leaders of school choirs and orchestras to register with the music department of the People's Commissariat for Military Affairs and where none existed they should be immediately formed and the pupils taught *The Internationale* and *La Marseillaise* in preparation for May Day. If necessary, orchestra leaders and teachers could be supplied by the music department.

After Oktogon, the next junction on the Avenue, the Köröndo (circular in shape, hence its name in Hungarian—the 'Circus'), was at the time the site of four imposing statues depicting military figures from Hungary's past—Miklós Zrínyi, István Bocskai, Gábor Bethlen and János Pálffy. Unsurprisingly, on 1 May 1919 all four statues were covered by architectural structures supporting large globes. The idea was presumably that the memory of national military personalities should be forgotten and replaced by an internationalist outlook, albeit that the message was put across in a rather simplistic manner. The symbol of a globe representing internationalism appeared elsewhere in the city, but some citizens seem to have reacted with characteristic Pest humour, regarding them as representing the new people's commissars and calling them the *vörös hólyagok* (a slang term meaning the red blockheads).[7]

The internationalist atmosphere on Andrássy Avenue was more concretely expressed by the presence of the many foreigners who marched along its length. Years later Mariska Gárdos, a journalist in 1919, would recall thinking that the 'international march' along the avenue was one of the day's 'most impressive' sights. The idealism and romanticism of her account is clear:

> Hearing news about the outbreak of our proletarian revolution, workers groups set out so that by our side they would enjoy the workers' power, and if necessary defend it with us with weapons … On the demonstration you could see side by side, arm in arm, Italians, Austrians, Turks, Serbs, Romanians, Bulgarians, Czechs and others. Thousands of Russian prisoners of war stuck here after the world war also took part in the celebration. They were not able to fight for the Great October Socialist Revolution in their own homeland, but after the formation of the Hungarian Soviet Republic they immediately held a large meeting and offered their work and preparedness for struggle. Now they marched, one and all, as a living symbol of proletarian internationalism—with

7. Dr József Hollós, 'Első szökésem' (My First Escape). In: Petrák (1978), p. 510.

> reddening faces, the light of happiness in their eyes, in their hearts the cheerfulness of accomplishment.[8]

Vörös Újság reported that there were also French participants, Germans with lots of children on lorries, as well as Poles, Slovaks and Jewish workers with flags sporting Hebrew inscriptions.

Naturally it wasn't only groups of foreigners who marched along Andrássy Avenue. There were plenty of Hungarians, too, in the main grouped according to their place of work, their employment or profession, or the industrial district in which they worked or lived. Thus theatre workers, including actors and actresses, walked together in their own group with their own placards, as did teachers, civil servants and film studio employees, along with film stars of the day. The latter group had a cart drawn by six horses on which there was a huge mock-up of a film reel, several metres in diameter and decorated in various colours. At the side, like characters in a film about medieval times, there were heralds dressed in red. Some of the groups had their own bands.

One large vehicle was filled with books like a mobile bookshop or library, and there was a large flag with the inscription 'Proletarian Literature'. The report in *Vörös Újság* didn't specify which books were deemed suitably proletarian.

Among the manual workers a contingent appeared from the giant metal and iron works on Csepel Island, just to the south of Budapest. Representing one of the largest working-class constituencies with a tradition of militancy, they came with floats decorated in red on which were 'statues' of industrial equipment. One lorry carried a workers' choir, while an ironworker wearing a red cloak rode on a horse at their head.

Perhaps most 'decorative' of all were the workers from the city's huge abattoir and other meat industry works. They came with a red carriage drawn by six oxen. On one side a huge ham, sausages and crispy baked sweetbread were hanging. A slogan read: 'The bourgeoisie lived like this up to now, and from now on this is how the proletariat will live!' Another slogan reading 'The proletariat lived like this, and now this is how the bourgeoisie will live' was accompanied by a small chunk of black bread and a large bone.

Archive film indicates that the marchers were dressed in their Sunday best and some of the better off, like the actresses, even turned up in their furs. As each group passed by they waved to the cameras and smiled, indicating that the event, as planned, was more of a celebration than a protest. As they reached the end of Andrássy Avenue they came in sight

8. Gárdos (1964), p. 48.

of the huge Millennium Monument. What they saw must have seemed quite astounding.

Since 1932 the area where the Millennium Monument stood (and still stands) has been known as Heroes' Square. It is one of Budapest's most impressive locations and approaching it along the avenue, the grand, almost super-human scale of the square cannot fail to impress. With its massive expanse flanked by the imposing neo-Classical buildings of the Museum of Fine Arts on one side and the Hall of Arts[9] on the other, and with its Millennium Monument, comprising a tall central column and two curved colonnades with statues at the rear, Heroes' Square is one of the most remarkable and striking public spaces in Europe, on a par with Trafalgar Square in London, Place de la Concorde in Paris and Palace Square in St Petersburg.

The monument was originally planned for Hungary's 1896 Millennium Celebrations, organised to mark what was believed to be the thousandth anniversary of the arrival of the Magyars or ancient Hungarians in the Carpathian Basin, but it took a number of years to complete.

The plan envisaged a double life-size statue of the Archangel Gabriel holding the Hungarian crown at the top of the 36-metre central column, while at the bottom there would be equestrian statues of Árpád, the chieftain who led the Magyar tribes into the Carpathian Basin in 896 or thereabouts, plus six of his fellow leaders. To the rear, between the pillars of the two colonnades, there were to be 14 statues, all bar one of which were to represent monarchs who had ruled Hungary over the centuries, including Habsburg rulers.

At the beginning of 1919 most of the statues were in place, apart from the six leaders of the ancient Hungarians who were due to accompany Árpád and one of the planned 14 statues of the two colonnades. Then in early April, within two weeks following the formation of the Soviet Republic, the five statues which depicted Habsburg rulers—Ferdinand I, Charles III, Maria Theresa, Leopold II and Franz Joseph—were removed from the monument. That of Franz Joseph, which showed him in military uniform, was smashed to bits.[10]

---

9. Today known as the Kunsthalle.

10. After the 1919 events the five Habsburgs were put back with a new statue of Franz Joseph, this time in coronation robes. Then in the years following the Second World War they were removed again and replaced by statues of noted figures who had struggled against Habsburg rule. The place of Franz Joseph, for example, was taken by Lajos Kossuth, the leader of Hungary's anti-Habsburg 1848–49 War of Independence. Among the post-1945 statues replacing the Habsburgs two of them (those of István Bocskay and Gábor Bethlen) were moved from the Köröند, where in 1919 they had

The imagery in the form of statues remaining on the Millennium Monument was now entirely national with no direct trace of imperial rule. However, for the May Day celebrations the entire monument—the massive colonnades as well as the huge central column—was concealed by red covering. The famous slogan from *The Communist Manifesto*, 'Workers of the world unite!' appeared along the top of each colonnade, while at either end were large decorative placards produced by the artist Béla Uitz. One represented the urban proletariat, the other the peasantry and in case it wasn't clear there were also texts proclaiming the meaning of the images.

The central column was transformed into a giant red obelisk and at the bottom, in place of the now hidden equestrian statue of Árpád, there was a giant, white plaster sculpture of a bearded Karl Marx flanked by a miner on one side and an iron worker on the other. Thus now Marx and the proletariat had taken centre stage in what was no longer—at least for a day—a Hungarian national monument.

A number of newspapers at the time reported that the Marx statue had been sculpted by György Zala. If that is true, it is rather intriguing since Zala was one of Hungary's most prominent sculptors of the pre-1914 era and had been closely associated with the Millennium Monument and its statues. The equestrian statue of Árpád and the figure of the Archangel Gabriel were both by Zala, as were other statues of the monument. It must have been rather painful for him to see his statues covered in red, with one of them being 'replaced' by Karl Marx. Did he really create the Marx composition?

György Borbás notes in his 1999 overview of the life and works of Zala that the Marx statue was prepared in Zala's studio, but he doesn't say whether Zala was involved or not. Perhaps the truth is close to the somewhat ambiguous situation implied by Zala's fellow sculptor, Zsigmond Kisfaludi Strobl, who recalled in his memoirs that the Karl Marx composition was made 'under György Zala's direction'.[11]

Perhaps a degree of pressure, even intimidation, was involved. In his book about his father, the son of the sculptor Alajos Stróbl records that Zala was later reproached for his involvement with the Marx statue. Zala would respond with a question: 'What would you have done if armed soldiers had burst into your studio and announced that the statue had to be made?'[12]

A speakers' platform was erected in front of the Marx statue and one witness, László Wessely, a Communist Party youth activist in 1919, would

been covered up for the May Day events! No alterations were made to the monument following the political changes of 1989–90.

11. Kisfaludi Strobl (1969), p. 74.
12. Stróbl (2003), p. 171.

recall that from there 'the three most popular actresses of the time', Sári Fedák, Emma Kosáry and Gizi Bajor, sang revolutionary songs and 'kitschy recruiting numbers' based on Hungarian folk tunes. József Hollós would also recall Sári Fedák participating 'with heart and soul' in the May Day events, commenting that she was even 'the most devoted recruiter for the Red Army'. However, his reflections published decades later also note that she would become a 'similarly ardent supporter of the [post-1919] counter-revolutionary governments'.[13]

Mihály Stróbl writes that during the May Day demonstration his father, Alajos, found himself on a lorry with Sári Fedák and other theatre personalities. He recalls that his father was the only teacher at the Art College to participate in the march. 'My father wasn't averse to the workers' regime and he, too, fell under the spell of the events. He declared that he was also a manual worker and had never been pampered.'[14]

In their lengthy reports of the May Day events both *Vörös Újság* and *Népszava* said the façade of the Hall of Arts to one side of the Millennium Monument was covered by Bertalan Pór's massive canvas *A vörös hadsereg* (The Red Army). The claim is repeated elsewhere, for example in Lajos Kassák's memoir of the 1919 'Commune', as he and others called it.[15] This is intriguing since in an interview given many years after 1919 Bertalan Pór, an active member of the Arts Directory during the Soviet Republic, recalled how he was, indeed, working on a huge, eight-metre-high canvas for May Day, which was to decorate the façade of the Hall of Arts, though he doesn't say what theme was depicted, apart from mentioning a slogan at the top reading: 'Forward for your wives and children!' In the event, however, according to Pór nature intervened and his work was completely destroyed by a huge storm which raged before the May Day celebrations![16]

As the marchers passed the Millennium Monument they entered the City Park, one of the largest and most popular public parks in Budapest and one of the 'playgrounds' of the metropolis. Here could be found garden restaurants, circuses, a zoo, a fun fair, the massive thermal Széchenyi Baths and the striking Vajdahunyad Castle, a complex of different architectural styles found in Hungary, which had initially appeared in a temporary form during the Millenary Celebrations of 1896. As today, in 1919 part of the complex housed the Hungarian Museum of Agriculture. According

13. For the recollections of Wessely and Hollós, see Petrák (1978), pp. 251 and 511.
14. Stróbl (2003), p. 171.
15. Kassák (1983), p. 575.
16. For Pór's recollections see Kende & Sipos (1989), p. 119.

to *Népszava*, the façade of the museum was decorated with a big picture representing 'proletarian agriculture'.

Around the lake in front of the Vajdahunyad Castle Marx's name appeared in huge red letters and rising from the water there were various artistic creations providing a picturesque spectacle. Using the present tense, though writing much later, Lajos Kassák thought it was a 'kitschy, sentimental hodgepodge, but today these monsters advertise the predominance of the people's power and of justice'.[17]

Another of the large buildings in the City Park was the Iparcsarnok (Trade Hall). Constructed in 1885, this was a huge edifice which housed major exhibitions. It stood not far from the Vajdahunyad Castle and there was an open space in front, suitable for large gatherings and speechifying. Many of the marchers headed there on 1 May 1919.

In front of the Trade Hall there were statues of Lenin and Engels, and the façade was draped in red with allegorical images and slogans galore: 'Workers of the world unite! … Long live the proletarian dictatorship! … Long live Lenin, the leader of the world proletariat!' One text was more than a simple slogan and tried to express a whole world view: 'The carved saints have brought more misery to the world than the living.—What human beings don't build is not theirs.—The more essential the work, the more respected the worker.—The revolutionary people is like melted metal, it purifies itself. Long live the communist world revolution! Long live the communist 1st May! Whoever doesn't struggle with us, we oppose.—Let the bourgeoisie tremble at the communist world revolution!'[18]

The last phrase echoes the final paragraph of *The Communist Manifesto* and though it omits to add what followed, namely the well-known slogan about proletarians having nothing to lose but their chains and having a world to win, it seems quite natural and understandable, that in the context of the 1919 Soviet Republic the famous text of Marx and Engels should have been quoted in that way.

But what of quoting Trotsky? Given the history of the Stalin-Trotsky rift and all its practical and theoretical implications, it is easy to forget today that there was a period when Leon Trotsky was highly regarded by revolutionaries who looked to the Bolshevik experience for inspiration. So it shouldn't be surprising that on 1 May 1919 one of the prominent members of the Revolutionary Soviet Government, the Commissar for Internal Affairs Jenő Landler, himself a left-leaning Social Democrat, quoted Trotsky in a rousing speech delivered in front of the Trade Hall. His words were reported by the newspaper *Vörös Újság* on 3 May:

17. Kassák (1983), p. 575.
18. Quoted in *Népszava* and *Vörös Újság*, 3 May 1919.

> Comrades! As Trotsky said: 'For the proletariat to conquer power and be able to hold on to it doesn't depend on how many troops or guns there are, but whether the proletariat perceives how enormous, great and sacred is the cause for which it might have to make a sacrifice.'[19]

Landler was prepared not only to point to examples from Russia but also to put Budapest and its workers on an equal level with Moscow and its proletariat:

> Today the significance of Budapest in world terms is roughly the same as it formerly was for Moscow. Today the whole of Europe is looking at us. Today the fate of the European working class lies in the hands of the Budapest proletariat. Let this proletariat show an example. Let it show that it has self-consciousness and a revolutionary spirit. Let it give an example to the world and then the Budapest proletariat will fulfil the obligation of its great world-historical duty.

Mariska Gárdos would recall that the Barocaldi Circus in the park was also nicely decorated. A tunnel-like tent with red flowers and green foliage formed the entrance and there were inventive plaques, inscriptions, statues and paintings. A huge black catafalque was inscribed with large lettering: 'Here lies capitalism. May it rest in eternal peace!' A lion was lying on top, as if wanting to prevent capitalism from rising from the dead. In its mouth there was a white sign with red letters reading: 'There is no resurrection!'

Gárdos, at the time a reporter for *Vörös Újság*, was due to give a speech in the circus. She was met at the entrance by the 'comrade stewards' who introduced her to the circus director, 'Monsieur Barocaldi' (actually an Italian). As she began her speech she heard the Monsieur whispering loudly to his business manager sitting next to him in the unmistakable accent of Budapest's Francis Town district: 'Jesus, what a voice this woman's got!'

'I didn't have time,' says Gárdos, 'to pay further attention to the conversation, since I had to continue with my celebratory speech. But I understood that the circus director was surprised by the strength of my voice, given my appearance, since at the time my weight in kilos was not much more than the number of my years, namely 34.'[20]

Elsewhere in the park attempts were made to provide some entertainment. For example, there were plans to erect a stage in the playground

---

19. This wasn't a totally isolated incident. For example, the 26 June 1919 issue of *Népszava* carried an advertisement for new publications. One of them was Trotsky's *Work, Discipline and Order*.
20. Gárdos (1964), p. 49.

area behind the Vajdahunyad Castle where variety and cabaret acts would take place to amuse the crowds. Artists from the Royal Orpheum and the Municipal Cabaret were scheduled to appear, though as if to emphasise that politics would never be far away, *Vörös Újság* pointed out in its 27 April issue, that between the acts there would be political speakers making propaganda.

An awful lot had been done to make May Day in Budapest something special. What is remarkable is that so much had been organised in so short a time. By 1 May the Council Republic had been established for only six weeks. Today the type of celebrations organised for May Day would be expected to take much longer to prepare, perhaps even up to a year, if not more. How did they manage it? Clearly enthusiasm was an important element. People were swept along by the feeling that perhaps a new world really was being created. The enthusiastic use of street art as political propaganda echoed developments in Russia, but in some ways it prefigured the latter's highly organised agit-prop art, since in 1919 Russia was still embroiled in a civil war.

Yet enthusiasm alone cannot explain the amazing feat of preparation that lay behind the May Day events. There was also planning, strict organisation and, presumably, a degree of coercion. It was perhaps significant that in early April the person put in charge of overseeing the preparations for 1 May was Tibor Szamuely, someone not usually associated with cultural matters. In fact Szamuely is usually remembered as one of the 'hard men' of the Council Republic.[21] However, he did have knowledge of artistic matters, partly because his wife, Jolán Szilágyi, was an artist, and partly because a number of his official commissions in 1919 had a cultural connection.

Szamuely gave an interview to *Fáklya* (Torch), the official paper of the Commissariat of Education and Culture, which was published on 20 April under the heading 'Cultural Propaganda in the Red Army'. At that point Szamuely was in charge of such propaganda. In the interview he asserts that military organisation includes leafleting to distribute information and propaganda, the use of libraries, films and images, and he points out that companies of actors were being formed to give theatre performances at the front and in the rear.

---

21. See the section on dictatorship and terror in Chapter 11. Before the First World War Szamuely worked as a political journalist and was associated with the Social Democratic Party. During the war he fell into Russian captivity. Like Béla Kun, he agitated among Hungarian prisoners in support of the Bolsheviks. He returned to Hungary in early January 1919 and joined the Communist Party and the staff of its *Vöros Újság*. The following month, when Kun and others were arrested, Szamuely, who remained free, became a leading member of the Party, which now operated for a while in an underground fashion.

Szamuely was clearly a busy man. When the interview was published, in addition to his duties in connection with the army, he was already the chief organiser of the 1 May celebrations, one of the heads of the central housing committee and (from the previous day, according to the newspaper) in charge of dealing with issues concerning war invalids.

In principle, responsibility for the 1 May events devolved down to others. Thus the noted poster artist Mihály Bíró was officially appointed to head the preparations in relation to sculpture, architecture and painting. However, in practice that wouldn't have stopped Szamuely from intervening in artistic matters, as the following rather amusing anecdote recalled by Bertalan Pór indicates.

Pór relates how Tibor Szamuely once telephoned him to say a poster was needed to portray the following themes: 1. The land belongs to those who till it! 2. The factory belongs to those who work in it! 3. The power belongs to those who struggle for it! Work and Struggle! Pór told Szamuely that as a member of the artists' directory he was fully occupied and didn't have the time, to which the latter replied that it was a very important matter and that he had to have the placard by the following morning, so he should go home and make it.

'I went home and did it,' says Pór, adding that for someone like Szamuely it was absolutely normal to dictate the theme for an artist.[22]

In her memoirs, published in 1966, Jolán Szilágyi recalls that Szamuely often visited the Fészek Club, a popular haunt of artists, writers and journalists. He came home one evening and told her: 'I talked with your artist friends and criticised them for not painting pictures with revolutionary themes.' The artist Ödön Márffy apparently responded: 'We've already made our special revolution.' Szamuely laughed, she says.[23]

Film-makers were also getting geared up for 1 May. The 26 April issue of *Vörös Film* (Red Film) enthusiastically described how the documentary newsreel workers were preparing to record for posterity Budapest's first May Day celebration under the proletarian dictatorship. All available camera operators would be stationed to capture the atmosphere on Andrássy Avenue, in front of the Millennium Monument and elsewhere in the city. Others would be following events from moving vehicles. It was expected that two thousand metres of film would be used to record the events, after

---

22. Bertalan Pór—reminiscences; manuscript in the PTI Archives, PIL 867.f. (11), p. 114, p. 1. Reproduced in: Kende & Sipos (1989), pp. 118–21.

23. Szilágyi (1966), pp. 79–80. Márffy had been a member of The Eight, a group of influential avant-garde artists active prior to 1918.

which the compiled documentary would be shown throughout the week in the six largest cinemas of Budapest.[24]

As 1 May approached, the word went out to the general public regarding what to do and what to expect. Even concerning trivial matters, a degree of implied coercion is evident. A 25 April decree declared that all flags in Budapest, with the exception of those that were purely red or black, had to be surrendered within 24 hours to a specified flag collection point. Compensation—'in so far as it is necessary', the decree stressed—would be given. People surrendering flags with undesirable colours could receive a red flag in exchange.[25] An awful lot of red flags were produced for the May Day celebrations, so perhaps it is understandable that the decree was issued by the People's Commissariat for Social Production.

Another decree, this time from the Revolutionary Governing Council (in effect the new government since 21 March) and dated 29 April, urged citizens to put red carpets on balconies and hang red drapery on windows. Women intending to join the May Day march were encouraged to wear a red dress or hat. People were told to stick to the official routes and obey whatever orders were given. There would be first aid centres marked with a green flag and places where drinking water would be available, though all participants were urged to take some food and drink with them. Private vehicles would be banned after 8 a.m. and trams (some of which were decorated with images and slogans) would only be running in the early morning and evening. At the various meeting places only the officially appointed speakers would be allowed to make propaganda. Finally and somewhat ominously, the decree warned that anyone disturbing the peace would find themselves arraigned before a revolutionary tribunal.

Although Andrássy Avenue and the City Park were focal points during the 1919 May Day celebrations, they were by no means the only places to receive festive decoration and to attract large crowds. For years the large square in front of Hungary's massive parliament building (today called Kossuth Lajos Square) had been a traditional place of protest for the labour movement. The struggle for the right to vote, including female suffrage, was a hallmark of Hungarian labour politics in the pre-1914 era and the big square in front of the parliament building was the scene of many demon-

24. For more about the newsreels and what was actually filmed on May Day, see Chapter 6.

25. Flags with the national colours (red, white and green) or depicting the Hungarian crown or other, previously official insignia would have fallen into the 'undesirable' category.

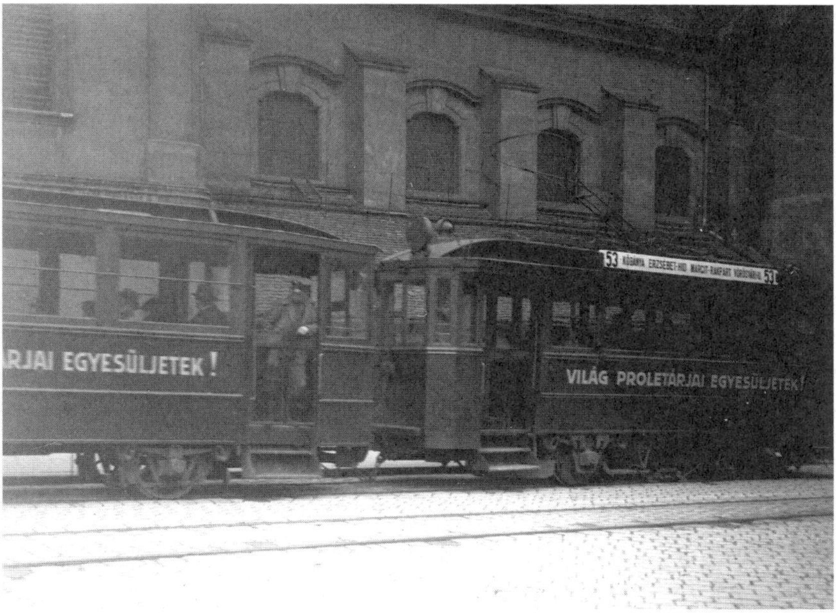

Figure 2.2 The texts on this tram quote the famous slogan: 'Workers of the World Unite!'

Photo: FORTEPAN/Frigyes Schoch

strations as the Social Democrats and their allies persistently agitated for universal suffrage and the secret ballot. The square was also the scene of several mass rallies at the end of the First World War, in particular on 16 November 1918 when Hungary's independence from the Habsburgs was proclaimed and the country was declared a republic. Thus on 1 May 1919, 'the first free May Day', as it was called, it was no wonder that the area around parliament received some special treatment.

There were busts of Lenin and Karl Liebknecht and reliefs of Sándor Petőfi and György Dózsa. Petőfi was a radical poet who played a prominent part in Hungary's 1848 anti-Habsburg revolt. He was to become what could be described as Hungary's 'national poet', yet he could be authentically interpreted as a 'leftist' due to his strong internationalism and support for the common people. Dózsa was a soldier of the border fortresses in southern Hungary who became a leader of a peasants' revolt in 1514, 'the most bloody and ferocious rural revolt' Hungary has ever experienced, according to historian János Bak.[26]

Sándor Petőfi had once written that György Dózsa was the 'most glorious man in Hungarian history', saying that he hoped that one day a statue

26. János Bak, 'The Late Medieval Period, 1382–1526'. In: Sugar et al. (1994), p. 78.

would be erected to the peasant leader, modestly adding 'perhaps mine will be next to it'.[27] A relief, especially a temporary one put in place for May Day 1919, is not the same as a permanent statue—but what a prescient idea.

There was a richly decorated platform in the square for afternoon performances, with many of the city's well-known actors taking part. Scheduled for 3 p.m. during the celebrations was the unveiling of János Istók's statue *Munka* (Labour). *Az Est* reported that there were 5,000 people present.

Highlighting labour and the working class—as opposed to what were seen as the antics of the bourgeois representatives who had hitherto occupied parliament—was echoed on the south side of the building, where a huge equestrian statue of Count Gyula Andrássy, a former prime minister of Hungary and foreign minister of the Austro-Hungarian Dual Monarchy, was entirely covered by a structure resembling a Greek temple. Designated the 'House of Work'—presumably as a counter-point to the Houses of Parliament nearby—the edifice was designed by Zoltán Bálint and Lajos Jámbor, two noted, early 20th-century Hungarian Art Nouveau architects, and featured allegorical images by graphic artists Géza Faragó and Andor Székely. A slogan proclaimed 'All Glory to Labour!'

At each end of the structure there were copies of a statue depicting a soldier marching forward, one hand balancing a rifle on his shoulder, the other hand raised in the air. They were the work of Zsigmond Kisfaludi Strobl and illustrate that not all the statues and busts displayed prominently around the city had been specially commissioned for the May Day celebrations, since the soldier had been modelled well before the Council Republic was established in March 1919.

In his memoirs, *Emberek és szobrok* (People and Statues), Kisfaludi Strobl recalls an amusing story about the origin of the 'Chrysanthemum Soldier', as his statue was called—the reference being to Hungary's revolutionary upheaval in late October 1918 when mutinous soldiers wore a white chrysanthemum in their caps.

During that upheaval Kisfaludi Strobl encountered a group of soldiers not far from Budapest's Eastern Railway Station who were singing and shouting slogans.

> 'Come to my place and I'll make a statue of you,' he said to one of them.
> 'What on earth for?' was the response.
> 'I've got some pálinka,' the sculptor said.
> 'Then I'm coming!' replied the soldier.[28]

---

27. László Deme, *The Radical Left in the Hungarian Revolution of 1848*. Boulder, East European Quarterly, 1976, p. 12.
28. Kisfaludi Strobl (1969), p. 68. Pálinka is Hungary's fiery fruit brandy.

Kisfaludi Strobl remarks that May Day 1919 produced a lot of work for sculptors.[29] He says he made three copies of his 'Chrysanthemum Soldier' and he also participated in the celebrations on the day. Two of his copies stood by the specially constructed 'House of Work' near parliament. The third was placed by the entrance to the tunnel running under Castle Hill. *Népszava* referred to that one as a 'Red Soldier', meaning a member of the Soviet Republic's recently formed Red Army. As indicated above, this was a mistake—deliberate or otherwise.

The entrance to the Castle Hill tunnel was also decorated with the huge depiction of a red, naked muscular figure wielding a large hammer. The latter was based on a well-known image created by the poster artist Mihály Bíró. It had often appeared in the publications and on the posters and placards of the Social Democrats, and had assumed almost iconic status as an emblem of the Hungarian labour movement.

In Kossuth Lajos Street and Kígyó (today Ferenciek) Square in Pest there were six busts on columns. Lenin and Liebknecht were among those represented. A triumphal gateway had been formed at the side of the square nearest Elizabeth Bridge—itself full of flags with its columns covered in red. There were also two of those ubiquitous red globes, perched on top of structures erected to hide two statues which had obviously lost their appeal in 1919. One was of Péter Pázmány, a seventeenth-century Catholic archbishop, while the other depicted István Werbőczy (c 1458–1561), a jurist and statesman who drew up the so-called *Tripartitum*, a codification of customary law which entrenched the privileges of lesser nobles and, with harsh laws, kept commoners in a state of disenfranchisement for centuries.

In Deák Square, one of the major junctions of central Pest, yet another statue was completely covered. This one had only been there since 1915 and was in fact Budapest's earliest large-scale, First World War-related monument. The work of sculptor Ferenc Sidló, it took the form of a medieval knight mounted on a horse, lance in hand. Carved from wood, it was covered with bronze 'leaves' nailed to the structure, bearing the names of those who had donated funds to charities helping the war wounded. Officially entitled the 'Statue of National Generosity', it was also known as the 'Statue of Victory'.

For May Day 1919 the statue was covered with a temple-like structure in front of which was a raised tribune. There were flaming torches and rev-

29. In her 1981 study (p. 623), art historian Nóra Aradi makes the following interesting observation: 'The majority of sculptors participating in the decoration of Budapest for 1 May ... chose to follow the traditions of heroic monuments or portraits, and this style was employed for the figures of revolutionaries, too.' In contrast, much of the visual imagery on posters was rather more avant-garde.

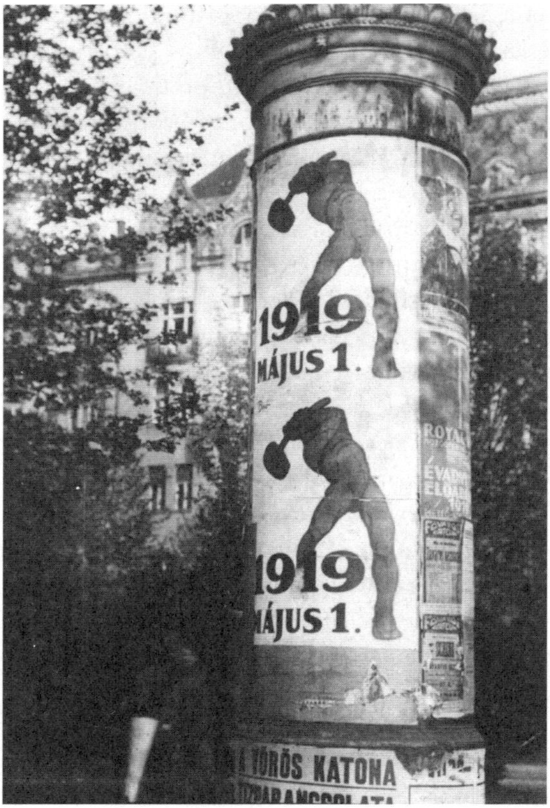

Figure 2.3 Images of the hammer-wielding figure appeared countless times in 1919.

Photo: FORTEPAN/László Péchy

olutionary images, as well as busts of Ervin Szabó and Lenin. As noted in the previous chapter, Szabó was a leading theorist of the Social Democratic Party, albeit a rather interestingly unorthodox one in that he aimed to unite Marxism and anarcho-syndicalism.

Ervin Szabó had opposed participation in the First World War, as Lenin had in Russia, which presumably made him an attractive figure for the commissars in 1919, but it is intriguing to speculate whether, given his interest in anarchism and libertarian socialism, he would have supported them had he still been alive during that year. Ilona Duczynska, who had got to know him well during the war, thought not. 'I cannot imagine him participating in the 1919 Hungarian Republic of Soviets,' she would later recall.[30] Yet in 1919 Hungary's Bolsheviks seemed to have no problem with

30. Quoted in McRobbie (2006), p. 69.

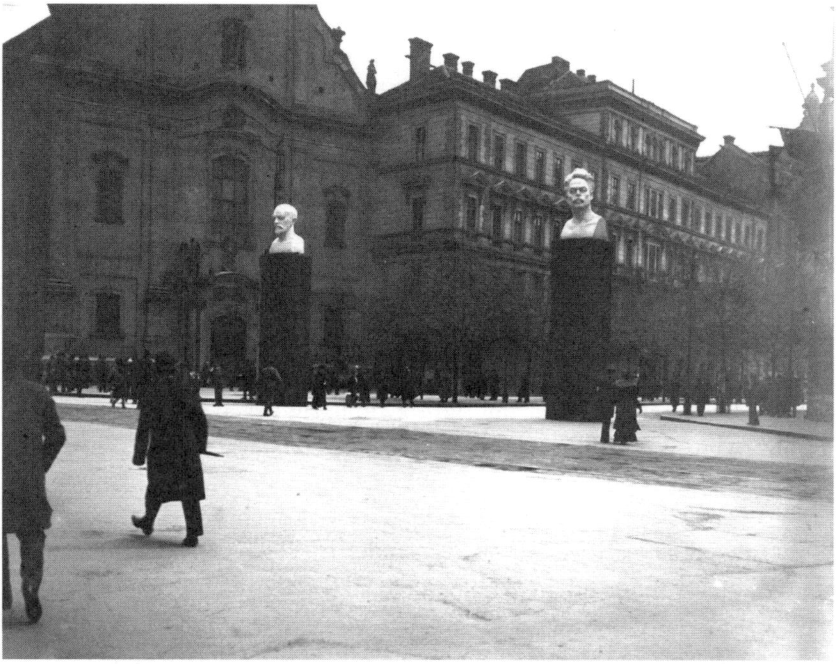

Figure 2.4 Busts of Lenin and Liebknecht in what is today Ferenciek Square. The May Day events celebrated the hoped-for dawn of universal equality, but it was clear that some people were deemed worthy of being placed on a very high pedestal.

Photo: FORTEPAN/Frigyes Schoch

him—perhaps reflecting the practice whereby dead 'heroes' can be much more easily appropriated and manipulated than the living.

While much activity on May Day 1919 in Budapest was concentrated on the Pest side of the city, particularly along Andrássy Avenue and in the City Park, there were also major events across the river, on the Buda side of the Danube. One of the focal points there was the large park area called Vérmező, or Field of Blood, which lies below Castle Hill on its west side. The name refers to the execution here in 1795 of the so-called Hungarian Jacobins. Led by Ignác Martinovics, they were a group of radicals inspired by the French Revolution and its ideals.

On 1 May 1919 a huge symbolic sarcophagus was erected in the park bearing the name 'Martinovics'. On each side there were platforms for speakers and throughout the park there were other stages for performances, shows and games. The Field of Blood was designated as a gathering point for workers on the Buda side. As *Népszava* over-enthusiastically reported, the 'entire Buda-side working people gathered here'. Archive film shows that in the course of the day different groups of people, some with their own bands, marched together through the park in formation. Inevitably, there was also a red column with a bust of Lenin.

On Gellért Hill the statue of St. Gellért, which stands overlooking the Buda end of Elizabeth Bridge, was covered in red and yellow, while the curved colonnade behind the statue was decorated with red drapery. Below, just above street level, there was a huge allegorical picture under the inscription 'Work and Paradise shall be Yours'. The image depicted a worker with a hammer wearing a Phrygian cap, a woman and children all proceeding towards an idyllic landscape, where there was a bearded figure reading under a big tree.[31] To the left there was a naked male figure, a fiery sword in his hand, while on the right a similarly naked male figure with flaming sword was striking down the figure of a bourgeois fleeing with a bag of money.

In his 1999 essay, Boldizsár Vörös suggests that the bearded figure might be interpreted as Karl Marx, possibly under the Tree of Knowledge, and that the intended meaning of the covered statue above and the allegorical image below was clear—don't expect happiness or Paradise to come from either the heavens or the saints, but produce it for yourselves with work and study, and—as the two sword-wielding figures suggest—if necessary, with armed struggle as well.[32]

A location for some special events on 1 May 1919 was Margaret Island, which lies on the Danube just to the north of Margaret Bridge. Over the centuries preceding 1919 the island had fulfilled a variety of functions—a royal hunting ground, a home for religious orders and an exclusive playground for the wealthy. The municipality bought the island in 1908 and placed it under the management of the Budapest Council of Public Works. Visitors were charged an entrance fee, which doubled on Sundays and holidays. Then during the Soviet Republic the island was declared a free public park, open to all. For May Day Margaret Island was given a special function—it became a children's paradise. Lots of fun activities were arranged, including races, games and competitions. There were also shows, clowns, musical performances and storytelling. A ballet group from the Opera House came to provide entertainment. Children were brought in droves for the day. As they entered the island they were greeted by a large

---

31. The red Phrygian cap was a symbol of liberty during the French Revolution. Images of the cap often appeared in the iconography of 1919. Some sources say that on 1 May a red cap covered the Hungarian crown at the top of the cupola of the Royal Palace on Castle Hill. The palace itself, like many other buildings, was decorated in red.
32. See the website listing in the bibliography—Vörös (1999).

statue of the 'Proletarian Mother', decorated with red carnations. Behind it a huge triumphal gateway had been constructed bearing the inscription: 'Children, the future is yours!' *Vörös Újság* would estimate that over 10,000 children attended the Margaret Island events.

Apart from the fun and games, no doubt a major attraction was the food provided. Bread rolls, sweets and cakes were distributed free of charge. 'Pastry cakes for children,' announced *Népszava* in its 1 May edition. 'Today the people's commissariat for public supply will distribute 1200 kilos of dry almond pastries and 10,000 pastry cakes among children through the good offices of the Friends of Children Association.' Some reports referred to the association as the 'Friends of Proletarian Children'. Either way, archive film shows kids stuffing themselves with glee. Some of the children are scruffily dressed; others appear to be wearing their Sunday best.

The ever-present Mariska Gárdos made an appearance as a speaker at Margaret Island on top of her many other commitments during the day. 'What did I say to the young people on the island?' she asks in her memoirs published over half a century later. First of all, she recalls, she spoke about the world of the upper classes who had appropriated the island for themselves alone; how well-to-do children, nannies speaking foreign languages and well-dressed ladies and gentlemen had made the island their realm, a place where the proletariat couldn't enter. But now, she told her young listeners, the beauty of the island was all theirs. She told them they had the right to enjoy all the beauties of life, not just the island. What was needed was to study and work with all one's heart and soul for proletarian honour.

It started to rain, slowly at first but then there was a downpour. 'But this didn't cool the burning enthusiasm of the young people one bit,' she remembers. 'The crowd didn't thin out. Who would pay attention to such an insignificant thing at that time!'[33]

The mainly light-hearted activities on the island that day were well organised and had good intentions, reflecting one of the most positive aspects of the short-lived Soviet Republic, namely the attention paid to improving children's welfare.

Yet entertainment, games and competitions weren't designated only for the children who went to Margaret Island. For example, in the early morning on Andrássy Avenue, before any marchers had appeared, there were running races for adults in which more than 30 groups of ten participated. Apart from sports events in different parts of the city there was also

33. Gárdos (1964), p. 49.

much general merry-making throughout the day, though no alcohol was on sale. It all culminated in an evening fireworks display.

Needless to say, not everyone was pleased with the 'red' events of 1 May. The writer Cécile Tormay was one who wasn't, though that's not surprising given her ultra-conservative political views.

'The new saviours of the world promised the millennium for this day,' she wrote in her memoir *An Outlaw's Diary*.

> On a blood-soaked land the blood-maddened masses are streaming towards the final battle which is to bring them an utterly unattainable victory. Red flags unfurled in a storm of blood are floating under a sky painted red by incendiary fires. ... Moscow has sent its propaganda gold ...
>
> *Panem et circenses!* There is no bread, the capital faints for lack of food, so let there be a circus for the people. The last rags are falling from the backs of the destitute millions, so let the town be garbed in red ... even the electric trams have been painted blood-red ... red columns, red flagstaffs and flags, wreaths, five-pointed stars. A sickening red disguise over the deadly pallor of the Hungarian capital.[34]

Tormay gives some detailed descriptions of what different parts of Budapest looked like on 1 May, but her report has to be read with a certain scepticism, if only because—as she herself says—she wasn't in Budapest on May Day. Nevertheless, her disgust at the events comes through quite clearly and no doubt there were many others who shared her views, even her blatant anti-Semitism, presumably fuelled by the fact that many of the Soviet Republic leaders were of Jewish descent.

'The demon of the Revolution is not an individual, not a party, but a race among the races' are the words she uses to introduce a section of her book which can only be described as a demonic, anti-Jewish diatribe.[35]

At the same time there were some left-wing activists who didn't look at everything through rose-tinted spectacles, and in this sense Lajos Kassák's reflections are interesting:

> Maybe this day really was a turning point. The day before yesterday it seemed the system couldn't be saved from collapsing and now the fires of hope are burning bright. But maybe all this is just a delusion. The sound

34. Tormay (1923), pp. 108–9.
35. Ibid, p. 59. In 2012 a bust of Cécile Tormay was unveiled in central Budapest, as was a memorial plaque on a building where she used to live.

> of rejoicing has drowned out the cannon thunder of opposition and all the red decoration has hidden the shades of bitterness and destitution.[36]

The difficulties that Kassák highlights were obvious to the authorities, too, at least in the sense that they acknowledged the overwhelming problems caused by the military situation. Even on 1 May, *Fáklya*, the official mouthpiece of the cultural commissariat, devoted a full two-thirds of its front page to a report under the heading 'Atmosphere at the Front', and page one of its next issue gave more prominence to the Revolutionary Governing Council's mobilisation decree than to the May Day events.

Despite all the problems, they called it 'the first free May Day', meaning that this was the first time the traditional workers' celebration on 1 May in Budapest was held at a time perceived to be one of workers' power. Certainly those in power in May 1919 believed they were ruling on behalf of, and in the interest of the proletariat, but whether they actually were and whether the proletariat was actually in power (as opposed to a coalition of two political parties being in power) is open to question, and thus the concept of 'the first free May Day' is debateable. What is a fact, however, is that the 1919 events were the last May Day celebrations in Budapest for a long time.[37]

---

36. Kassák (1983), p. 576.
37. To a large extent due to the reaction which set in after 1919, there was no May Day demonstration until 1930. That took place amidst increasing militancy in response to the unfolding world economic crisis and its effects on Hungary. It prefigured a huge demonstration along Andrássy Avenue and in the City Park on 1 September 1930, which was the biggest labour movement protest to take place in Hungary during the 1920s and 1930s, though its background and circumstances were quite different from what had happened in 1919. See Bob Dent, *Hungary 1930 and the Forgotten History of a Mass Protest*. Pontypool, Merlin Press, 2012.

3
Poster Power

During the 1919 Hungarian Soviet Republic, the poster functioned as the propaganda means par excellence. Its striking power of expression and exhortation involving red, with figures in dramatic poses was recognised as being worth more than a thousand words. Revolutionary placards were everywhere, on almost every wall of almost every street. The quantity is difficult to imagine today. A large proportion were in colour, and red certainly dominated. Each had a clear message to convey and pictorially was simply presented. Some of Hungary's leading painters and graphic artists, including Bertalan Pór, Mihály Bíró, Róbert Berény, József Nemes Lampérth and Marcell Vértes contributed to this art.

The monumental Hungarian poster art of 1919 has arguably attracted more attention outside Hungary than any other artistic manifestation of the Soviet Republic.[1] No wonder—the striking posters with minimal text literally speak for themselves. They can be understood without having to acquire much knowledge of the Hungarian language, the lack of which has prevented widespread attention being paid to other aspects of 1919 in Hungary on the part of many scholars. Be that as it may, Hungarian political posters of 1919, in terms of images and intention, can be justifiably compared to the much more well-known early Soviet poster art.

In Hungary, the radical cultural leftist and activist Lajos Kassák had identified some specific characteristics of the poster even well before the Soviet Republic was declared, and even before the 1917 Russian Revolution.

> The good poster is always borne in the spirit of radicalism—its creator wishes to make it break through a sluggish mass or a hostile current—and for this reason it leaps on to stage as an absolute force on its own, and never as part of a mass simply to record something. By its very nature it has the properties of an agitator, but in its essence it is never forced within limits ... The new painter is a moral individual, full of faith and desire for unity! And his pictures are weapons of war![2]

---

1. For example, in 2011 the Museum of Modern Art in New York staged a six-month exhibition entitled *Seeing Red: Hungarian Revolutionary Posters, 1919*. See also Mansbach (1991), pp. 57–63.

2. Lajos Kassák, 'A plakát és az új festészet' (The Poster and the New Painting), *MA*, vol 1, no 1, November 1916. English translation from Willett et al. (1980), pp. 112–13.

Elsewhere in Europe the significance of the poster, the widespread use of which had been facilitated by the development of lithographic techniques, had also been recognised along with its social and even political implications. For example, in 1897 the prominent French art critic Roger Marx declared:

> Posters are understood and appreciated by everyone, irrespective of age; they appeal to the whole populace ... The poster has replaced, in the street, the decorations previously to be found on the exterior walls of palaces, and on the walls and ceilings of cloisters and churches. The poster is mobile, ephemeral art, just what is needed during a period when people are avid for popularization, hungry for change. The art of the poster is no less important and no less prestigious than the art of fresco ...[3]

In a similar manner, Anatole France once referred to the poster as the 'fresco of the poor'.[4]

In 1919, soon after arriving in Hungary, the American reporter Crystal Eastman was struck by the political images, particularly the recruiting posters, she encountered in the streets of Budapest.

> Next morning in Buda-Pesth [sic!] I found the newsstands, the pillars, the walls, every blank space, shouting with revolutionary posters. It seemed to me that Por [sic!] and the other Commissars of Propaganda, in the two short months of their work, had put the National Security League, the American Defense Society and all the other patriotic poster designers of America wholly in the shade. The revolutionary placards are all red, almost wholly one color. They are everywhere, on every wall of every street—enormous sheets many of them, some good drawings, some bad; very daring and simple; all emphatically modern. One is a great bold red figure running with a flag—'To Arms!' There is a soldier charging with a bayonet—'He who is not with us is against us!' 'Save the Proletariat,' 'Defend the Revolution,' 'Join the Red Guard!'– these are the phrases repeated again and again—but never a word about Hungary, never a note of nationalist appeal.[5]

---

3. Quoted by Claire Frèches-Thory in the catalogue of the exhibition *Toulouse-Lautrec* at the Hayward Gallery, London, 1991–92, p. 377. Published by the South Bank Centre.
4. Quoted by Zsuzsa Gonda in the catalogue of the exhibition *The World of Toulouse-Lautrec* at the Museum of Fine Arts, Budapest, 2014, p. 16. Published by the Museum of Fine Arts.
5. Crystal Eastman, 'In Communist Hungary', *The Liberator*, Vol. 2, No. 8, August, 1919, p. 9.

Eastman's observation about the lack of nationalist appeal is interesting and, as will be seen, perhaps valid in terms of the posters themselves, their images and texts. What is more debatable is to what extent the recruiting efforts implicitly, albeit perhaps subconsciously, did actually appeal to a nationalist sentiment or—expressed in another way—to what extent, irrespective of the intention, was the genuine and widespread response on the part of different social segments of Hungarian society based on national sentiment.

Posters produced with the aim of recruiting for, or urging support for the Red Army were among the most striking and memorable, and they have often been reproduced in works about the Hungarian Council Republic. In the sense of aim and visual impact, they are the equivalent of the famous First World War varieties of Alfred Leete's classic British poster *Your Country Needs You*, featuring a pointing Lord Kitchener, or Dmitry Moor's similarly classic 1920 recruiting poster of Russian Civil War times, *You: Have You Volunteered*? which features a Red Army soldier, pointing at and exhorting the viewer.

One of the most iconic recruiting posters of 1919 was Róbert Berény's *Fegyverbe! Fegyverbe!* (To Arms! To Arms!), which portrays the upper part of a sailor leaning forward, clearly striding from left to right with arms raised and outstretched, one behind, the other in front of him. In the fist of the latter, the sailor is clutching a large red streamer, or possibly the corner of a large red flag, which is floating in the air above him. The determined look on the sailor's face, his mouth wide open indicating he is shouting, and the centrally placed, repeated text in capital letters stresses the urgency of the message. The landscape format, the unusual cropping of the figure and the arms outstretched in different directions amplify the energetic feeling of movement, while the sailor's strong fists and rather unnaturally oversized arm muscles signify, optimistically, the implied might of the Council Republic.[6]

Revolutionary sailors played a central role in many events of the Russian Revolution and the same was true in Germany and Hungary during the political upheavals following the First World War. In Hungary the Revo-

6. Unless otherwise indicated, the posters described in this section can be found in Aradi & Győffy (1979) and Gábor (1959). The red sailor of Róbert Berény's poster lived on, so to say, years later. In 1969 a monumental bronze statue, sculpted by István Kiss and based on Berény's dynamic image, appeared by the side of Budapest's City Park, marking the fiftieth anniversary of the Soviet Republic. The massive statue remained there until the early 1990s, when it was removed along with many other political monuments erected during the post-1945 decades to the newly-created Statue Park by the south-west perimeter of the capital. One of the collection's largest items, it can still be seen there today.

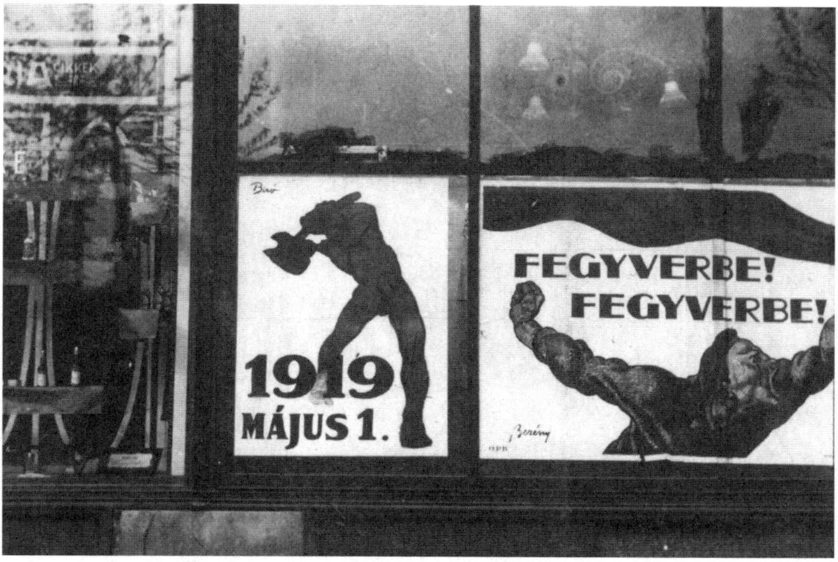

Figure 3.1 Mihály Bíró's 'Man with Hammer' and Róbert Berény's 'To Arms! To Arms!' were two of the most iconic posters of 1919.
Photo: FORTEPAN/László Péchy

lutionary Sailors' Brigade was one of the most combat-ready units of the Soviet Republic's armed forces.

Sailors feature prominently in Béla Uitz's poster bearing the slogan *Vörös katanák, előre!* (Red Soldiers, Forward!), though its pictorial composition, described by art historian Nóra Aradi as 'Constructivist-Expressionist', is rather different from Berény's work.[7] Four bulky sailors, stylized rifles on their shoulders dominate the foreground. They are marching in step to the right, though their legs appear somewhat out of proportion and at an angle which gives the appearance that they could almost be sitting. Each figure has a determined facial expression, though only one is looking forward, albeit slightly to the side. Two appear to be casting glances at each other, while the fourth is looking to the left, as if to survey the surrounding crowd. Behind the four figures there appears to be a mass of people, probably also marching sailors. Only their heads are visible and only one clearly so. That figure also has a determined expression and the face is the only one in the composition looking sternly ahead, directly at the viewer. Apart from the colour of the slogan, rendered with capital letters, red is not predominant in this image. There are just touches of red on the sailor's clothing. The overall impression projected is one of unity and steadfastness. There is no

7. Aradi & Győrffy (1979), p. 9.

over-optimism here, let alone triumphalism. The difficult military situation the Soviet Republic found itself in is clearly manifest.

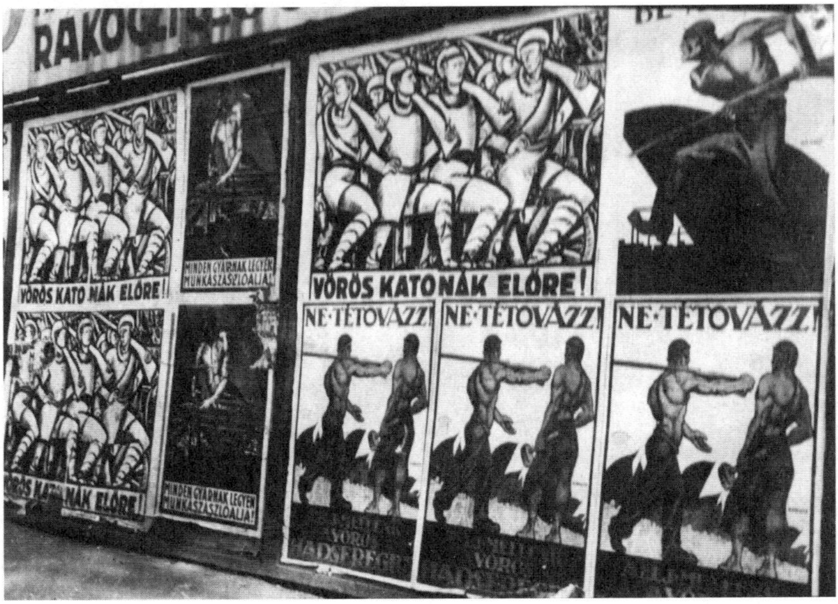

Figure 3.2 Citizens were bombarded with images and slogans. Dominant here are three copies of Béla Uitz's 'Red Soldiers, Forward!' Two posters towards the left bear the slogan 'Let every factory have its own worker's battalion!' Three at the bottom declare: 'Don't hesitate!' and 'Stand by us in the Red Army!' while much of Ödön Dankó's 'Join the Red Army!' can be seen at the top on the right.

Photo: FORTEPAN/László Péchy

Exactly the same slogan, 'Red Soldiers, Forward!', appears at the top of a poster by János Tábor. Here red is definitely predominant. The text, in red capitals, and the fabric of a massive, unrealistically large red flag dominate the upper space, while the lower part features two thick-limbed, naked figures, rendered in dark green, striding to the left, their mouths wide open, as if they are shouting the slogan. Indeed, here the slogan is given in quotation marks. One figure is gripping the flagpole; the other holds a weapon. Below them are more weapons and flags, all pointing to the left. In the distance there are factory buildings with tall chimneys, signifying the proletarian nature of the struggle.

Ödön Dankó's *Be a Vörös Hadseregbe!* (Join the Red Army!) also has red text and an oversized red flag prominently positioned, though in this case in the central space and behind a large, semi-naked figure striding to the left while clutching a fairly realistic-looking rifle with bayonet fixed. The facial expression is determined, angry almost, and here, too, the figure appears to be shouting. The muscular man portrayed is a blend of soldier and proletarian, but as if to emphasise the latter and stress the nature of the struggle, once again we see factories and smokestacks in the distance.

Another of Dankó's posters is even more emphatic in stressing the proletarian nature of the struggle. It features a similarly bare-chested man, behind whom is a large red flag and again below there are factories and smokestacks. The black lines of the emitted smoke are being blown horizontally to the right, in contrast with, although as if to emphasise, the movement of the figure who is positioning himself and about to swing some kind of bludgeon, or maybe it's the neck of a rifle, to the left in order to destroy a large pile of bags stuffed with coins and topped by a crown. The two parts of the slogan at the top, *Védd meg!* (Protect it!) occupy the upper corners of the image, while the lower text, again rendered in red and with capitals, reads: *A proletárok hatalmát* (The Power of the Proletariat).

Returning to the recruitment theme, a poster by Árpád Bardócz, who was known in the 1910s for his decorative commercial posters, also carries the slogan about joining the Red Army, but his image is quite different from those of Berény, Uitz and Dankó. Here the text at the bottom is in red and with capitals, but the central space is occupied by two youths shouting, calling out to a large mass of civilians portrayed in the distant background and sketched with indistinct detail. One of the youths is holding a pole with a mass of colourful flowers, ribbons and other adornments. There is also a red flag draped from it. It is clearly a maypole and similar poles can be seen above the heads of the crowd in the distance. The location of the scene could be Margaret Island or the City Park in Budapest, or indeed any other place where crowds gathered on May Day in 1919.

It was on 2 May 1919 when the Budapest Workers' Council proclaimed the slogan *Be a Vörös Hadseregbe!* (Join the Red Army!) and, as seen, the slogan was taken up by poster designers. Among those was Jolán Szilágyi, whose dynamic image of a red soldier holding a gun while actually crossing the entire globe may seem rather grandiose in concept, but it reflects the internationalist ideas of Hungary's Bolsheviks. Indeed, at one point the idea was for the Hungarian Red Army to break through its opponents' lines and link up with its Russian equivalent. However, that was not to be.

Another poster with a recruiting theme, by Jenő Erbits, shows one worker, a gun balanced on his shoulder, approaching another who stands motionless, a hammer in his left hand and an enquiring look on his face. The text at the top, in large red capitals proclaims: 'Don't hesitate!' Below the two figures the words read: 'Stand by us in the Red Army!' Echoing what was in reality a massive wave of volunteering by workers, in the background we see a huge crowd of people with red flags marching across the width of the poster. Most appear not yet to be in uniform.

The text of one recruiting poster, by the painters József Nemes Lampérth and János Kmetty, consisted simply of the exhortation *BE!* in large letters, though the meaning was obvious (Join!). The poster depicts a red flag-bearing man (another one with unnaturally large arm and shoulder muscles) who in this case is not rushing anywhere but leaning backwards, a look of anticipation and determined preparedness on his face. He is holding a sword, though its point is held downwards. With his large boots and the fact that he is shown standing above an undulating landscape implies this might be aimed at the country's peasants, who are being exhorted to join the Red Army and defend the land.

A recruiting poster by the equally renowned artist Bertalan Pór, a member of the Arts Directory in 1919, stands out among others. Here we return to the theme of armed sailors, but the small group of them with Cezanne-like figures, which dominates the left side of the space, does not give an entirely solid impression of strict unity of purpose, although they are all clearly moving off, apparently with some specific intention. However, they actually appear a little disoriented and are looking in different directions, one of them upwards at the red flag he is holding. Another, clutching a gun is looking back and up at what is in effect the central feature of the image, a female figure rising, almost floating above the sailors and pointing forwards over their heads. The image is slightly reminiscent of Delacroix's famous 1830 painting *Liberty Leading the People*, though Pór portrays a somewhat older-looking woman with a more concerned expression on her face, holding in her left arm a baby at her breast. Interestingly, the slogan at the bottom of the poster—'Forward for your wives and children!'—is not in red, but black, and is rendered in the form of handwriting not block capitals.

In parallel with explicitly recruiting posters, there were also others aimed at generating support among the population for the armed forces of the Soviet Republic. One, by an unknown artist, depicts a youthful soldier from behind, gun slung over his shoulder and haversack on his back, as if ready to depart for the front. His right arm is outstretched and his hand is on the shoulder of a solid-looking brawny worker standing rigidly and staring determinedly out of the poster at the viewer. The worker is standing behind an anvil and in his left hand he holds a hammer. In the background is one of those ubiquitous large red flags. The slogan in red at the bottom of the poster simply says: 'Proletarian, don't abandon the Council Republic!' Perhaps here there's a touch of the desperation which crept in after the Red Army began to suffer defeats.

One of the most unusual and therefore striking posters of 1919 is by Marcell Vértes, a graphic artist and illustrator who years later would become noted in the West, among his other roles, as a costume designer for films.

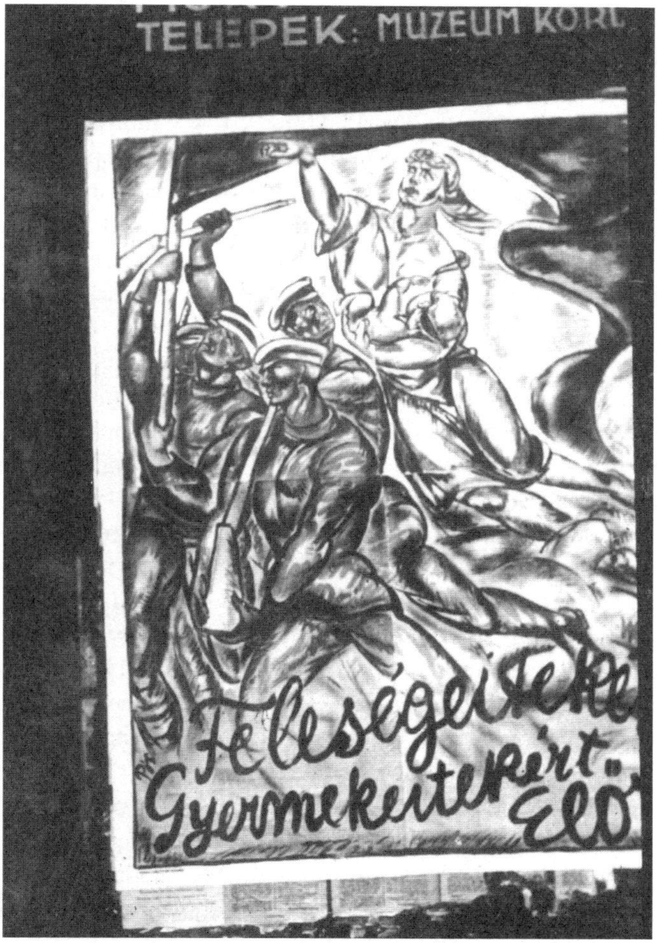

Figure 3.3 The female figure points the way—forward!
Photo: FORTEPAN/László Péchy

The poster depicts a young soldier in uniform apparently holding in his left hand a maypole, colourfully decorated with flowers, ribbons and a red flag. The soldier is motionless and appears to have just stepped out from behind the maypole, though we still can't see his full figure. In contrast with the flowers in his hat, the look on his face as he stares at the viewer, albeit steadfast, is rather melancholy. The simple text in red capitals to his side has few words: 'With me or against me'.

The propaganda art of 1919 was by no means confined to recruiting and related matters, though the volume of posters produced on that theme reflects the central importance of the issue at the time. There were also posters involving a general political theme and others which dealt with quite specific topics.

An example of general propaganda is Bertalan Pór's *Világ proletárjai egyesüljetek!* (Workers of the World Unite!), the famous slogan of the *Communist Manifesto*, which reflects the internationalist aspirations of the Council Republic. However, this is no prefiguration of Soviet-style Socialist Realism, it rather betrays a romantic element. Two naked, Cezanne-type figures, gracefully striding to the left, each bearing aloft a red flag with gentle folds, are looking not at the viewer or to the future, but directly at each other. In a modern interpretation, their poses and the clearly seen expression on the face of one figure, might suggest that they are gay lovers. Be that as it may, or may not be, the two figures are far from the traditional, muscular proletarian images encountered in so many other posters of the time. There is a combination here of a traditional slogan and traditional red flags with something much more avant-garde.

Another naked figure, albeit one more 'proletarian', featured on a poster aimed at promoting Hungary's May Day celebrations in 1919. The image was already well known in Hungary. According to Hungarian poster historian Katalin Bakos, Mihály Bíró's famous red *Man with Hammer*, which she describes as a mixture of Hercules and Vulcan, was published in early 1912 as a poster advertising *Népszava* (People's Voice), the newspaper of the Social Democratic Party. The massive figure wielding a hammer, dramatically representing the might of the proletariat in the class struggle, was set against a background of an enlarged front page of the paper from 1911.[8] The figure soon became a recognised emblem of the Party, its newspaper and publishing house, and eventually of the broader labour movement as a whole. The image was used again in 1913 with a similar mix—this time the background was the front page of *Népszava*'s 1 January edition.

Bíró's *Man with Hammer* appeared once more in 1914, though this time in chains, struggling with armed gendarmes. The *Népszava* title could be seen in the background, but the page was blurred. The idea was to protest against censorship and in favour of press freedom. Then in 1918, during the Chrysanthemum Revolution and beyond, it appeared widely again, as it did during the period of the Soviet Republic, particularly in connection with the May Day events. On that day, too, a number of temporary statues depicting Bíró's figure appeared in different locations of Budapest.

Nóra Aradi writes that the man with hammer image became internationally renowned. It was used on the cover of a 1922 strike pamphlet in China, and subsequently also appeared in Britain and Italy.[9]

---

8. Bakos (2007), p. 62.
9. Aradi (1974), p. 5. The image even appeared on the cover of the 1965 Penguin paperback edition of John Berger's novel *A Painter of Our Time*. However, perhaps that

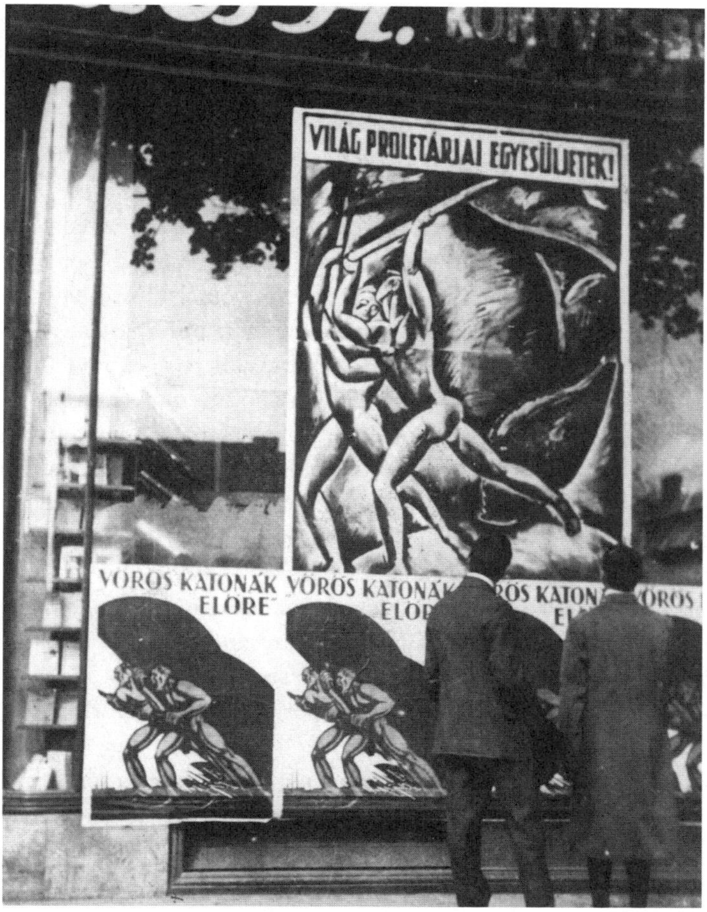

Figure 3.4 Two men appear to be examining Bertalan Pór's massive poster. The slogan at the top is the often repeated 'Workers of the World Unite!' The posters below show János Tábor's 'Red Soldiers, Forward!'

Photo: FORTEPAN/László Péchy

Some of the posters of 1919 were directed at the home front, particularly at emphasising the new relations of, and boosting of production. One dramatic poster by Imre Földes and Gusztáv Végh proclaimed: 'Prosperity springs from social production.' Above the slogan a factory worker stands by a large item of industrial equipment, which is operating at full speed, as indicated by the sparks emanating from it. The man is looking out of the window, gazing at a scene completely dominated by the colour red. The sky is red, a pleasant little house has a red roof, the lawn in front is

---

is not so surprising, since the book is about a Hungarian artist who had been forced to leave Hungary after the events of 1919.

red, sunflowers have red heads, and a woman, a red kerchief on her head, is sitting with two children, one in a red dress. All three are looking at a book with a red cover. This red colour overkill stands in sharp contrast to the factory interior, portrayed in monochrome, but the message is clear—work hard in the new conditions and your family will live a good, fruitful life.

Red also features prominently in one of János Tábor's posters. We see the back of a half-naked man, a red cap on his head and a red seed bag slung over his shoulder, striding across a field in the act of sowing. The red text reads: 'Proletarian! The field is already yours!' However, in reality the Hungarian Soviet regime did not follow its counterpart in Russia of instituting 'Land for the Peasants!' Agricultural collectives were established in some parts of the country, but there was no attempt to implement a policy of general land distribution. State ownership was preferred—not that very much could be accomplished, given that during the period of the Commune much of the country was a battlefield, as the Red Army fought against encroaching Romanian and Czech troops.

Another poster with an agricultural theme, the work of Ernő Barta, features a healthy-looking peasant woman standing in front of a cornfield. Her arms are spread and raised high, her palms are open. She is looking to one side, and her pose and facial expression seem to indicate she is calling people to join her. That would match the poster's slogan: 'Work ... because the bread is running low!'

Sometimes cultural progress became a poster theme, reflecting the importance the new political authorities attributed to raising the cultural level of ordinary Hungarians. Echoing the above-mentioned image of a woman and two children reading, a poster by István Azary-Prihoda featured a broad-shouldered worker, seated. His hammer is on the floor, its long handle resting against his leg. His shirtsleeves are rolled up and in his hands he holds an open book, which he is gazing at studiously. At his side, on tiptoe and with his head resting on one of the man's shoulders, a child is leaning over and also gazing down at the pages of the book. The text asserts that books are available from the house concierge in residential buildings, indicating that culture was for the workers, and was publicly and directly available.

Uplifting is a term which can be applied to many of the 1919 posters, though a more common characteristic is that they were exhortative, employing simple images and direct, easily understandable texts to encourage people to join or support the Red Army, to develop production and stand by the radical changes underway.

As already seen, in many cases red was the dominant, even overwhelming colour. That is not surprising, since by 1919 red had been associated with social revolt, rebellion and revolution for well over a century. The red flag appeared as a political symbol during the French Revolution and it reappeared time and again in periods of upheaval—during the Europe-wide revolts of 1848, at the time of the Paris Commune, during the 1905 Russian Revolution and again in 1917 in Russia. The song *The Red Flag* was adopted by workers' movements in Britain, Ireland and the US from the 1890s, and as noted above, in Hungary Mihály Bíró's red hammer-wielding figure had been an emblem of the labour movement since before the First World War. No wonder the colour red appeared again in 1918–1919, and no wonder the Hungarian capital was spectacularly decked out in red on 1 May 1919.

One very specific theme of propaganda poster art in 1919 concerned the prohibition of alcohol. This might seem surprising, yet the labour movement in Hungary, as elsewhere, had for many years included a vibrant segment of activists promoting a teetotal lifestyle. The well-worn slogan 'Drink is the curse of the working class' and its many variants were based on the perception that alcohol consumption led to impoverishment, degradation and ruin, and—politically speaking—diverted workers from the struggle to improve their condition. In short, alcoholism was seen an evil of capitalism, fuelling the oppression and exploitation of the working class.

The strength of this feeling in Hungary is illustrated by something that is perhaps even more surprising, namely that on 22 March 1919, the very day following the declaration of the Soviet Republic, the second decree adopted by the new Revolutionary Governing Council—after declaring martial law and introducing the death penalty for taking up arms against the new regime, and for theft and looting—involved a ban on alcohol. The serving and consumption of alcohol was forbidden. Anyone trading in the alcohol business would have their property confiscated and be subject to a large fine. Consumers of alcohol would also be fined and could find themselves liable to be imprisoned for up to one year.

These harsh measures were backed up by a propaganda campaign involving posters. For example, a dramatic image by Imre Földes with the slogan 'Every alcoholic drink leads to ruin!' depicted a horror-stricken woman holding a child and trying to pull back a stupefied, drunken worker, bottle in hand, from a railway track as a train approaches at full speed. A similar message was conveyed by Ferenc Lejava's 'Every Glass is Deadly Poison!' which showed a drunken man clutching a bottle and holding up a glass in another. A skeleton behind him is pouring something into the drunk's glass. The same artist produced another poster with the slogan 'Alcohol and Prostitution are the Murderers of Humanity!'

Another large poster consisting of text only in red and white letters, all in capitals, loudly proclaimed: 'Alcohol kills, stupefies and reduces you to destitution! Conscious workers, sensible women and rational thinking youth struggle against alcohol with all their might.'[10]

As with this example, not all the posters of 1919 bore pictorial images. Many were simply reproductions of texts, carrying proclamations of the Revolutionary Governing Council or decrees issued by various People's Commissariats and other bodies. Some functioned in a traditional manner, transmitting information to the public, such as theatre programmes or concert schedules, even if sometimes the message wasn't so 'traditional'. One, for example, announced that free education courses for people who were illiterate were being organised in Budapest's eighth district. Another text, referring to Budapest's many thermal and other baths which had been opened to the public, exhorted people to keep clean! 'The baths are yours!' it pronounced, urging people to use them.

By and large, the poster artists seemed happy enough to turn their skills into means of propaganda. Róbert Berény, for example, wrote to the People's Commissariat for Education and Culture on 10 May saying he would see to all tasks associated with being a member of the Arts Directory without any special remuneration.[11]

Needless to say, during the Council Republic the publication of posters was subject to censorship. This was not new for Hungary. There had been poster censorship prior to October 1918 and the Chrysanthemum Revolution. Then during the Károlyi regime there was no censorship, but it was reintroduced during the Soviet Republic.

At one point in 1919 Lajos Kassák was involved with censoring posters, which was rather odd since, as he himself admitted, he had always and in every way been an opponent of censorship. He claims he was given the task after having been persuaded by Zsigmond Kunfi, the People's Commissar for Education and Culture, to work for the cultural commissariat.[12] Whether Kassák could have refused the appointment is not clear, but he set about his task with energy and, apparently, enthusiasm, marking with a blue pencil the proposed posters which could be published and with a red

10. Munkácsi (1959), p. 16.

11. Szíj (1963), p. 121.

12. Kunfi was a key figure in Hungary's cultural world of 1919. A leading Social Democratic politician, before the war Kunfi edited the party's journal *Szocializmus* (Socialism) and wrote for its newspaper *Népszava* (People's Voice). He had been a grammar school teacher and had worked as a translator. As an intellectual, a university graduate with a degree and a doctorate, he was unusual among the SDP's mainly trade union party leaders. After the war, which he had opposed, he joined the Hungarian National Council and was a member of Mihály Károlyi's government. From January 1919 he was minister of education, a post which in practice if not exactly with the same name, he maintained after the Council Republic was formed in March.

one those which could not. (One might have thought that at the time red would have been the positive colour!)

Kassák says that most of the posters he rejected were insignificant from an artistic point of view and had been produced for commercial purposes in an old style. However, he also had a dispute with one of the most noted political poster artists of the time, Mihály Bíró, who was closely connected with the Social Democratic Party and whose image of a huge, red, hammer-wielding figure had become an icon of the labour movement.

From his account of the dispute, it's not particularly clear what Kassák found objectionable in another of Bíró's posters. He simply asserts it had an 'ambiguous tendency', whatever that might mean. What is clear is that there was a sharp difference of opinion between the two noted left-wingers.[13] Perhaps Kassák was relieved when, soon after, he was moved from his position and assigned to the theatre socialisation committee where it appears (see Chapter 7) he had a more relaxed and tolerant attitude as a political minder.

Today, finding examples of the innovative poster art of 1919 is not easy. Postcard reproductions of some of the striking images of 1919 used to be readily available in bookshops up to the late 1980s, but no longer. In addition, there used to be a Museum of the Hungarian Labour Movement in one of the wings of the former Royal Palace on Budapest's Castle Hill, which concentrated to an extent on the 1919 period and displayed some posters. However, the whole exhibition tended to conflate and confuse 'labour movement' and 'Communist Party', so perhaps it is not surprising it has disappeared. The Hungarian National Museum in Budapest also used to have a substantial section about 1919, including its poster art. After the political changes of 1989–90 a new permanent exhibition was installed in the museum, the part about revolutionary 1919 being reduced dramatically.

13. For his account of being a poster censor, see Kassák (1983), pp. 511 and 516.

4

Art for the People

As in many other fields, the new authorities in 1919 tried to change the formal structures of the fine arts world and to introduce new sets of ideas and goals. Gyula Benczúr, a well-established painter and representative of academicism, was dismissed from his post as director of the School of Fine Arts. A Directory for Arts and Museums was established, headed by art historian Kálmán Pogány. Its members included the painter Róbert Berény, the sculptor and graphic artist Béni Ferenczy, the designer Lajos Kozma, the art historian Frigyes (Frederick) Antal, the art historian and years later deputy director of the Courtauld Institute János (Johannes) Wilde, and the sculptor Pál Pátzay. Its tasks involved reforming education in the arts—particularly with a view to spreading culture among workers and opening up possibilities for worker-artists—taking works of art into the public domain, as well as assisting artists experiencing financial difficulties by purchasing their work.[1]

Like other fields of endeavour where great changes were envisaged, the Hungarian Soviet Republic didn't last long enough for any major structural changes to be implemented, take root and flourish. Yet, as elsewhere, certain things were achieved, including the appearance of a number of 'free schools' for the arts. Two quite contrasting such schools were those run by Károly Kernstok in Nyergesújfalu and Béla Uitz in Budapest.

Nyergesújfalu is a village by the Danube to the northwest of Budapest. The school there was led by the painter Károly Kernstok, who had a studio and villa in the village. Kernstok had a long-standing connection with Nyergesújfalu. As a small child he had been sent there to live with his maternal grandparents.

In the 1890s Kernstok studied in Munich and at the Julian Academy in Paris. His early works reflected critical realism with titles like *Socialist Agitator* (1896), *Agitator in a Factory Canteen* (1897) and *Hauling Boatmen* (1897). Later, after a period of *plein air* painting and another trip to Paris

1. Krisztina Passuth & Júlia Szabó, 'Chronology of Events', in: Willett et al. (1980), p. 41.

in 1906, he moved towards postimpressionism. He was a leading member of The Eight and mixed in radical intellectual circles.[2]

Kernstok had expressed his views about the social role of art already before the First World War. Writing in 1912, he asserted that 'in the future when the artist will use his creative power directly to fulfil the needs of uncorrupted souls, he will no longer be the mercenary of the priesthood or any other class ... The artist will occupy the highest rung of the social ladder where ... he will provide direction for the mass psyche. His work will be that ray of light that will penetrate the vast jungle of society, to convey light and shade, depth and splendour.'[3] That reflected Kernstok's view that art had a social (and therefore political) role to play, though it wasn't a resounding, clear-cut political manifesto for the arts.

Lajos Kassák would recall that Kernstok was 'a fine, interesting figure'. He saw in him 'a mixture of a little bit of an aristocrat, a little bit of a gypsy, part unkempt Hungarian and part French bohemian; a real artist type, and in matters of life possibly the most far-sighted person in the artists' community.'[4]

Somewhat more critically, Bertalan Pór, who had also been a member of The Eight and who in 1919 headed the painters' section of the Arts Directory, once commented: 'Every Communist knew very well that Kernstok wasn't a revolutionary. Kernstok had the mentality of a Social Democrat.'[5]

Perhaps it is therefore not surprising that Kernstok was prominent in cultural politics during Hungary's post-war, but pre-Soviet period, when Mihály Károlyi was the premier and later president, and the Social Democrats played a leading role. Yet it's not so surprising that he also remained fairly prominent after 21 March, being entrusted with heading one of the free schools supported by the new authorities.

Kernstok's school in Nyergesújfalu attracted many budding artists from Budapest who had already been involved with earlier free schools for the arts, such as the one in Haris Close in the city centre, which had been established in 1917. It was Kernstok's personality which drew many of them to study and live in Nyergesújfalu. In a letter written four decades

---

2. The Eight (*A Nyolcak*) was an influential avant-garde movement of painters established in late 1909. Their events often involved representatives of modernist literature and music.
3. 'A művész társadalmi szerepe' (The Role of the Artist in Society), *Huszadik század*, vol. 1, 1912. Quotation from an English translation by John Bátki in: Benson & Forgács (2002), pp. 129–32.
4. Kassák (1983), p. 384.
5. Kende & Sipos (1989), p. 119.

later, one of the students, Mária Goszthonyi, still had strong memories of Kernstok:

> Károly Kernstok was the most brilliant individual I have ever known. He was highly cultured, progressive in everything, thinking deeply about social matters. He was outstandingly amusing and intellectually stimulating. We young ones adored him. He was our ideal. For us he wasn't only a master but an apostle as well, an apostle of all beauty, of everything exalted, of noble, uplifting thought. This is how he remained in our memory. The outstanding atmosphere generated by our master's personality made the summer school in Nyergesújfalu unforgettable.[6]

Viktória Dombai was among those who moved to Nyergesújfalu from Budapest, where she had been an artists' model at the Haris Close school. She has left an account of daily life in the new environment:

> The members of the colony lived together. Apart from painting and drawing, they cultivated the land. Our daily routine was as follows: early morning hoeing and weeding, then breakfast from 7 to 8; from 8 to 11 painting and from 11 to 1 bathing in the Danube; lunch was between 1 and 2, and from 2 to 4 there was relaxation or more bathing; from 4 to 7 painting, then work in the garden; dinner was at 8. After dinner we would sing or read.[7]

Dombai's future husband, the artist Gyula Derkovits who later would become famous, was also drawn to Kernstok's school in Nyergesújfalu. However, due to his health, he couldn't participate in all the colony's activities.

> Derkó (that was his nick-name) was often missing due to his lung problem. He was often lying down. We fed him on a milk diet and looked after him together. In the daytime he painted in his room and if he came into the garden towards evening he hummed softly and spoke little.[8]

Kernstok would frequently visit Derkovits in his room and carefully look at his sketches, giving him encouragement to continue working. It was in sharp contrast to the experience Derkovits had had at the Haris Close school. One afternoon when the noted József Rippl-Rónai was the master

6. Quoted in Bodri (2000), p. 122.
7. Derkovits, Gyuláné (1954), p. 31.
8. Ibid., p. 31.

there, Derkovits was drawing when the former approached and without a word spent at least five minutes drawing over the latter's work. When he put the charcoal down a typical Rippl-Rónai drawing remained. 'Gyula ungraciously removed the drawing, packed his things and quietly left. He didn't turn up at the school again for a long time.'[9]

In contrast, according to Viktória Dombai, the time Derkovits spent at Nyergesúfalu in 1919 was the happiest period of his life. The apparently idyllic atmosphere was also noted at the time in a report appearing in *Figáró*:

> Seventy or eighty children, boys and girls, are sitting in front of their easels, and amidst them is the nude model, like an immoveable statue … only the scraping of charcoal can be heard and every now and then master Kernstok speaks softly as he pauses behind the back of one or the other of his pupils, correcting, explaining ... 'Here I feel myself,' he confessed to me during a break when the model, wrapped in a fur coat, was smoking by the stove, 'as if I were taking part in an experiment, or on some distant planet. It's a completely different world, this. Here people aren't jostling around or shouting, but working. And with what innate gifts! … Look, the model is standing again, what splendour! As if she'd been excavated from an Egyptian pyramid.'[10]

However, not everyone was entirely impressed. Tibor Szamuely paid a visit to Nyergesújfalu. He went to visit Béla Kun's wife and family who were holidaying there and he also took a look at the artist's colony. On his return he gave a detailed account of his experiences to his wife.

'You are right,' he said, 'I have respect for Kernstok, and there are a lot of genuine pupils there, as well. But there are also pretentious, stuffy, over-enthusiastic, snobbish posers. These "Tolstoyans!" I'd really like to throw a hand grenade into their midst.'[11]

There clearly was a certain 'Tolstoyan' atmosphere at the artists' community. Indeed, Mária Goszthonyi actually read aloud to the others from Tolstoy's *The Gospel in Brief*. Kernstok gave talks about Buddha and Derkovits, departing from portraying working-class figures, drew nudes set in the idyllic surroundings.[12]

---

9. Ibid., p. 29.
10. Quoted in Molnos (2008), p. 17.
11. Szilágyi (1966), p. 110.
12. Gréczi, Emőke, 'Az a bizonyos ötven nap Nyergesújfalun' (Those Fifty Days in Nyergesújfalu), *Artmagazin*, 2014, no. 4, pp. 38–43. http://artmagazin.hu/artmagazin_hirek/az_a_bizonyos_otven_nap_nyergesujfalun.2609.html?pageid=119 (accessed 3 July 2017).

Thus perhaps it is surprising that, according to Viktória Dombai, Szamuely visited Nyergesújfalu several times, always staying until late evening. She would recall one occasion early on when they all went down to the Danube embankment to watch the setting of the sun. From the other side of the river they could hear some singing in Slovak. Szamuely suggested that they sing something, too. Only Dombai did so. After she had finished he thanked her and then asked if she knew *The Internationale*, which she did, as did the others, so they all sang—except Szamuely, who just listened attentively as he sat taking in the fine view.[13]

Reaching out to workers

Another of the free schools supported by the new regime was headed by the artist Béla Uitz. Uitz was born in 1887, one of several children in a peasant family. He worked for three years as a metal worker then in the pre-war period studied at the Applied Arts School, followed by the Fine Arts Academy. He was one of The Eight and also among those anti-war artists in the circle around Lajos Kassák. His drawings and critical articles often appeared in *MA*, which he co-edited for a while. During the 1919 Council Republic, as a member of the Arts Directory he planned monumental murals for parliament, created striking recruiting posters and was involved with the decoration of Heroes' Square for May Day.

Uitz, who would later spend many years in the Soviet Union where he was a Communist Party member, had a much more 'hard line' approach to art and society than Kernstok, as is clearly reflected in the title of one of his polemical writings, 'We Need a Dictatorship!' which appeared about three weeks after the Council Republic was declared. Its opening paragraph leaves no room for misunderstanding his position:

> Dictatorship is needed in painting as much as it is needed in today's society. Among painters the revolutionary artists stand opposed to the reactionaries, artists with revolutionary social views stand opposed to those with a bourgeois humanist worldview who believe in patching things up. The latter are worse than the most reactionary artist, because their delaying tactics and reforms give time for the reactionary art and worldview that was defeated and weakened by the revolution to recover its strength. The only art needed by the dictatorship of the proletariat is art with a social revolutionary worldview. ... We must have a worldview and we must have revolution—for only the

13. Derkovits, Gyuláné (1954), p. 30.

consuming flames of these two can annihilate compromise, spinelessness and unethical behaviour.[14]

Uitz goes on to reject the concept of *l'art pour l'art*, asserting that 'art is a creed … something to give one's life for'. Genuine art of necessity has a revolutionary character and creative power. Its task is the uplifting and advancement of citizens and developing new cultural needs, for which the 'sole means' is 'a dictatorship, an intellectual dictatorship'.

Given his views, it is no wonder that the school led by Béla Uitz was called The Proletarian Fine Arts Apprentice Workshop. The name appeared as the title of a *Népszava* (People's Voice) article in early May, which outlined its goals.[15] The article began by pointing out that proletarian children barely received more than a few years of elementary schooling and had virtually no chance of entering any higher institute of arts education. This represented a great loss to the whole of humanity since there were many workers in mines and factories who had the potential to become outstanding sculptors or painters. With the liberation of the proletariat this was all going to end, and now the Arts Directory was setting up a Fine Arts Apprentice Workshop for talented young workers. Initially, the new institute would accept 20–30 full-time students who would not have to work elsewhere. Others would be able to participate in evening courses and those showing the most ability would be able to join the full-timers. Béla Uitz had been appointed director of the workshop, while József Nemes Lampérth and Ferenc Medgyessy, 'both among the most outstanding Hungarian artists, who had been excluded by the war-profiteering bourgeoisie with impossibly bad taste from all serious work', would head the departments of painting and sculpture, respectively. Premises for the new institute had been allocated in the Danube embankment mansion of Gyula Andrássy.[16]

In an interview given in Moscow in 1968 Uitz recalled his activities during the Hungarian Soviet Republic.[17] He said that in 1919 he was a member of the directory and the trade union and, unlike others, he had no desire to teach at the Academy. He rather wanted to establish a proletarian

14. 'Diktatúra kell!', *Vörös Újság* (Red Gazette), 10 April 1919, p. 8. Quotation from an English translation by John Bátki in: Benson & Forgács (2002), pp. 225–7.
15. 'Proletár képzőművészeti tanműhely', *Népszava*, 4 May 1919, p. 10.
16. Gyula Andrássy the younger (1860–1929) was the last foreign minister of the Austro-Hungarian Monarchy, though he only occupied the post during its final days. In 1919 he was one of the leaders of the counter-revolutionary Anti-Bolshevik Committee established in Vienna. His father (1823–1890) had also been foreign minister of the Monarchy.
17. Béla Uitz—reminiscences; manuscript in the PTI Archives, PIL 867.f. U-14, pp. 5–6.

fine arts study course for young workers. His own life had been hard and his aim was to help beginner artists. He was also keen on physical fitness and health, and would go to Margaret Island with his pupils every week to do exercises.

He mentioned Sándor Ék, who did indeed attend Uitz's workshop. Ék was born in 1902, one of many children of a working-class family. He became a shipyard apprentice and later worked in an aircraft factory. In late 1918 he joined the Communist Party, soon after its formation. The following year, he registered for the Red Army and although he was initially rejected (he was 16 years old at the time) in view of his drawing skills he was put in touch with the Proletarian Fine Arts Apprentice Workshop. In his memoirs Ék recalls that at the school about one-third of the participants were studying sculpture with Medgyessy, while the others, who were more interested in painting, were divided between Uitz and Nemes Lampérth. As a 'scholarship' he received the average pay of a young skilled worker.[18]

He says that he and his fellow students were familiar with Futurism, Expressionism and Cubism from reproductions, but did not know much about Dada and the Surrealists. Nor, interestingly, were they acquainted with the Russian Supremacists or Constructivists, and neither did they know of Malevich or Tatlin, or the arts generally during the Civil War and years of War Communism in the early Soviet period.[19]

An interesting picture of Uitz and his school has been left by Lajos Kassák. He notes that the students were young workers—active as shoemakers, tailors, metal workers, carpenters, factory girls, seamstresses and the like. According to Kassák, Uitz managed the school as if it were a master's workshop of classical times with the pupils being like apprentices, who might one day become masters themselves. He thought that the young people had probably only had a few years of schooling and that their artistic skills were intuitive. Thus they needed some general cultural education. Uitz was a keen sports fan and would go with his students to Margaret Island to swim and do exercises. 'He loves his pupils and they love him,' Kassák says.[20]

Not all accounts have been so sympathetic. One observer would remark that the experience of the school was a rather sad one. 'There was no

18. Ék (1968), p. 50.
19. Ibid., p. 52.
20. Kassák (1983), p. 580. Sándor Ék confirms that they went to Margaret Island, though adds that apart from exercising they also practiced drawing in the open air. Like many artists Ék left Hungary after the fall of the Council Republic. From 1933 he lived in the Soviet Union and during World War II was noted for his anti-Fascist posters, which in style were linked with the traditions of Hungary's 1919 poster art. He returned to Hungary after the war.

teaching or learning to speak of. Fuzzy-headed lads with black finger nails and young women with flimsy blouses received an abundant daily allowance, which was precisely why they had applied.'[21] According to this critic, there were few who were punctual, taking their cue from their teachers who regarded getting their pay as more important than teaching the proletarians entrusted to them. Needless to say, this harsh view was penned after the fall of the Council Republic.

At one point there was a plan to move Uitz's school from its riverside location to Sváb Hill above the city, where a number of villas housed an artists' colony and school under the direction of the painter Géza Bornemisza, a former pupil of Matisse. It seemed a better environment, but it didn't really suit Uitz, who wrote a letter of complaint to *Vörös Újság* in the form of a short report about the place. According to Uitz, its 'bourgeois leaders' didn't really want him to bring his school because he would have appeared in the company of people wearing blue workers' clothing, rather than with dilettante female pupils. He wanted to bring it to the attention of the authorities who supported the Sváb Hill operation that 'public cultural institutions were badly needed, but not public institutes governed by caste culture'.[22]

So much for young workers perceived as the most talented. As for the rest, one plan to further their artistic education was outlined in an article in *Fáklya* on 8 May, according to which there would be organised group visits to museums where specialists would introduce the youthful proletarians to the different displays. Breaking with previous practices, these introductions to the arts would begin with the applied arts, rather than the fine arts, since the former were closer to the lives of young people.

However, the fine arts were by no means neglected in terms of attempts to raise the cultural level of the proletariat, as exemplified by a truly large-scale exhibition staged in Budapest in June.

The exhibition of the century?

It sounds like a curator's dream—an exhibition of over 500 works of art, including paintings by internationally renowned artists such as El Greco, Goya, Delacroix, Millet, Manet, Courbet, Pieter Brueghel the Elder, Constable, Cézanne, Pissarro, Gauguin, Rossetti, Renoir, Van Gogh,

21. Ernő Margitay, 'Vörös művészeti politika' (The Politics of Red Art), *Magyar Iparművészet*, 1919, 3–10, pp. 50–63.
22. *Vörös Újság*, 27 July 1919, p. 6. The letter was published on the back page 'without commentary'.

Matisse, Monet, Degas and Jan Steen, not to mention Hungarians such as Mihály Munkácsy, Paál László, Pál Szinyei-Merse, Bertalan Székely, Miklós Barabás, Károly Lotz, József Borsos, József Rippl-Rónai, Károly Ferenczy and Simon Hollósy—all presented at the same time.

Yet, surprisingly perhaps, such an exhibition was indeed staged during the 1919 Hungarian Soviet Republic. It opened on 14 June at the large Műcsarnok (Hall of Arts) in what is today called Heroes' Square. A clever marketing manager—if such had existed at the time—might have called it, with some justification, the exhibition of the century.

What may not be surprising is that the exhibition could be organised because the works of art in question had been sequestrated from private owners and collectors and 'socialised', as the rather dry title of the exhibition clearly indicated—*First Exhibition of Art Treasures Taken Into Public Ownership*.

There were twelve exhibition rooms in all. The first one contained 50 works, nine of which were by El Greco and included versions of his *The Disrobing of Christ*, *The Apostle Saint Andrew* and *The Agony in the Garden* (also known as *Christ on the Mount of Olives*). All bar one of these El Grecos had belonged to the renowned art collector Baron Mór Herzog. Other paintings he had owned also appeared in the exhibition, including works by Goya, though he wasn't the only collector who had been targeted. The noted collectors Marcell Nemes and Baron Ferenc Hatvany had also had their works confiscated.

Room 7 contained the largest number of works (76), almost half of which were by Bertalan Székely. Unsurprisingly, there were large numbers of works by other Hungarian artists. One room had 19 by Szinyei Merse, another 17 by Munkácsy and twelve by Paál, while a third had 24 by Rippl-Rónai.

Apart from paintings, wall tapestries, statuettes and miniature portraits were also on display. Entry was free for workers on production of a trade union membership card and a series of talks was planned 'to introduce proletarians to artistic pleasures, from which they had been systematically excluded by the nefarious, stupid old world', as *Vörös Újság* put it. The paper noted that the works of art were not socialist or communist, but in its lengthy article it described the different schools represented by the exhibited artists, noting that the El Grecos were something special, the type of which were rarely found outside Spain.[23]

23. 'A szocializált műtárgyak első kiállítása' (The First Exhibition of Socialised Artworks), *Vörös Újság*, 18 June 1919, pp. 7–8. The emphasis on 'first' indicates that other such exhibitions were also planned for the future.

Népszava was equally upbeat, stressing similar themes regarding how in the past the wealthy had been able to use their money to obtain art exclusively for their own benefit and enjoyment, but that now the socialised works of art could be enjoyed by all. It emphasised the richness of the displayed works and it, too, highlighted those by El Greco.[24]

The message was repeated in the introduction to the exhibition's catalogue, published by the Műcsarnok sometime after the official opening. 'The capitalist social system, the two main pillars of which were physical and spiritual beggary, systematically excluded the masses from the truly great beauties of life,' it declared, adding that the new social system aimed to reverse that. It admitted that the catalogue only gave minimal information about the artists, their schools and the names of paintings (intriguingly, it also provided the name of each painting's former owner), but that for further information visitors could turn to the guides permanently on hand. It also promised that 'a brief printed guide to art history would soon be at the disposal of comrades' and that for trade unions giving advance notice special guided tours could be organised.[25]

Had the works of art been surrendered willingly by their owners? That seems unlikely, though in a journal article published in 1962 the noted art historian Krisztina Passuth claimed that, by and large, art collectors were not as opposed to public ownership as were factory owners. She gives little evidence for that assertion in her article, though there is the suggestion that some collectors might have assumed that at least the artworks would be safe if held in storage by the Museum of Fine Arts. She also pointed out that the idea, at least, of public ownership of art had started to be worked out already in the pre-Soviet Republic, Károlyi period by the art historians Kálmán Pogány, Antal Frigyes and others.[26]

Nevertheless, it seems that some people were clearly not keen to relinquish their art treasures. Writing in 1969, György Lukács, who in 1919 was a people's commissar concerned with cultural matters, stated the following: 'If I remember correctly, the Brueghel picture that can be seen in the Museum of Fine Arts was the property of one or other of the Counts Batthyány. When our people went to collect the art treasures in his mansion, this picture couldn't be found. Our Commission immediately

---

24. 'A köztulajdonba átvett műtárgyak kiállítása' (Exhibition of Artworks taken into Public Ownership), *Népszava*, 15 June 1919, p. 8.

25. The catalogue bore the same title as the exhibition and the introduction was signed simply 'The Artworks Socialisation Committee'.

26. Passuth, Krisztina, 'A köztulajdonba vett műkincsek kiállítása 1919-ben' (The Exhibition of Art Treasures taken into Public Ownership in 1919), *Művészet*, III, no. 8 (1962), pp. 12–13.

inquired about it, and our people knocked and knocked till finally they found the walled-up painting.'[27]

On the other hand, there is some indication from other sources that certain collectors might have been happy enough for the works in their collection to become publicly owned. In her reminiscences, the former teacher and art enthusiast Jolán Kelen, who in 1919 headed the Child Care Department of the People's Commissariat for Education and Culture, recalls that Ödön Rippl-Rónai, the younger brother of the noted painter József, 'donated to the proletarian state' his art treasures, which he had spent a lifetime collecting, saying: 'I have no right to keep between four walls that which was created for the whole of humanity.' When she asked him whether he wouldn't miss this well-loved, familiar beauty when he went home he replied: 'I can always see them in the museum.'[28]

Kelen was present at the opening of the exhibition, the contents of which—as she recalled in her published memoirs—she found remarkable and wonderful. The same sentiment appears in her unpublished reminiscences, but there she adds the interesting observation that, in her view, what had been taken from the homes of wealthy nobles didn't include much of value, mainly bad oil paintings, hunting scenes and 'portraits' of dogs and horses, whereas what was really valuable was found in the mansions of the financial aristocracy, hidden away in metal lockers.[29]

Someone else who visited the exhibition with enthusiasm was another Jolán, Jolán Szilágyi. Herself an artist, she was pleased to find that the exhibition was a symbol of 'culture and art for the working people'. Szilágyi went with her husband, Tibor Szamuely, a prominent communist regarded as one of the most notorious, hard-line figures in the leadership. Perhaps reflecting that subconsciously, Szamuely's favourite was one of the El Greco

27. Quoted in Fekete & Karádi (1981), p. 96. In 1919 Lukács was a prominent political figure in the arts world and he appears frequently in this book. Born in 1885, he was the son of a wealthy Jewish family. His father rose from a poor rural background and by 1906 was a bank director. Before the First World War, Lukács was intellectually influenced by people such as Georg Simmel and Max Weber, and he was looking forward to a university career in Germany, where he spent much time. During the war in Budapest he was a leader of the Sunday Circle, an intellectual group which discussed literature and philosophy, and sponsored events involving avant-garde figures in music and literature. The war radicalised Lukács and after some hesitation and soul searching, he joined the Hungarian Communist Party in mid December 1918, rising quite quickly to prominence in the Party when Béla Kun and other leaders were arrested in February 1919 and held in prison for some time.

28. Jolán Kelen—reminiscences; manuscript in the PTI Archives, PIL 867.f. K-48, p. 10.

29. Ibid., p. 10.

paintings, a portrait of Cardinal D. Ferdinando Niño de Guevara, Spain's Grand Inquisitor at the start of the 17th century.[30]

The exhibition was officially opened in the afternoon on 14 June, a Saturday, by People's Commissar György Lukács. Years later, in a conversation with two historians in 1968, Lukács recalled the exhibition and its opening. He said that with the help of art historians an inventory had been drawn up of all the important private art collections in Hungary and that it wasn't long before all the great art treasures in the country had become state owned. As for his speech at the opening, he said he had outlined one of the basic principles of socialisation as follows: 'Our task was to gather together everything which was of value from an art historical perspective irrespective of art styles so that it would be in the hands of the state. The fate of the different styles would depend in the future on the cultural level of the proletariat. At some point we will arrive at a situation where the proletariat itself can say which heritage it will accept and which it will not.' He went on to say that with this he wanted to emphasise that the proletarian dictatorship, as he put it, was far from regarding any particular trend as being official.[31]

In a filmed interview of 1971, Lukács returned to the issue again, highlighting the role of the art historians in 1919. 'They played an outstanding role,' he said:

> combining radicalism with expert knowledge. We integrated this into the cultural policy of the dictatorship in the way I indicated at the inauguration of the exhibition of socialised art treasures. That is, we take over into state—i.e. proletarian—ownership every valuable work of art; and the time will come when the proletariat will be in a position to declare what it considers, and what it does not consider, as its own.[32]

According to Jolán Kelen, Béla Kun was due to give a celebratory speech at the opening. She says he turned up, but all he said was: 'I'd like to see the factories socialised like this!' She thought he was right, but that what he said didn't seem appropriate for the occasion.

A month and a half later, at the time when the Soviet Republic fell, Kelen met her friend, the art historian Hugó Kenczler, who had headed the committee tasked with requisitioning works of art. He had with him a

---

30. Szilágyi (1966), p. 103.

31. Lukács (1987), p. 546. What Lukács recalled he said at the opening of the exhibition tallies with the report of what he said published the following day, 15 June 1919, in *Pester Lloyd*. For the actual text of that report, see: Ibid., p. 225.

32. Quoted in Fekete & Karádi (1981), p. 105. Note the optimistic (or perhaps naïve?) view equating state and proletarian ownership.

small Rembrandt, which he had taken home. 'I couldn't sleep all night,' he told her. 'I was looking at this wonder non-stop. It lit up my room. Do you know what happiness that was?' She asked him where he was taking it now, and he replied: 'Back to the museum. Let not the workers of the Council Republic have any stain on their hands.'[33]

33. For the stories about Kun and Kenczler, see Kelen (1976), p. 148.

5
Cultural Polemics

Lajos Kassák features in a number of chapters in this book. This reflects his participation in a variety of activities during the Soviet Republic and his involvement with different fields of the arts. It also makes Kassák—quite interestingly—difficult to pin down into any one category.

Kassák was born in 1887, in Érsekújvár (then in Hungary, today the small town of Nové Zámky in Slovakia, 25 km from the present Hungarian border). The son of a Slovak pharmacist's assistant and a Hungarian washerwoman, Kassák failed his primary school exams and became a fitter's apprentice. He worked in Győr and Budapest as a metal worker, occasionally getting involved in the organisation of strikes. In 1909 he embarked on a European journey, much of it on foot, which would take him through Austria, Germany, Belgium and France. After his return to Hungary he wrote about his experiences of the journey, the people he had met and life at the bottom of society. A rebellious, anarchistic view of the world remained with him for much of his life.

In November 1915 Kassák launched a journal called *A Tett* (The Deed), which aimed to be a forum for the avant-garde. It was also anti-war and in October 1916 it was banned by the Hungarian authorities. Almost immediately Kassák began publication of another journal on the same lines, albeit slightly more 'artistic', called *MA* (Today). It, too, had a chequered, but somewhat longer career. *MA* was a literary and art journal, publishing short stories, poems, literary and theatre criticism, art reproductions and reviews of exhibitions. It also had a publishing arm and a gallery. Furthermore, the *MA* circle was involved with organising literary evenings, lectures and concerts. In summer 1917 *MA* even opened a drama school under the direction of the playwright and critic János Mácza. After the Chrysanthemum Revolution of October 1918, *MA* carried an increasing number of critical articles about the role of art in society. All its activities involved a strong element of promoting social change.

Both politically and artistically Kassák was always a radical internationalist—art historian András Zwickl calls him 'one of the most outstanding advocates of international modernism in the twentieth century'.[1] It was

1. Mansbach et al. (1991), p. 232.

perhaps inevitable that in 1919 he had clashes with the political authorities and the established cultural circles, as well as with orthodox left-wing political leaders.

Kassák was a supporter of the Council Republic, participating in the work of the cultural commissariat, although he was at odds with some of its aspects. You can see the differences brewing in what was written by Kassák even months before the Soviet Republic was proclaimed on 21 March 1919, for example in his 'Proclamation for Art!' which appeared in November 1918. It gives a good idea of Kassák's forceful, even bombastic style—which no doubt appealed to some and repelled others—while at the same time hinting at rifts which were to come.[2]

> Times are running amuck. What was, exists no more; but take care, because the future might also rapidly turn into a has-been in the bungling hands of the present ... The young student, the hunchbacked workingman, the soldier whose lungs have been shot through, all shine with the torchlight of their conscious commitment, while you who embarrassingly pose as artists would settle for dancing to the most trivial music while howling for compromise!

Kassák claims that since Hungary's 1848 revolution against the Habsburgs and its radical poet-leader Petőfi, it is only the artists around *MA* who have been able to blossom into full-grown maturity. It was only they who opposed 'the general drunkenness' leading to the war.

> We in our desolation embraced our creative brothers anywhere in this sinking world. The censorship of the dastardly ruling class throttled us in our holy infancy! Yes, they with the assistance of so-called 'artists', squelched us ... But we have resurrected, because our blood is the blood of the masses who possess the future ...

Next comes an inkling of future tension:

> We proclaim that art cannot tie itself down to any one party or social class! For any special interest group is bound to be cursed with blindness beyond a certain point, and every prescribed programme ossifies into legal paragraphs. Our lot is never to be contented! ... Our socialism manifests itself in art. Cast beyond all political parties and economic

2. Lajos Kassák, 'Kiáltvány a művészetért!', *MA*, special issue no. 1, (November 1918). Quotations from an English translation by John Bátki in: Benson & Forgács (2002), pp. 213–14.

> class interest, we coil the springs of unbounded desire aimed at life ... Our vocation is not to provide entertainment, but to incite action ... Our art is the anarchy of synaesthesia ... Long live Anarchy, where the order of precedence is still unborn! Death to all new forms that are new only to cover up the same old essentials!

Finally, after all this hyperbole, there come some rather prosaic demands. The first, on behalf of artists, painters, sculptors, actors and writers, is simply the demand to be heard. The second is that in place of the former ministry of religious affairs—'which in a new social system has no rational or practical justification'—there be a new cabinet post of minister of arts, by the side of the minister of education, for the moral and material support of the arts. Not exactly a revolutionary suggestion! But this was early days and there was more to come.

In the month following publication of the aforementioned article, Kassák had another outburst under the title 'Onward on Our Way'.[3] In it he moaned: 'For us the revolution has petered out before it had a chance to ripen in a creative force, for lack of a receptive soil—the educated will of the one and only revolutionary element, the proletariat.'

Kassák lambasted the Social Democratic Party, which was a major force behind the Károlyi regime, for operating in the spirit of compromise, and he urged the masses to break with it—in effect, with their own party. There were no particular concrete demands this time, but the role of 'new art' was highlighted. Again there was a hint of future tension. 'We want a socialist art,' wrote Kassák, 'but, again let us emphasise, one that is beholden to no external directives.'

In January 1919 *MA* published an article by Árpád Szélpál with the explicit and provocative title 'Revolutionary Art or Party Art?'[4] He defined art as 'the intuitive positioning of the self in the cosmic context, or rather the synthesised expression of this in sensory forms'. For Szélpál revolutionary art meant that the synthesis was accomplished with the aim of changing existing worldviews, their advancement and continual recharging with ever more progressive content. In contrast, Party art meant that 'the synthesis is a revolutionary programme turned conservative, because the goal of realising a specific programme becomes, instead, one of preserving a political party'. This was quite an insight for the time, anticipating the

3. Lajos Kassák, 'Tovább a magunk utján', *MA*, vol. 3, no. 12 (20 December 1918), pp. 138–9. Quotations from an English translation by John Bátki in: Benson & Forgács (2002), pp. 171–3.
4. Árpád Szélpál, 'Forradalmi művészet—vagy pártművészet', *MA*, vol. 4, no. 1 (26 January 1919), pp. 4, 9–10. Quotations from an English translation by John Bátki in: Benson & Forgács (2002), pp. 216–19.

degeneration of self-styled revolutionary political parties both before and after they have gained power.

Szélpál asserts that the true artist is characterised by a refusal to be satisfied and constant searching, and by 'the struggle with the self, with artistic problems and against programmes that have fossilised into rules'.

Yet another 'proclamation' was made the following month. This time the medium was a speech delivered by Kassák on 20 February, which was published in *MA* only later, in April, after the declaration of the Council Republic.[5] The occasion for the speech was the founding of the Budapest Group of Activists. Kassák defined Activism as essentially meaning 'direct action', but he continued: 'I wish to invest the term with a larger sense, the spontaneous and infinite revolutionary force of the oppressed for self-liberation. The Budapest Group of Activists was constituted on this basis and it wishes to continue working toward the destruction of all forms of government and all party dictatorships for the revolution of the individual.'

Intriguingly, this emphatically anarchist beginning is later mixed with more classical Marxist phraseology, making Kassák's approach almost a combined prefiguration of 1960s utopianism and New Left ideology. Yet parts of it are entirely traditional. 'It is undeniable that the salvation of the world depends upon the proletarian revolt,' he asserts, and he even accepts that the 'first productive result' of revolution is the dictatorship of the proletariat, but adds, perhaps paradoxically, 'we wish to emphasise that we are militantly critical of all dictatorships.'

Once more in his anarchist or libertarian mode, Kassák declares: 'The revolution organised by parties is not the true revolution ... The value of life lies in the neverending revolution of the individual, far beyond the speculative revolution conducted by political parties.' Whether Kassák was a Marxist, or to what extent he was, is debatable. What seems quite clear is that he was no Bolshevik, in the Leninist sense of highlighting the leading role of the Party. No wonder he was to set to clash with Hungary's Bolsheviks in 1919, almost irrespective of whether there were differences in their views about art itself.

After the Council Republic had been declared on 21 March 1919, Kassák had doubts about the whole project. He reminded his colleagues how much the Communists had criticised the Social Democrats for accepting ministerial posts in Károlyi's bourgeois government, and now they were in a pact with the Social Democrats themselves. Without thinking, Kun and his followers had taken over a government which was already bankrupt. They

5. Lajos Kassák, 'Activism', *MA*, vol. 4, no. 4 (10 April 1919), pp. 46–51. Quoted excerpts are from an appendix to Levinger (1985/1986).

had not conquered it, but received it as a gift, since at the time there was no one else but them willing to live with such power.

Kassák thought that the communist leaders, having done a deal with the Social Democrats had abandoned their own programme and thus it was as if they had dug the grave of the revolution. The Communist Party was not prepared for being able to hold power on its own and at the same time Kassák reckoned the Social Democrats were thus stronger. 'I reckon this revolution is a cheap show,' he concluded, 'and that the pact is to no purpose …'[6]

There was some dissension within Kassák's circle about this and whether the workers had actually assumed power—an idea dismissed by Kassák. Despite his doubts, however, it didn't stop the group working out a plan at the end of March detailing at some length what they would like to do in the future, with the hope that their activities would be supported, financially and with other means, by the new regime. It was an ambitious plan involving continued publication of Hungarian and foreign writings in Hungarian translation, organisation of seminars on the arts, exhibitions, propaganda matinees with drama, music and dance, as well as book publications.[7]

In the early days of the Soviet Republic, the question was also raised whether editing *MA* should be given up and the group present itself at the service of the Party. This, too was dismissed by Kassák who argued they should continue their work as they always had.[8] Actually, the issue of the status of *MA* during the Soviet Republic became a bone of contention at the time and the argument continued after the Republic had fallen. Clearly Kassák did not regard *MA* as the mouthpiece of either the new government or the new Party formed by the merger of the Communists and Social Democrats. At the same time, its rhetoric about art and revolution seemed to imply that, while supporting the Council Republic, albeit critically, only Kassák and his circle really knew what revolutionary art was all about, indeed what revolution itself was all about.[9] This standpoint and independence clearly rattled the new regime. Maybe this is why the authorities made an attempt to take over *MA*, at least that is how Kassák would later recall the incident.

6. Kassák (1983), p. 497.
7. *A MA művészcsoport munkaterve* (Plan of work for the MA arts group), reproduced in: Csaplár (1987), pp. 150–2.
8. Kassák (1983), p. 498.
9. The impression that the *MA* circle believed that their views really ought to be regarded as official is most clearly implied by the thoughts of Béla Uitz, a painter and a co-editor of *MA*, as presented in his article 'We need a dictatorship!' for which, see the previous chapter.

Kassák says that one afternoon he got a telephone call from József Révai, then an assistant editor of *Vörös Újság* (Red Gazette), the Communists' daily newspaper.

Addressing him as 'Comrade Kassák', he said a decision had been made to classify *MA* as the Soviet Republic's literary journal. Kassák was suspicious and asked directly what he had in mind: 'Do you want to change the journal's orientation, its editorial style? What exactly do you have in mind?'

Révai said it was about making *MA* the official literary journal of the Soviet Republic. An editorial committee would see to the editing, but Kassák would remain as head of the committee. Kassák indicated that it was what he suspected, but he would turn down the offer, explaining he was only willing to edit the journal if it remained in the hands of the same group of people who were currently involved with it. He added that 'Comrade Révai' well knew his views about such 'editorial committees'.

The response was sharp. Révai wanted to apply pressure and, shouting down the line, demanded in the name of the Council Republic: 'So you want to rebel against the decision?'

'I didn't say that,' retorted Kassák.

> I just don't want to accept the role that's been meted out to me. ... Thank you, but I don't want to be an official editor. Close down the journal or take it away from me, you have the means for that, but I will only edit it if it remains within its present framework.[10]

On that note the conversation ended. However, the idea that *MA* already was some kind of official mouthpiece, perhaps simply because of its claims to being revolutionary, must have been commonly held. Indeed, on 15 April the Social Democratic weekly *Az Ember* (Man) published an article by Pál Kéri attacking the official literary policy, strongly criticising Lukács and others for being too favourable towards *MA* and its circle, which Kéri believed included people who were muddled, incompetent and philistine.[11]

The following day, *Vörös Újság* responded in its 'Communist culture' column with an article attacking Kéri entitled 'Suppress the Cultural Counter-revolution'.[12] On the same day Ferenc Göndör, the editor of *Az Ember*, joined in the fray, defending Kéri and attacking the *MA* group in an article published in *Népszava* (People's Voice) under the heading 'Who wants to be the dictator of proletarian literature?'[13] Finally, cultural

---

10. Kassák (1983), pp. 520–1.
11. Pál Kéri, 'Máca!', *Az Ember*, 15 April 1919, pp. 5–6.
12. 'Letörni a kulturellenforradalmat', *Vörös Újság*, 16 April 1919, p. 7.
13. Ferenc Göndör, 'Kik akarják diktálni a proletárirodalmat?', *Népszava*, 16 April 1919, p. 7.

commissar György Lukács, in an attempt to set the record straight once and for all, categorically denied that *MA* was an official mouthpiece of the Soviet Republic.

'The journal *MA* is not, nor will it be, an official organ of the People's Commissariat for Education and Culture,' was his first point in a quite lengthy statement entitled 'By Way of Information'.

> The People's Commissar for Education and Culture is not going to officially support any kind of literature tied to a particular line or party. The Communist cultural programme only makes a distinction between good and bad literature, and is not prepared to throw out Shakespeare or Goethe on account of their not being socialist authors. But neither is it prepared to let loose dilettantism in art, under the pretext of socialism. The Communist cultural programme stands for the highest and purest art reaching the proletariat and is not going to allow its taste to be corrupted by editorial poetry badly used for political purposes. Politics is only the means, culture is the goal.[14]

In the event, the leadership of the united Party sided with Lukács with the result that publication of *Az Ember* was suspended for a number of weeks on the grounds that it had published *ad hominem* criticism of a people's commissar.[15]

Lukács returned to a similar theme many years later. In an interview recorded in 1971 he claimed that Kassák's ambition:

> had always been to be appointed official poet to the Commune, but I did not believe the Commune had any need of an official poet. Representatives of every shade of opinion that can be tolerated under communism should write freely, and if one ideology prevails over the others, well and good. I always took the side of Kassák and his friends when the Social Democrats and the trade union bureaucrats launched a campaign to destroy them. I did not allow them to be gagged. But equally, I would not allow them to be granted official recognition.[16]

As indicated in the previous chapter in connection with the huge exhibition of confiscated artworks, and in the sections of this book dealing with film, theatre and writers, the Commune, in line with Lukács's view, had a fairly neutral official view about different artistic tendencies, but note his

14. György Lukács, 'Felvilágosításul', *Vörös Újság*, 18 April 1919, p. 4.
15. József (1969), p. 72.
16. Lukács (1983), p. 62.

expression above asserting freedom for every shade of opinion 'that can be tolerated under communism'. Who was to define what that would mean?[17] In the event, the 1919 Commune didn't last long enough for it to turn out fully what might be tolerated and what might not (though see below in relation to *MA*).

Returning to Lukács and Kassák, the former admits that 'Kassák probably did not like me any better than I liked him'.[18] Lukács acknowledges he had his own reasons. He did not like Kassák's poetry and he certainly didn't like his self-proclaimed revolutionary aloofness from all parties. One alleged incident recalled by Kassák particularly riled him.

In his memoirs Kassák asserts that on one occasion Lukács strongly tried to persuade him that cultural activists, including Kassák himself, had a duty to go to the front to fight for the Soviet Republic. Kassák emphatically disagreed, arguing that his responsibility and that of others like him was to remain on the home front and employ their skills there. He claims that Lukács, irritated, pulled a gun out of his pocket, placing it on the table between them. He had a wild look on his face. But he adds that the scene wasn't so much intimidating, rather something provoking laughter. Nevertheless the tension remained and they failed to agree.[19]

Regarding this incident, Lukács interprets Kassák as saying in his memoirs that he, György Lukács, tried to force him to go to the front at the point of a revolver, something he completely denies, calling it 'nonsense'. Then, rather revealingly he adds:

> If Kassák had gone to the front as a political commissar and turned up in my territory, I would have sent him back home ... When I was there—and this I can vouch for—it was crawling with ultra-left communists. I sent them all home without exception. I had no need of them. I chose my subordinates from among the decent Communist workers in the army.[20]

Lukács did indeed spend some time at the front as a political commissar and it seems from his comment that he took it for granted that he would

17. One is reminded of the astute exchange in Lewis Carroll's *Through the Looking Glass*.
'When *I* use a word,' Humpty Dumpty said, in rather a scornful tone, 'it means just what I choose it to mean—neither more nor less.'
'The question is,' said Alice, 'whether you *can* make words mean so many different things.'
'The question is,' said Humpty Dumpty, 'which is to be master—that's all.'
18. Lukács (1983), p. 62.
19. Kassák (1983), pp. 598–9.
20. Lukács (1983), p. 61.

have been Kassák's superior there, able to issue him with orders, even if they had both been political commissars. Certainly, while at the front Lukács had no qualms about the use of measures even more extreme than sending people home, such as the execution of deserters from the Red Army as a means of enforcing discipline. 'In war fugitives and traitors must be shot,' he told the American reporter Crystal Eastman in 1919.[21]

But to return to the incident with Kassák, was the issue involving Lukács's revolver—whoever's memory was correct—a small matter of no major concern, or something reflecting broader differences? Kassák and Lukács were both similar and dissimilar, a familiar recipe for potential conflict. One was born into poverty, the other the son of a wealthy banker. Both had made their way through life as outsiders, though while Lukács was at home in university and intellectual circles, Kassák was self-taught. Both perceived the need for revolution, though they differed in what they meant by that and how it was to be achieved. By 1919 Lukács had become a 'Party man', while Kassák remained essentially a radical non-party activist. Both had a deep interest in, and firmly held views about politics and culture, though their views differed. Both displayed a certain self-righteous dogmatism vis-à-vis their own position. Tension between the two was perhaps not inevitable, though quite understandable.[22]

A more widely known, because often referred to, clash concerned Kassák's *Letter to Béla Kun in the Name of Art*, which was sparked off by a comment made by Kun at the June national congress of the Hungarian Socialist Party, the first such congress of the united party. In a speech delivered on 13 June, the second day of the conference, Kun made some remarks about the need for workers to produce a new intellectual life and new culture. He asserted that these were not represented by *MA*, which he described as 'a product of bourgeois decadence'.[23]

Kun's brief but politically vitriolic comment about *MA* was strange in that it was rare for Kun to get involved in cultural matters, if only because he was primarily tied up dealing with the military situation and international relations. Kun's biographer, György Borsányi, indicates that generally he approached different writers with good will and could be 'extremely

---

21. Eastman (1919), p. 9.
22. David Kettler (1971, p. 92) quotes a letter he received in 1962 from Ilona Polanyi (née Duczynska), in which she boldly asserts: 'Kassák was avant-garde in literature; Lukács cannot by any stretch of the imagination be regarded as having sympathies (or even understanding) for modernism in literature … Further, Kassák had his roots in the masses, in the working class, and his appeal to them was very strong; Lukács had hardly any appeal to the workers, they didn't know what to make of him … They were poles apart.'
23. *Vörös Újság*, 14 June 1919, p. 5.

tolerant'.[24] Only with Kassák did he have a public incident over literary policy.[25] Be that as it may, the incident generated a sharp polemic from Kassák's pen, the text of which was published in *MA* on 15 June and also printed as a separate pamphlet for general distribution.

In his response to Kun, expressed in a very respectful though forceful manner, Kassák first describes the history of *MA*, how its predecessor, *A Tett*, had taken an anti-war stand, had published critiques of the Social Democrats and bourgeois writers, and how it was quickly banned. Kassák points out that until 21 March 1919, *MA* also had a negative reception from bourgeois society.

He then emphasises that his group welcomed the proletarian revolution and pointedly remarks that while Kun was still active in Russia before returning to Hungary he and his friends were already agitating for Communism. In the early days of the Károlyi regime, they were calling for a communist Soviet Republic and many people in the *MA* network personally welcomed Kun after he had arrived from Russia. Kassák then goes on to repeat the *MA* worldview, 'which precludes affiliation with the interests of any political party ... [since it is] beyond party politics, beyond national or racial ideologies'.

As if to emphasise *MA*'s internationalist and revolutionary credentials, Kassák then calls Kun's attention to a number of renowned radicals 'whose art is in the same spirit as ours', some of whom had texts in the current issue of the journal—for example, the Frenchman Henri Gilbeaux, Franz Pfemfert, the editor of the Berlin periodical *Aktion*, the Czech Ottokar Brezina, Alexei Remisow, an associate of the Futurist writers in Russia,

24. Borsányi (1993), p. 190. Although the original, Hungarian-language edition of Borsányi's biography first appeared in May 1979, a full ten years before the country's political changes got fully underway, it was by no means an uncritical, let alone adulatory portrait of Kun. In fact, soon after its publication and when copies were already being sold, further distribution was banned and all unsold copies withdrawn, the apparent reason being that it was too critical! According to Borsányi, who tells the story in the introduction to the later, English-language edition, the then Party leader, János Kádár, was sent the book with 'an outraged note attached'. Kádár was displeased, apparently since it countered the then official view of Kun. Borsányi says that the day after Kádár was replaced, in May 1988, the book reappeared in the shops and sold out within a week. He doesn't indicate who authored the outraged note, but Paul Lendvai (2003, p. 372) says that 'Kun's family protested at Party headquarters and allegedly also at the Soviet embassy ...' and that the Central Committee had all unsold copies of the biography withdrawn. He adds that they were 'pulped overnight', which contrasts with Borsányi's story.

25. Yet it wasn't the first time the two had clashed. Before the formation of the Soviet Republic they had had a face-to-face disagreement, which seems to have revolved around Kassák's desire to keep his distance from the Communist Party. See Kassák (1983), pp. 472–3.

Romain Rolland, Franz Merhring and Anatoly Lunacharsky, at the time and for many years to come the Soviet People's Commissar for Education. In particular, Kassák highlights the propagation of the 'new art being realised in posters' on the part of Lunacharsky, 'a man who is hardly your bourgeois decadent'. Kassák draws to a close with a rather barbed comment, though on the surface one expressed in a polite manner:

> I respect you as one of the greatest among politicians, but allow me to have my doubts about your competence in the area of art. On this point we, whose political outlook—or more correctly worldview—is blameless from the viewpoint of the liberation of the proletariat ... are therefore most qualified to pass critical judgement in matters relating to our profession.[26]

Reflecting on the incident, György Borsányi, in his biography of Kun published in English in 1993, remarks that:

> Later generations may well wonder: in which Communist country could a writer attack the top man of the 'party-state' in a pamphlet published legally by himself, yet retain his office even after that? This minor episode goes to prove that the ethics and norms of the Communists in 1919 were rather different from their ethics after 1945.[27]

The remark is interesting and curious at the same time. First, it does not appear in the earlier, Hungarian-language edition of Borsányi's book. Second, Kassák himself acknowledges that publishing the pamphlet was illegal.[28] He doesn't explain why that was so but, as we will see, he was officially reprimanded for issuing the text. Third, even if a 'minor episode' cannot itself prove a major point, Borsányi's substantive emphasis about differences between 1919 and the post-1945 years arguably has some merit—not to mention any comparison which could be made with the Soviet Union under Stalin. Nevertheless, Borsányi fails to add that shortly after Kassák's *Letter to Béla Kun* appeared, his journal *MA* was officially banned.

Or was it? That is how Kassák puts it quite bluntly in his memoirs written years later, saying the ban was by government decree.[29] Over the years, it has often been repeated that *MA* was outlawed as a result of

26. Lajos Kassák, 'Levél Kun Bélához a művészet nevében' (Letter to Béla Kun in the Name of Art), *MA*, vol. 4, no. 7 (15 June 1919), pp. 146–8. Quotations from an English translation by John Bátki in: Benson & Forgács (2002), pp. 230–3.
27. Borsányi (1993), p. 190.
28. Kassák (1983), p. 595.
29. Ibid., p. 614.

Kassák's response to Kun. However, Kassák acknowledges that after the *Letter* had been published in *MA*, nothing happened for a couple of weeks, and indeed the next issue of the journal duly appeared on 1 July, apparently without any interference. But on that same day an official communication was addressed to Kassák upbraiding him for having published the separate pamphlet without authorisation for use of the paper or the print shop.[30] According to Farkas József, a few days later József Pogány, who was now a leading figure in the cultural commissariat, issued a decree to the effect that, in view of the paper shortage, all existing newspapers and journals would require a new authorisation for publication, but in the view of József there was never any indication that permission to continue publishing *MA* would not be granted.[31]

That may well be true and in fact during an earlier wave of restrictions initiated against newspapers and journals in mid-May, when a number of publications were closed down allegedly due to a paper shortage, *MA* emerged quite well. From its 15 May issue it now appeared twice a month, instead of just once, and it contained 35 pages, double its average number of pages in the first four months of 1919. On the other hand, the *Letter to Béla Kun* affair might well have finally turned the leading comrades in the commissariat fully against Kassák and his journal. What is clear is that the next edition of *MA*, which in line with its then frequency was due to be published in mid-July, did not appear.[32]

In a letter addressed to the authorities and dated 8 July 1919, Kassák indicates that his understanding was that *MA* had been suspended due to the paper shortage. He pleaded to be allowed to use some paper which already had the *MA* masthead printed on it, since it otherwise could not be used—apparently to no avail.[33] In his memoirs, he further says that by mid-July he had put together a booklet about the new art, which he would have liked to get published. He took the page proofs to show the cultural commissariat. Pogány looked through them, tore them up and threw them into the waste paper basket, saying: 'Not one more line of yours can be set in type and printed!'

'With that categorical pronouncement,' says Kassák, 'they dealt with us once and for all.'[34]

30. For the text of this, see Csaplár (1987), p. 153.
31. József (1984) p, 245. For more about Pogány and his earlier activities, see 'A second Bonaparte' in Chapter 7.
32. Nor did any further issues, at least not in Hungary, but that was due to the collapse of the Soviet Republic. Later, Kassák revived publication of *MA* during his exile in Vienna.
33. For the text of the letter, see Csaplár (1987), p. 154.
34. Kassák (1983), pp. 614–15.

6
The Silent Screen Talks Politics

It is often asserted that the passing into state ownership of the film industry in Hungary in 1919 was the world's first such politically motivated nationalisation. That may seem surprising given that the Bolsheviks had been in power in Russia since November 1917. The formal truth of the statement is based on the fact that Lenin's decree nationalising the film industry in his country was issued only in late August 1919, sometime after the fall of the Hungarian Soviet Republic.

When nationalisation actually occurred in Hungary depends on which event or events are highlighted, in that it took place as a process involving a number of steps. In the evening of Saturday, 22 March, just one day after the proclamation of the Soviet Republic, a mass meeting of cinema industry personnel took place in the large hall of the Royal Apolló cinema in central Budapest. All branches of the profession were represented—scriptwriters, camera operators, directors, actors, actresses and others. A proposal in favour of the public ownership of film enterprises was agreed and an administrative body, known as the Directory, was elected to oversee the industry, at least for the time being.

As time went by matters became more complicated, since a number of different bodies were created to manage the film industry. Nevertheless, the mass meeting can be said to represent the start of nationalisation in Hungary.

Formal nationalisation occurred on 8 April when the Revolutionary Governing Council in its Decree XLVIII declared the state ownership of film studios, laboratories and distributors, as well as cinemas, irrespective of the number of employees in each enterprise. A 'Central Managing Council for the Socialised Cinema Enterprises' was charged with putting the decree into effect, and a political commissar plus two production commissioners were delegated to the body.

The decree spoke of former managers being allowed to continue their work. Though apart from the Central Managing Council, there was also mention of monitoring activities on the part of the industry's workers' councils.

The government decree appeared on the front page of a new publication, *Vörös Film* (Red Film), the first issue of which was dated 12 April 1919.

The same issue included another decree issued by the Central Managing Council for the Socialised Cinema Enterprises, which went into more detail about the nationalisation process.

On 19 April *Vörös Film* reported that the Central Managing Council had established its own seven-person Directory, which was to be the final decision-making body for all questions relating to the industry, albeit in consultation with the political commissar and listening to professional advice. Then on 25 April this body set up a new one, the so-called Arts Council, responsible for judging the appropriateness of proposed films.

And so it went, in a manner not untypical for the Soviet Republic—a bureaucratic structure of overlapping institutions established from above in the name of popular socialisation. A Central Managing Council decree of 15 May even abolished the existing workers' councils and called for new elections, since they were deemed not to have been established in an appropriate manner, i.e. not in accordance with regulations of the Revolutionary Governing Council.[1]

One wonders what might have happened if the original Directory established by film industry professionals during the night of 22–23 March had been left to work out its own version of public ownership without the interference of the new political authorities.

As it happened, that wasn't to be and the government-appointed political commissar, Béla Paulik, a former prisoner of war in Russia and Bolshevik convert who had no film industry experience, was quick to make his mark with an address entitled 'To My Fellow Workers', published on the front page of *Vörös Film* on 12 April. His opening words were: 'The socialisation of our enterprises, as surely every comrade knows, is advancing at a fast pace.' He urged his readers to continue the process so that the fruit of their labour would be to the benefit not of the capitalists but the liberated workers. The time would soon come, he asserted, when the industry would be entirely and appropriately centralised. The workers would be paid more, an honest wage, but in the meantime production work must continue.

Paulik signed himself as the 'political commissar' and was clearly more interested in the politics and organisation of the industry than in the content of films. Another appointed colleague of his, Júlia Komját, dealt more with matters of film aesthetics, engaging in debate with professionals in the pages of *Vörös Film*.

Paulik's political zeal came to the fore with a decree of his published on 7 May in large lettering, taking up an entire page of a special issue of *Vörös Film*. He announced that all workers in the socialised film industry were required to register for military service. Those who were ill or disabled

1. Garai (1969), p. 58.

had to produce written evidence supplied by military doctors within 48 hours. Previous medical evidence would not be accepted as valid. Those in special positions such as in the workers' councils or trade unions also had to produce written evidence within 48 hours. Women, men over 45 and those under 18 were exempt from conscription. Anyone not fulfilling their 'proletarian duty' satisfactorily in accordance with the decree would be deemed not fit to consume bread in the proletarian homeland and would lose their jobs. At the end of this decree Paulik signed himself not only as political commissar but also 'battalion commander'.

The decree followed an announcement of the day before, signed by Paulik, according to which the 'entire workforce of the cinema profession had decided to enter the Red Army' and, as a special unit, to go to the front under the command of political commissar Béla Paulik to 'defend the proletarian dictatorship'. For the time being, the production of new films could not be commenced.[2]

All this was probably a step too far for the Revolutionary Governing Council and, indeed, in a matter of days Paulik announced that on the basis of instructions from higher authorities he was disbanding the special film workers' battalion. He himself was put in charge of the shooting of newsreel footage at the front and organising film screenings for front-line troops. In effect, the position of external political commissar was thus dissolved.[3] The centralised management of film production remained, though there was more emphasis on artistic concerns and the appropriate allocation of resources.

What films were planned and what films were actually made during the 133 days of the Hungarian Soviet Republic? In view of the circumstances, the external military threat and the internal domestic chaos, the answers are quite remarkable.

In its first issue, published on 12 April, *Vörös Film* gave a report about the plans. It began by asserting that new times demanded new films, productions which were not designed to fit the old, false capitalist ideology, but were in tune with the new revolutionary era. Perhaps it is surprising, therefore, that what was deemed worthy was the creation of screen versions of what were by then already 'classics' of literature. The new programme of planned films listed in *Vörös Film* included adaptations of works by well-known, popular Hungarian writers such as Mór Jókai, Kálmán Mikszáth, Mihály Vörösmarty, Sándor Bródy, Géza Gárdonyi and Ferenc Molnár. Among foreign classics scheduled for film adaptation were works by Zola,

2. *Vörös Film*, 6 May 1919. In: Garai (1969), pp. 54–6.
3. Magyar (1967), pp. 34–5.

Goethe, Dumas, Tolstoy, Ibsen, Hugo, Gogol, Gorky, Stendhal, Dickens, Shaw, Mark Twain and even Charlotte Bronte. Beyond these, the report stated, there would be some lighter productions, such as adaptations of operas or tales by Hans Christian Andersen.

One of the most bizarre plans was surely one referred to by Zsolt Kőháti in his history of Hungarian silent films. Apparently at one point the idea arose of making a major film (shot partly in Odessa and the Crimea) based on *Diana Barrington*, by the Anglo-Indian writer Bithia Mary Croker. The novel is a romance set in India and the proposal was that Lenin, played by an actor, would feature in the film, since the production would immortalise his 'entirely romantic youth'![4]

Needless to say, this and other more realistic but also ambitious plans were not fulfilled in their entirety, but what was achieved was impressive. Erzsi Garay lists 20 feature films which were completed during the Soviet Republic, a further 15 which were all but completed and two agit-prop films.

Among the 35 completed or almost completed films were adaptations of Edward Bulwer-Lytton's *Night and Morning*, August Strindberg's *Miss Julie*, Upton Sinclair's *Samuel the Seeker*, Maxim Gorky's *Chelkash*, Alexandre Dumas's *Francillon*, Charles Dickens's *Oliver Twist*, Victor Hugo's *Marion Delorme* and Israel Zangwill's *Merely Mary Ann*, just to mention some foreign works chosen. Not surprisingly, the films tended to have strong social content, portraying the injustices and inequalities of class-ridden societies.

Among other films produced in the period, *A baba* (The Doll), based on a work by Sándor Bródy, had an anti-clerical theme. *Mária Nővér—A legnagyobb bűn* (Sister Mária—The Greatest Sin) was about a convent school where one of the pupils is seduced and made pregnant by a Hussar officer billeted there during the war. *A dada* (The Nanny), another Bródy adaptation, gave a representation of the life of Hungarian peasants. There were also non-political adventures and some comedies. *Tilos a csók* (No Kissing) was a burlesque about an imaginary country where kissing is illegal. No one obeys the law, which leads to amusing complications.[5] Could this have been an indirect comment on the prohibition of the sale and consumption of alcohol introduced very early on by the Revolutionary Governing Council?

In his history of Hungarian cinema, John Cunningham asserts that 'most Hungarian film-makers supported the revolution' though he adds that 'in

4. Kőháti (1996), p. 138.
5. Most of the films made in the period have not survived. The brief descriptions given here are from Nemeskürty (1974), pp. 46–7.

some cases this may have been a simple matter of expediency, a desire to carry on making films'.[6]

There could also have been other reasons. Sándor Zöldi was a technician who found himself in charge of film production at the Star Film Studio. 'Some of the writers and actors were quite passive,' he would later recall, 'which caused quite a lot of bother for me, or rather the production process. But they were successfully persuaded to work, partly through convincing arguments and partly through their stomachs. With the help of some higher authorities, the studio established a group for organising food supply and despite the difficult circumstances I was able to ensure quantities of fat, flour, sugar and other items for the staff.'[7] Obtaining film stock was a more difficult matter, but Zöldi managed to get some in Vienna, where he had travelled on a false passport.

Whatever the motivation, directors and others who had previously worked regularly in Hungarian film production continued to make films. In addition, the possibilities arose for talented assistants to direct their first films. For example, Sándor Pallos, an assistant cameraman at the Corvin film studio, directed *Chelkash*, the first of a planned series of adaptations of Gorky's stories. However, Pallos's career would end in tragedy. In the autumn of 1919 he fell victim to the post-Commune 'White Terror' and was tortured to death.[8]

A so-called Proletarian Academy was set up in early April, headed by the writer and stage manager Dezső Orbán. Among its aims was helping develop the talents of young writers and others in the film industry and expressing new tendencies in film-making. Out of this came the film *Tegnap* (Yesterday), written and directed by Orbán in collaboration with Lajos Lázár.

A workman lives in a room rented from the director of a factory where he is employed. He is allowed to use only a small part of the luxurious villa and grand park. The workman falls in love with the neglected wife of the boss. The affair is discovered and the workman is driven out, while the lady is to be divorced, which her husband was planning anyway.

Perhaps not surprisingly, the workman is a revolutionary who is making propaganda at the factory and agitating for a strike. Ideological lectures are given and leaflets are printed, but the army is called in and the workers are defeated. In his despair the hero kills the manufacturer and escapes from the country.

---

6. Cunningham (2004), p. 20.
7. Sándor Zöldi—Reminiscences; manuscript in the PTI Archives, PIL 867.f. Z-43, p. 3.
8. Nemeskürty (1974), p. 49.

István Nemeskürty regards the film, which survived, as a noteworthy achievement from the point of view of direction, considering its close-ups, camera movements, cuts and montages.[9] However, in 1919 it got a poor reception.

At its meeting on 8 July the Central Managing Council for the Socialised Cinema Enterprises passed a resolution which was quite condemnatory of the film, saying: '…an average kitschy film was produced, which only differed from the average bad film by bad taste, lack of culture and high-flowing but confusing naivety … It is simply a poor film, based on an impossible script, produced without any artistic flair. … Those comrades who initiated this experiment will find themselves with a new position in the profession.'[10]

It was a harsh judgement, but at the same time it is interesting to note that not everything emerging from a newly established body bearing the sacred title of 'Proletarian' was going to be automatically accepted.

As well as politically appropriate films, the authorities wanted to see well-made films, and sometimes films that were simply for amusement. A statement in *Vörös Film* on 10 May, at the time of Béla Paulik's attempt to mobilise film workers for front-line duty, declared: 'During the transition, for the time being motion pictures have no other aim than to entertain people in their hundreds of thousands … Cinemas must keep on functioning!'[11]

Yet when they were functioning there was also some regulation about who could attend them, specifically in relation to young people. The Hungarian Soviet Republic took the issue of children's upbringing and welfare, both physical and mental, quite seriously and there was an effort made to discourage young people from attending film shows. Indeed the People's Commissariat for Education and Culture issued a decree on 7 June banning children under 14 years of age from attending cinemas, with the exception of those places set aside for screening special films for young people. Yet even before that some places had been enforcing a minimum attendance age of 16, and on 8 May the presidium of the Budapest Central Council of Workers and Soldiers had decreed that children under ten should not attend cinemas, theatres and other places of adult entertainment.[12]

Such moves were not popular with everyone. In a letter published in *Vörös Film* in late April a certain Mihály Gerl complained that this was the wrong approach, despite the fact that many films were inappropriate for children or not understandable for them. He claimed he had seen dozens

9. Ibid., p. 51.
10. *Vörös Film*, 13 July 1919. In: Garai (1969), pp. 115–16.
11. Quoted in Magyar (1967), p. 35, n. 42.
12. The decree is reproduced in Garai (1969), p. 57.

of youngsters hanging around outside cinemas 'with tearful eyes' their small coins pressed in their hands, hoping to get inside. He also claimed that the ban on youngsters also deprived many proletarian women of their one and only entertainment of the week—going to watch a film on Sunday afternoons—since they had no one to whom they could entrust their children.[13]

What were the reasons for the ban? At the time, cinemas in Hungary were not the places they are today. Films were screened in places which had been adapted in an ad hoc manner to accommodate the new technology. These included coffee houses, nightclubs, beer halls, basement cellars and even tents at flea markets.[14] Many dingy 'cinemas' were located in the less salubrious districts of the city and no doubt many were unhealthy, smoke-filled places, not fit for children, as indicated by a report in *Vörös Film* on 10 May, according to which five cinemas were being transformed for children, which involved their refurbishment (for example, with small seats and low benches), but also their complete cleaning and disinfection.

The five new cinemas opened in different areas of Budapest in early June with the names 'Andersen', 'Snow White', 'Gulliver', 'Sleeping Beauty' and 'Grimm'. The plan was to have a children's cinema in every district of the capital. Meanwhile, setting the example, these new places would show three types of films: educational films, fairy tales and stories, and humorous material, including cartoons.[15]

Korda and Curtiz

It may seem surprising to many people familiar with their later international fame that two of the leading film personalities active during the Hungarian Soviet Republic were Alexander Korda, who in 1942 became the first film director to receive a British knighthood, and Michael Curtiz, the director of one of Hollywood's most popular and highly-regarded films, *Casablanca*.

In 1919 the then 25-year-old Sándor Korda, as he was known, was already a well-established figure of Hungarian cinema, as a producer, director, film critic and film magazine editor. Immediately after the formation of the Council Republic he became a member of the film Directory, and as the weeks went by he continued to make films.[16]

---

13. *Vörös Film*, 26 April 1919, pp. 2–3.
14. Pongrácz (1998), pp. 5–11.
15. Garai (1969), p. 304.
16. As mentioned above, the meeting from which the Directory emerged took place in the Royal Apolló cinema, which was located in the Royal Hotel, at the time Korda's place of residence. Thus he didn't have to go far to attend the meeting!

Different authors have given different interpretations of Korda's political views and involvement. In his 1959 biography, Paul Tabori is at pains to play down any political commitment Korda might have had to the Council Republic and to emphasise his distance from the communists. He writes that one evening at the Café Balaton Korda described to friends how the Communist film bosses wanted to force him into making a propaganda picture, but that he had refused. Korda, he says, played for time and managed to avoid the commission. However, the date of this café encounter is unspecified and no source is given. Moreover, Tabori makes no mention of the films Korda did direct during the Soviet Republic, each of which had a political angle—not that there were many.

Of the three films Korda worked on during the period one, *Fehér rózsa* (White Rose), was an adaptation of a romantic novel (called *Halil the Pedlar—A Tale of Old Stambul* in its English translation) by the noted Hungarian writer Mór Jokai, which was based on a rebellion of 1730 against Sultan Achmed III.

The other two were clearly also political and 'appropriate' for the times. *Yamata* was about a black slave's revolt against a cruel master, while *Ave Caesar!* told the story of a gypsy girl abducted for a Habsburg prince. The lead actor in both was Gábor Rajnai who had played a patriotic young officer in Korda's *The Officer's Sword Knot* made during the war. The political times had indeed changed.

A nuanced position somewhere between Korda the 'socialist' and Korda the 'anti-communist' is adopted by his nephew Michael, who describes his uncle as 'joining mildly in the revolutionary fervor'. He even has some kind words to say about Béla Kun, who, he asserts, 'lacked the single-minded ruthlessness of Lenin' and was 'a rather gentle and humane person, as revolutionary leaders go'. Perhaps he was influenced in that by his uncle's views, since he quotes him from later years as saying 'Kun wasn't nearly as bad as people had made him out to be'.

Nevertheless, another later comment of his uncle perhaps gets closest to the point: 'Film people must make film if they're going to earn their bread, whatever the government.'[17] In other words, applying that to the situation of total nationalisation in 1919, anyone who wanted to work in the film industry had to adapt to the existing structures.

Unlike many others in the film industry, Sándor Korda remained for a while in Hungary following the fall of the Council Republic at the beginning of August 1919. However, two months later he was arrested and taken from his suite at the Royal Hotel, where he had been living for a number of years, across the Danube to the Gellért Hotel. The hotel was

17. For these comments of Michael and his uncle see Korda (1979), pp. 60–3.

being used as a base by supporters of Miklós Horthy who were keen to round up those they perceived as 'Bolsheviks', as well as their followers.[18] The building allegedly had rooms set aside as torture chambers.

The precise reasons for Korda's arrest are unclear. Paul Tabori implies it was a case of mistaken identity, but Michael Korda indicates the order came from Horthy himself after he had viewed the films his uncle had made during the previous months. Either way, he wasn't held for long, but the circumstances of his release are even more mysterious. The simplest story is that Korda's wife Mária and others were quick off the mark and kicked up a fuss, reigning in the assistance of Jenő Heltai, a well-known writer who had links with the authorities. A more complicated version includes the curious involvement of a certain Brigadier Maurice, 'variously described as the representative of MI-5 in Budapest, the British government's secret link to Admiral Horthy and as an adventurer, profiteer and speculator'.[19]

Whatever happened, the experience of his arrest appears to have sealed his fate. By early November Sándor Korda had left Hungary and was in Vienna. He would not return to his home country. Hungary's loss, however, would prove to be a gain for the American and British film industries.

Like Korda, in 1919 Mihály Kertész (the future Michael Curtiz of *Casablanca* fame) was a well-known figure of Hungarian cinema, already having been involved with well over 40 films. Having first started out as an actor, in 1913 he went to Denmark and immersed himself in cinema techniques by working at the Nordisk Studios. Returning to Hungary, he became a prolific director, but he also contributed to the literature of cinema aesthetics.

Unlike Korda, his name does not usually feature as one of the members of the 1919 Directory of Film Arts,[20] but according to a decree published in *Vörös Film* on 26 April he was appointed to the so-called Arts Council, one of several bodies established during the Soviet Republic to oversee film production. This one was charged with monitoring the scripts submitted

18. Admiral Miklós Horthy was one of the leaders of the counter-revolutionary forces. As Regent, he would become Hungary's political figurehead not long after the fall of the Commune—a position he retained up to October 1944.

19. Korda (1979), p. 67. According to Tóbiás (1980, p. 27), on 22 April 1951 the British Sunday newspaper *The Observer* carried a report about the involvement of a British officer in Korda's release and escape from Hungary. What the article—actually a general profile of Korda—simply said in connection with this incident in 1919 (by no means the main theme of the piece) was: 'A British official helped to secure his release.' Nothing more. (*The Observer*, 22 April 1951, p. 2.) Tóbiás says that Korda never either denied or confirmed the story.

20. He is not on the initial list published in *Moziviláq* (Cinema World) on 23 March 1919; for which see Garai (1969), p. 46.

for proposed films. Even earlier, on 19 April, the same publication had included Kertész in a list of six people assessing which films could be shot. In addition, one source says he was, like Korda, a member of the body deciding who could be included in the official list of 41 actors and actresses.[21]

There are some contradictions and unanswered questions concerning the activity of Kertész in 1919. István Nemeskürty, for example, writes that he had actually left Hungary in the spring of 1918, never to return, but a few pages later he acknowledges his membership of the Arts Council in 1919.

It is sometimes asserted that Kertész was appointed to be in overall charge of the newsreel films made about the massive celebrations held in Budapest on 1 May 1919, but what he actually did in that connection is not clear. Indeed, on 19 April *Vörös Film* reported that someone else, Oszkár Damó, would be in charge of the filming of the May Day demonstrations. However, one thing is certain—Mihály Kertész was the director of a strongly propagandistic film called *Jön az öcsém* (My Brother is Coming).

The film is a short, approximately ten-minute silent drama based on a poem by Antal Farkas, which appeared on the front page of *Népszava* on 26 March 1919. The poem has five eight-line verses all ending with the one-line refrain of 'Hurry, brother, Hurry!'

The film was made quickly, in a matter of days, and apparently was premiered on 3 April, barely two weeks after the proclamation of the Soviet Republic![22] Thus it was among the first films made during Hungary's 'Bolshevik' period and has even been described as 'one of the world's first agit-prop films'.[23]

The opening sequence shows a room interior. A workman is sat at a table reading a newspaper. To one side a woman (played by Kertész's wife, Ilona Kovács, later known internationally as Lucy Dorraine) sits at a sewing machine. On the other side a child is playing.

Suddenly the door opens of its own volition. The man gets up and goes to the door. All are looking concerned, but there's no one there. He returns to the table and continues reading. The room is poorly furnished, but on the wall there is a clock with a swinging pendulum, marking the passing of time. The intertitles tell us that the man's brother has been away for four years, but is coming back from Siberia 'flying a red banner and running'.

21. Magyar (1967), p. 37.
22. https://en.wikipedia.org/wiki/J%C3%B6n_az_%C3%B6cs%C3%A9m (accessed 6 July 2017). In his detailed study of Hungarian silent films, published by the Hungarian Film Institute in 1996, Zsolt Kőháti suggests that shooting of the film might have begun even before the proclamation of the Council Republic, which would be intriguing indeed. However, no evidence for this is offered.
23. Cunningham (2004), p. 20.

Now we see the brother, played by Oszkár Beregi, one of the most renowned Hungarian actors of the time, appear over the brow of a hill waving a red flag. 'The Carpathians echo his bugle call,' we are informed. Cheering crowds appear on the hillside.

We are told 'he was driven there [to war] by the leaden scourge of power'. And now, as if in a flashback, we see a crowd running up a hill, some are armed, some are falling. Beregi is standing, but as if reeling, finding it difficult to breathe. Then, lying in the snow, he appears to be almost at death's door.

Next he is in a prison cell, his arm is wounded and with the exaggerated gestures common to silent films he gives the impression of despair mixed with anger. He goes to the window and looks out. Suddenly, an image seems to appear on the cell wall. It's a text reading 'Workers of the World Unite', the famous slogan from *The Communist Manifesto*. Beregi examines the words and appears to be struck like St Paul on the road to Damascus. With a fixated look he spreads his arms wide, then clasps them to his chest. The next scene shows the exterior of the prison. Beregi climbs through a window and jumps down. He has escaped.

Having climbed over rocks, he makes a flag from a scarf and the stem of a bush. His look is determined. Now he is coming over the top of a hill, waving the flag and shouting. A crowd appears and lifts him up. He gives a rousing speech. Clenched fists are raised and the crowd moves down the hill, cheering and shouting.

Now we cut back to the room, where the man is still reading. The door opens and his younger brother appears with the flag. There is great rejoicing in the family. Then suddenly we cut to the interior of what appears to be part of a fine mansion, as if the revolutionary's family have been allocated better accommodation. They are all dressed in better clothes. Holding the child in his arms, the younger brother appears rather bemused by the new situation. They look out of the window and wave to demonstrators marching past, waving back. The revolution appears to have been victorious!

In the final sequence the younger brother is shown to have a newspaper in his jacket pocket. It is *Népszava* (People's Voice), the paper of the Social Democrats, not the Communists' *Vörös Újság* (Red Gazette). Whether this detail indicates that Kertész wanted to make a subtle point (or is simply a visual reference to the publication which had carried Antal Farkas' poem) is open to question.

All in all, the film appears as a simplistic propaganda message in praise of the communist leaders now in power, many of whom, like Béla Kun, were taken prisoner in Russia during the war, were converted to Bolshevism and returned to Hungary to establish the Communist Party in November 1918.[24]

It seems that *My Brother is Coming* was the only film Kertész made during the Soviet Republic, though one list of films being prepared but not completed in the period indicates that he was at one time directing a screen version of *Liliom*, based on the play by the popular Hungarian writer Ferenc Molnár, which is best known today as the basis for the Rodgers and Hammerstein musical *Carousel*.[25] That is corroborated by a short report which appeared in *Vörös Film* on 7 June 1919.

Kertész and his wife left Budapest for Vienna well before the fall of the Council Republic, probably in late May or early June. *Vörös Film* also reported on 7 June that he was already in the Austrian capital and that in an interview with *Der Filmbote* had expressed strong criticism of the Hungarian film industry and that political interference was ruining it. However, in a subsequent issue of the Austrian publication Kertész apparently distanced himself from the views attributed to him.[26]

It is often said that Kertész never returned to Hungary, but on 18 July 1931 *Az Est* (Evening News) ran an interview with him on the occasion of a visit he was paying to Budapest. He is quoted as saying that in 1919 'the outbreak of communism meant an end to the arts' and he claims he decided to leave. Without luggage or passport he took a train to Hungary's western border, where there was a minor altercation with some border guards. However, he says he was allowed to proceed after one of them recognised him. The introduction to the interview asserts that Kertész left Hungary within five days of the proclamation of the Council Republic. The implication is that this precise information came from Kertész himself, though it is not absolutely clear.

But if he did leave so early on, how could he have worked on *My Brother is Coming* or taken part in the Arts Council activities? Furthermore, a report in the 24 May 1919 edition of *Vörös Film* indicates that Kertész had recently participated in one of the cultural propaganda events held weekly at the Marx and Lenin cinemas in the provincial town of Kiskunfélegyháza.

Perhaps in 1931, when the official view in Hungary (indeed, a view commonly-held elsewhere) involved condemnation of everything and anything in connection with 1919, Michael Curtiz, as he was then known,

24. Subsequent to careful restoration work undertaken by the Hungarian Film Institute in 1999, *My Brother is Coming* was made accessible on the internet (with English subtitles). See, for example: www.youtube.com/watch?v=7DAiz_KoPFY (accessed 6 July 2017).
25. Garai (1969), p. 318.
26. Kőháti (1996), p. 151.

was inclined to cover his tracks and be less than forthcoming about his involvement with the cinema of the Hungarian Soviet Republic.

The red newsreel

One particular element of Hungarian film production in 1919 worth highlighting is *Vörös Riport Film* (Red Newsreel), a weekly cinema news report about current events. John Cunningham claims that these newsreels were 'probably the first of their kind in the world', which is strange since they were a continuation of newsreels screened in Hungarian cinemas prior to the Council Republic period. True, they tended to be strongly political, agit-prop films, but Dziga Vertov and others had been making such newsreels in Soviet Russia for some time.

The purpose of the newsreels was accurately captured by an article in the 26 April edition of *Vörös Film*. 'Primarily they have to serve propaganda purposes' by recording all the significant events of proletarian power. The films would also show the 'disgraceful, shocking conditions' in which the proletariat had lived, in contrast with the luxurious lifestyle of the bourgeoisie. Viewers could also see how formerly deprived children could now enjoy lively tea parties in the Park Club, which previously was 'the feasting place of the idle aristocracy'.[27]

Bálint Magyar says the newsreels were unlike documentaries in that they were one-sided and optimistic, with no deep analysis. Moreover, he adds that they threw no light on the 'spontaneous and systematic sabotage' and 'poisonous currents' which permeated the entire period of the Soviet Republic.[28]

What did the red newsreels actually show? Perhaps unsurprisingly, given the foreign intervention at the time, a large number of sequences deal with military matters, depicting recruiting, troops setting off for the front, or the situation after certain victories, such as the capture of Kassa (today Košice, Slovakia) in early June. The importance of the military situation is underlined by the fact that the entire content of six newsreels in a row during May and June dealt with military matters.

The scenes of cheerful, waving soldiers clambering on railway wagons to be sent to the front or marching off to engage with the enemy are uncannily reminiscent of similar enthusiastic scenes filmed in many countries across Europe at the start of the First World War.

---

27. Garai (1969), p. 222. The building of the former Park Club still stands at 34-36 Stefánia út, near Budapest's City Park.
28. Magyar (1967), p. 48.

Along with images of the troops there are many sequences showing the leading politicians of the time making speeches, sometimes in front of soldiers and sometimes in front of open-air, mass meetings of civilians in Budapest—the square in front of parliament was a favourite place for such demonstrations.

Then there are scenes of everyday life: people relaxing on Margaret Island, enjoying an open-air swimming pool, having a good time at the 'English Park' (the name of a fun fair by the City Park), enjoying music and food, or taking part in sporting activities. The idea is created that things have improved for ordinary people, thanks to the new regime.

Several sequences show children enjoying various activities, some of them newly organised, such as attending a fairy-tale matinee at the Orpheum,[29] playing in the City Park, being entertained at a circus, or arriving and singing (*The Internationale*!) at one of the newly opened children's cinemas.

One red newsreel includes scenes of children getting on trains at the Eastern Railway Station as they set off for a holiday at Lake Balaton. Then the twentieth in the series is all about adults and children enjoying life by the lakeside—relaxing as well as playing games in the sand. There are sequences showing the children's sanatorium at Balatonszabadi, children rushing into the water, and—the final scene of all—children building a sandcastle.

This was presumably not a deliberate allusion to building political sandcastles in the air, but as it happened that newsreel was the last in the series and was actually screened a couple of days after the fall of the Soviet Republic.

The biggest single project that the newsreel producers were involved in was the filming of the massive demonstrations held in Budapest on 1 May. Camera operators were placed at strategic locations across the city to capture the day's events—the rallies, the speeches and the demonstrations, as well as the entertainment and sporting activities. It was planned to use 2000 metres of film stock and the final product was well over twice the length of the usual newsreel.

Here again children featured prominently—being fed, playing games and engaging in various competitions on Margaret Island. Somewhat incongruously, these merry scenes of proletarian youngsters were immediately followed by a sequence showing members of what even the written insert in the newsreel described as 'the terror group', otherwise known as

29. The Royal Orpheum was a popular variety theatre. It stood on the site of today's Madách Theatre in Budapest.

the 'Lenin Boys', the regime's strong-arm enforcers. 'Bourgeois', the terror group's dog, is shown wearing a decoration, as if it had received an award.

Following this curious interlude (though one obviously deliberately inserted) the newsreel concludes by returning to more jovial scenes—May Day revellers enjoying a boat trip on the Danube, dancers in the City Park, a sausage-eating competition and, finally, cinema professionals at the tables in the garden of the Gundel Restaurant.

The 20 newsreels of *Vörös Riport Film* have been the subject of at least one academic study based on film aesthetics and film theory. Bruno de Marchi approaches the series as 'a documentary macrotext of the republic', one that is 'inspired by metanoia'. He refers to 'a denotative and a connotative reading' that can be applied to the sequences, and describes how the newsreels treat the proletariat as 'the omphalos of a new society'.[30]

The approach and the language may not be to everyone's taste, but at least we can make our own judgements since the newsreels produced during the time of the Hungarian Soviet Republic have been digitised and can sometimes be viewed online.[31]

30. De Marchi (1987).

31. The screenplays with the texts of the inserts are reproduced in Garai (1969), pp. 258–94.

7

Opening up the Auditoriums

In the evening on 21 March 1919, the day when the Hungarian Soviet Republic was proclaimed, a scheduled performance of Strauss's *Die Fledermaus* was underway at the sumptuous State Opera House on Budapest's grand Andrássy Avenue, when all of a sudden, in the middle of Act Two, set in the ballroom of Prince Orlofsky, unexpected guests arrived, but not with the intention of observing and appreciating the merriment on the stage.

A group of youths rushed through the auditorium towards the orchestra pit and disrupted the performance, loudly shouting that the Soviet Republic had been established. Not being accustomed to such public displays of political ardour at the Opera House, and no doubt being somewhat frightened, members of the audience fled towards the cloakrooms in the hope of making a speedy exit.

Total panic might have broken out were it not for the quick-witted action of opera singer Rezső Kornay, who came to the front of the stage, had the auditorium lights turned on and calmed the crowd, at the same time saying a few words about the political changes of the day. At that, the noisy intruders began to shout 'Long live the Soviet Republic!' with some of the audience following suit. The orchestra, also reacting smartly, loudly played *La Marseillaise*, and both audience and performers on the stage joined in—in so far as they knew any of the words. After all this, the performance of *Die Fledermaus* continued uninterrupted.[1]

In some ways the incident was a precursor of what was to come during the Council Republic period—a mixture of bombastic politics, fear, farce and the continuation, when possible, of normal activities.

Indeed, in the three months following the noisy incident of 21 March, the Opera House presented works by 'standard' composers such as Mozart, Bizet, Puccini, Verdi, Wagner, Gluck and Offenbach. Perhaps that is not surprising, since the everyday management of the enterprise by and large remained in the hands of the same people who had been running things

---

1. The story is related in Staud (1984), p. 128 and Gerencsér (1993), p. 19. A similar incident involving soldiers disrupting the performance at the Vígszínház (Comedy Theatre) on the same evening and proclaiming the formation of the Soviet Republic is recalled by Imre Gál. See Gál (1937), p. 7.

prior to 21 March. True, there were some changes. For example, there were special 'workers' performances' on Sundays, but they had already been a feature since late 1918.[2]

This type of continuity wasn't what the new regime was apparently intending. At the very first meeting of the Revolutionary Governing Council on 22 March, György Lukács, the Deputy People's Commissar for Education and Culture, spoke about removing theatres from private hands and transferring them to public ownership. There was no formal decree issued at the meeting, but the heading of an article in the following day's *Az Újság* (The News) clearly expressed what was taking place: 'The Nationalisation of Theatres'.[3]

The article reported that all privately-owned theatres in Budapest, as well as cabarets and music halls, were to become publicly owned and their management passed into the hands of the people's commissars for culture. A nine-member committee was to be established, the article continued, comprising writers, actors and theatre directors to work out all the details. The committee would determine the main directions of the theatres' programmes and that as far as possible these should include pieces reflecting revolutionary ideas and socialist tendencies. Failing that, classical works should be performed. In some theatres, during the intervals well-known Hungarian writers would give presentations 'of a revolutionary character'. The first 'lecturers', according to the report, would include Mihály Babits, Frigyes Karinthy, Dezső Kosztolányi and Ferenc Molnár.

On 24 March Zsigmond Kunfi, People's Commissar for Education and Culture, and his deputy György Lukács signed a decree which appeared as a poster with the heading 'From now on theatres belong to the people!'[4] The declaration included an announcement to the effect that the majority of theatre tickets would henceforth be allocated to workers and distributed via the trade unions at reduced prices. Some tickets would still be available at the usual prices from theatre box offices. As if anticipating that advantage might be taken of this dual-price system, the decree stressed that the low-cost tickets were intended only for workers. A couple of days later a new decree was issued, this time signed only by Lukács, which somewhat modified the situation. Now theatres themselves would also be able to sell reduced-price tickets, but strictly only to people with a trade union membership card. As an indication of how the commissars liked

---

2. Staud (1984), p. 128.
3. 'A színházak államosítása', *Az Újság*, 23 March 1919, p. 11.
4. The text of the poster is reproduced in Petrák & Milei (1959), pp. 176–7.

to meddle in the finest details, Lukács even specified the precise opening hours, morning and afternoon, for these 'workers' box offices'.[5]

According to Géza Staud, the system of workers-only tickets functioned for a while, but later a black market in tickets did indeed emerge.[6]

On 27 March the commissariat established a so-called theatre socialisation committee under the chairmanship of Béla Reinitz, a composer who for many years prior to and during the First World War had also been a music critic of *Népszava* (People's Voice), the newspaper of the Social Democrats. Reinitz was allocated responsibility for the Opera House and the National Theatre, while other venues were assigned to the other members of the committee, which included Béla Balázs and Lajos Kassák.

The same day saw the publication in *Vörös Újság* (Red Gazette) of a more general statement of aims for the theatre under the heading 'Theatre policy of the People's Commissariat for Education and Culture'.[7] The article stated that theatres had been taken into public ownership so that they could serve the interests of the proletariat, which to date had been forced to be satisfied with detective stories and sordid romantic dramas. Now they would be able to attain pure, artistic culture. Apart from transforming the economy, an intellectual transformation was also one of the most important tasks, particularly since the spiritual dominance of the bourgeoisie was one of the strongest means of economic enslavement. That domination was partly served by religious education in schools and partly by trashy cultural products.

'The theatre is the strongest means for the popularisation of art,' the article stated, 'because while a certain level of intellectual discipline is required for reading, the theatre with its illustrative power brings its public closer to understanding more complicated artistic concepts.'

Future theatre programmes would be assessed in terms of their educational value, but that could not be reduced simply to issues of political agitation. 'Every true work of art simultaneously bears revolutionary significance,' the article asserted. Equally important was the merging of so-called national culture and international culture. At the same time, efforts should be made to spread theatre art to provincial Hungary, which apart from a few large towns had so far been starved of it.

Although hoping that modern experimental works would soon be performed more widely, the article had to admit that for the time being theatres would have to work with what was available.

5. 'Rendelet a színházjegyekről', *Vörös Újság*, 27 March 1919, p. 4.
6. Staud (1984), p. 128.
7. 'A Közoktatásügyi Népbiztosság színházi programja', *Vörös Újság*, 27 March 1919, p. 7.

Also on 27 March, under the heading 'Revolutionary Presentations in the Theatres', *Az Újság* returned to the issue of noted writers giving brief political lectures during the intervals in certain theatres. The aim of these, the report said, was to raise revolutionary consciousness. In the middle of entertainment, writers and poets would take a few minutes to address the serious matters of life and the world of the future, which formerly was just a dream, but was now approaching as a reality 'with rumbling steps'.

According to the report, published just six days after the Soviet Republic had been proclaimed, Andor Gábor, Mihály Babits and Dezső Kosztolányi had already given such lectures and others doing so in the near future would include Frigyes Karinthy, Lajos Barta, Ferenc Molnár and Aladár Komját.[8]

It was one thing to have grandiose ideas about transforming the nature of Hungary's theatre world, but it was another matter to put those ideas into practice. Simply setting up committees of people perceived to be politically reliable to oversee the process wasn't enough. Even personality clashes could affect their work. Lajos Kassák would recall that the two Bélas (Reinitz and Balázs) who were prominent in the newly established theatre committee didn't work together well.

'The two people got on with each other only with great difficulty. Balázs clearly looked down on Reinitz, while Reinitz considered Balázs a clown and a poser. This hostile relationship went back a long way ...'[9]

Perhaps it helped that the committee members were allocated different theatres to 'look after'. Indeed, at an early meeting Reinitz declared that every theatre, cabaret and music hall should have its own political commissar. Kassák was allocated the Comedy and the Magyar theatres, which he soon visited. With his customary critical insight, he quickly started asking himself what on earth he was doing there.

> I had hardly looked around when I saw that it wasn't me who was needed, but a good financial manager. Why have a political minder here? The actors are friendly, but I can see they are mistrustful ... and if I want to avoid a conflict I have to realise that I should leave them in peace.[10]

Kassák was quite aware that the theatres had been put into an entirely new, difficult situation, that from one day to the next they had found themselves in a position of being beggars. 'Those directors who yesterday had been

8. 'Forradalmi előadások a színházakban', *Az Újság*, 27 March 1919, p. 7.
9. Kassák (1983), p. 527.
10. Ibid., p. 529.

managing their theatres profitably now have to turn to us for their working capital. They have no money for what they need and nothing from which to pay the actors' salaries.' It was 'a whirlpool', which could quickly cause chaos.[11]

Nevertheless Kassák continued his work on the committee, negotiating with various people, investigating complaints and trying to calm matters. The office was besieged by directors, producers, actors, musicians and singers, turning the place, in his opinion, into a public assembly point for all those whose ambitions were causing them misgivings, for those who were permanently dissatisfied, those who weren't quite sure which way the wind was blowing, those few who were actually interested in the political developments underway, but mainly for insatiable people looking for help and notorious extortionists wanting advances.

> Elderly actresses with a forlorn proletarian mask both requested and demanded a monthly pension. Young ones wanted a contract on the grounds that they had always placed their art at the service of the people's culture, while others who were known and significant on the stage ... were fighting for more and more advances.

Very few knew about and took seriously what had been happening recently in Hungary. 'Were they counter-revolutionaries?' Kassák asks himself. And he provides his own answer: 'They were no more Whites than they were Reds. They simply wanted to live, to ensure for themselves whatever they could in this temporary chaos.'[12]

Eventually Kassák came to the conclusion that matters were not going well for the theatre committee and that things were not functioning properly. No one in former positions wanted to take responsibility for anything and it wasn't possible to resolve the financial problems, nor ensure the standard of productions. 'Undoubtedly we faced united, quiet sabotage on the part of former owners, directors, actors and technical staff.'[13]

The financial problem was the most serious and most urgent task to deal with, and that wasn't restricted to paying salaries. The actors and particularly the actresses bombarded the committee for the means to enable them to obtain clothing, stockings, powder, rouge, face paint, eau de cologne, perfume and a thousand other things they insisted on. Reinitz was driven crazy by it all, says Kassák, and the situation was clearly unsustainable.

Eventually it was decided to call a meeting of the former owners and directors who were still in place, albeit with other job titles, to discuss what

11. Ibid., p. 530.
12. Ibid., p. 531.
13. Ibid., p. 545.

should be done (and what they were expected to do).[14] The meeting was addressed by Zsigmond Kunfi, the People's Commissar for Education and Culture, who for many years had been a prominent figure of the Social Democratic Party. In Kassák's view, Kunfi was no demagogue, rather someone who wanted to persuade his audience through reason. He was someone, he says, who always remained like a typical provincial teacher, who always dressed smartly and who always behaved somewhat awkwardly in public. Nevertheless, Kassák acknowledges, he was a first-class orator and one of his party's outstanding theorists. Kunfi had been given the culture portfolio during the latter half of the post-war Károlyi regime and again after the Soviet Republic was established.

Kunfi tried to win over those present with talk of culture and the arts, but according to Kassák they sat stiffly and behaved as if he wasn't talking to them. Then, stressing he would like to depart on a friendly basis and expressing the hope that the discussions would lead to peaceful cooperation, he thanked his audience and left the meeting—which Kassák suspected he was quite keen to do.

The meeting continued with Reinitz in the chair, Balázs and Kassák at his side. A workers' meeting in a factory would have been much easier, thought Kassák. He felt there was a wide gap between the two sides, even though Reinitz tried to focus on culture, rather than revolutionary politics.

Kassák and his circle around the journal *MA* organised their own presentations, independently of any established theatres, and they had been doing so since before the Soviet Republic was proclaimed. They weren't actually full drama performances, rather mixed-genre presentations involving dramatic elements, recitations, music and singing, all with a strong political theme. They were not always successful, as Kassák himself would admit. He records in his memoirs that at one point it was decided to organise a series of 'propaganda matinees' in the capital and the larger provincial towns. The first stage was Újpest, a working-class area which at the time was an independent township on the north side of Budapest.

> Sad memories are associated with the performance. The locals had only heard bad things about us, and now in vain did we appear before them with revolutionary poems and dramatic sketches. They reacted to the whole thing as a kind of comedy and giggled throughout the performance.[15]

14. Ibid., p. 546 ff. for what follows about the meeting.
15. Ibid., p. 513.

Greater success was apparently achieved with one of the '*MA* evenings', held at the Academy of Music on 2 May, which was announced two days before in *Fáklya* (Torch) as a 'demonstrative presentation for the revolutionary working class'. On the bill were poems, including works by Walt Whitman, and organ music. The same paper reported on 3 May that the performances before a full house had been greeted with unending applause. Kassák gave readings, the report said, as did the painter Béla Uitz, and the Opera House baritone Lajos Bársony also made an appearance with a song entitled *The Young Worker*.

A second Bonaparte

Perhaps one of the most unusual productions to be staged in 1919 was *Napóleon*, a three-act play about Napoleon Bonaparte premiered at the National Theatre in Budapest in mid May. Arguably the subject *per se* wasn't so unusual, rather the fact that the playwright, József Pogány, was more of a political activist than a dramatist.

Pogány was a member of the Social Democratic Party who, through his agitation and interventions, had managed to get himself elected as president of the Budapest Soldiers' Council in early November 1918, four months before the proclamation of the Soviet Republic. Prior to the war he had worked as a journalist and political writer. He also fancied himself as a literary figure and wrote *Napóleon* in that period, though according to his biographer the work was never performed until May 1919.[16]

By that time Pogány was a prominent leader of the new regime. With the formation of the Council Republic he had been appointed People's Commissar for War, but being aggressive and quarrelsome with his (equally aggressive) deputies, Tibor Szamuely and Béla Szántó, he was pressurised to resign after being in the post for barely two weeks. Yet, appointed as a Deputy Commissar for Foreign Affairs and being given important military positions, he remained a prominent and powerful personality, which may explain why his play was performed at the National Theatre.

The play depicted its protagonist as being somewhat reluctant to become emperor and, according to Géza Staud's listing of theatre performances during the Council Republic period, it was staged 17 times over a period of three weeks. As an indication of the mainly traditional nature of theatre programmes at the time, it alternated with classics such as *Richard III*, *Antigone*, *Hamlet*, *Romeo and Juliet*, *Faust* and *The Miser*.

Not surprisingly, perhaps, positive notices appeared in *Népszava* and Vörös Újság, and it seems from those that the opening night of *Napóleon*

16. Sakmyster (2012), p. 5.

produced enthusiastic applause. 'Of the performance and direction we can only write good,' enthused the latter.[17] One observer, however, would later assert that most applause came from holders of free tickets obtained from the trade unions and the Soldiers' and Workers' Council, and that the majority of the audience remained manifestly silent. Yet this commentator also thought that one of the performers, Imre Pethes, 'even during the proletarian dictatorship is still the best actor'.[18]

Other remarks were strongly negative, scathing even. Writing in the June 1919 edition of the progressive journal *Nyugat* (Occident), Miksa Fenyő asserted that 'József Pogány is no bard. At the most he is someone who gazes at the position from far away and very enviously … a truly boring writer entirely without personality.' The play itself was 'shallow', misleading about Napoleon and 'a very bad drama'.[19]

The conservative writer Ferenc Herczeg would comment in a volume published in 1921 that it 'heavy-handedly limped along with all the mistakes of the old sentimental school' and in the same publication theatre director Artúr Bárdos described it as a 'grotesque self-exposure' and 'pretty much worthless'.[20]

Even the left-wing Lajos Kassák couldn't contain his criticism years later. As he wrote in his autobiographical memoir:

> With his blustering manner and disagreeable postures, Pogány was generally mocked as a Napoleon himself, and it was precisely this premier which provided the opposition with new fuel for agitation. What unbounded shamelessness that someone in a leading position should appear before the public with an amateurish theatrical patchwork, and what unthinking philistines were those who gave permission for the performance.[21]

Soon after *Napóleon*'s stage premiere, Pogány himself provided further fuel for his detractors. He assumed imperial airs and began to hold elaborate banquets at his military headquarters by Lake Balaton. Writers, artists, actresses and others were invited to travel from Budapest on Pogány's private train. Alongside the parties with sumptuous food, they were entertained with horse races and excursions on the lake. These antics of the 'Red Napoleon' didn't go down too well at a time when many

17. *Vörös Újság*, 18 May 1919, p. 7.
18. Gál (1937), p. 144.
19. Fenyő, 'Pogány József—Napóleon', *Nyugat* (1919), No. 11; http://epa.oszk.hu/00000/00022/00268/07947.htm (accessed 4 July 2017).
20. Gratz (1921), pp. 700, 723.
21. Kassák (1983), p. 584.

people were starving and the regime was in danger due to foreign military intervention.[22]

What of the actors in all this? They were the theatre people most well known by the public and—almost by definition as actors—were people with a fine sense of the public mood, which in 1919 inevitably meant the political mood. Not surprisingly, interpretations about the role played by actors have differed, depending on who was writing or expressing an opinion and, in particular, when they did so.

The theatre director Artúr Bárdos, writing soon after the fall of the Soviet Republic, emphasised the corrupting influences and manipulation of theatre life witnessed in 1919. Actors needed to live and so sought roles and favours from those able to hand them out. However, that was a situation enforced from above as a result of the new political conditions (and arguably it had always been thus).

After 1945, however, and in particular in the post-1956 decades, the so-called Kádár era, when historians and others 're-visited' the 1919 Soviet Republic, the published views were much more positive and emphasis was given to the alleged active participation in and even enthusiasm for the then changes on the part of all sections of society, including actors. In a study published in 1962, for example, the literary historian Béla Osváth was keen to highlight that right at the start of the Soviet Republic period many well-known actors of the time participated in the Artistic Council, one of the new bodies established to oversee the theatre industry. He says that conditions for actors greatly improved, with actors' income differentials being much reduced and their unemployment rate falling considerably. Their material conditions as well as their moral esteem improved, he asserts, and there was no requisitioning of their apartments, some of which—those belonging to the well-known, better-off actors—presumably were quite grand. Osváth also claims that no actor got into any trouble, not even Szeréna Fáy who 'made derogatory remarks about proletarian power' and 'stirred up a nationalist atmosphere' at a meeting of National Theatre actors.[23] However, as this last observation clearly indicates, not all members of the acting community were of one mind or supported what was going on.

Indeed, on one occasion there was even a strike of actors. It took place on the evening of Sunday, 6 July, at the Király and Magyar theatres. The action was in protest at the attempt of József Pogány, who by then was in the cultural commissariat, to dismiss László Beöthy from his position as a

22. Sakmyster (2012), pp. 45–6.
23. Osváth (1962), pp. 104, 111.

director. The strike was supported by the musicians and other theatre staff, and an explanation was given by one of the leading actors to the audience whose members had turned up for the expected performance. They, in turn, walked out of the theatre in sympathy. However, nothing particularly dramatic resulted from the strike, one way or the other, as the following day saw the start of the summer break in the theatre programme.[24]

Dracula the union man

The names of Hungarian actors featuring in the literature on Hungary 1919 are likely to be unfamiliar to most non-Hungarians. However, there is one exception—that of everyone's favourite Hollywood Dracula, Béla Lugosi. Surprising though it may seem, Lugosi played a prominent role during the 1919 Soviet Republic, after the defeat of which he felt obliged to emigrate.

Béla Ferenc Dezső Blaskó was born in Lugos (today Lugoj in Romania) in 1882.[25] When he was 20 years old he changed his name to Lugossy and in 1911 he modified that to Lugosi. (In his early career as a film star in Hungary he used the stage name Arisztid Olt.) Béla's father, a baker who rose to become a small-town banker, died when he was just short of twelve years old.

His acting career took off mainly with repertory theatre in the provinces, and he made his debut at Budapest's National Theatre in early January 1913. In summer 1914 he enlisted in the army and spent 18 months on the Russian front, being wounded twice. He started out in films in 1917 appearing, for example, as the lead in *Az ezredes* (The Colonel), directed by Mihály Kertész (Michael Curtiz).

After the war, the break-up of the Habsburg empire and the autumn 1918 Chrysanthemum Revolution in Hungary, Lugosi 'threw himself into liberal causes, although he had never previously shown any political interest'.[26] On 2 December the Free Organisation of Theatre Employees was established with Lugosi heading the names of the committee members.

It seems he was proud of a trade union card he had kept from past times. Lennig indicates that before he became an actor he had attended an industrial school near his birthplace and later was an apprentice fitter. Other sources say he had worked in a mine. Either way, during the Soviet

24. 'Színházi sztrájk a kommün alatt' (Theatre Strike During the Commune), *Színházi Élet*, 7–13 September 1919, p. 6.
25. For this and other details about Lugosi's early life, see Lennig (2003).
26. Ibid., p. 32.

Republic period he was a prominent activist as the secretary of the National Trade Union of Actors, which was established on 7 April.

In the first edition of the revamped *Színészek lapja* (Actors' Journal), which appeared on 1 May 1919, Lugosi had an article about the history of the union's formation. In the same issue the director Sándor Hevesi wrote about 'The Real People's Theatre' and the noted actress Mari Jászai contributed a piece entitled 'An Actress as a Working Woman'. Jászai, 69 at the time, was a renowned member of the National Theatre and one of the most prominent personalities of Hungary's theatre world. The theme of her essay was not entirely removed from her own experience. She was born the daughter of a carpenter and from the age of ten worked as a nursemaid.

Elsewhere, Lugosi would recall that the post-war upheaval had induced the 'actor-slave' to come to his senses and speak out. 'The definite aim of my organising activity was the raising of the moral, economic and cultural level of the actors' society.'[27] According to Arthur Lennig, the minutes of the first congress of the actors' national trade union described Lugosi as entering the room to 'great cheering and applause' and saying 'I do not know Budapest and province actors, I know only actors and non-actors'. It was a reference to the discrimination and prejudice many actors in the provinces felt in relation to the Budapest theatre elite. He also urged all actors to join with other unions of technical workers and musicians so that together they could tackle the problems of the industry.[28]

In an article published in mid May 1919, Lugosi passionately contested the view that actors are not proletarians. 'What is the truth?' he asked.

> It is that 95 per cent of the actors' community has been more proletarian than the most exploited worker. After putting aside the glamorous trappings of his trade at the end of each performance, an actor had, with few exceptions, to face worry and poverty. He was obliged either to bend himself to stultifying odd jobs to keep body and soul together … or he had to sponge off his friends, get into debt or prostitute his art. And he endured it, endured the poverty, the humiliation, the exploitation, just so that he could continue to be an actor, to get parts, for without them he could not live. Actors were exploited no less by the private capitalist managers than they were by the state …The actor, subsisting on starvation wages and demoralised, was often driven, albeit reluctantly, to place himself at the disposal of the former ruling classes. Martyrdom was the price of enthusiasm for acting.[29]

27. Ibid., p. 32.
28. Ibid., pp. 33–4.
29. *Színészek lapja*, 15 May 1919. Quoted in Lennig (2003), p. 34.

Given his role and published views, it is perhaps no surprise that very soon after the collapse of the Soviet Republic Béla Lugosi decided to leave Hungary, crossing to Austria in early August 1919. He would eventually end up in the United States, where Hungary's loss would be Hollywood's gain.

As noted in Chapter 2, actors, actresses and other theatre workers participated together with their own section in the massive, celebratory demonstrations held on 1 May. The future internationally renowned playwright Gyula Háy, then almost 19 years old, would recall: 'They [the crowd on Andrássy Avenue] beamed with joy to see the most popular actors and actresses in the land dancing the csárdás on the backs of lorries.'[30]

They didn't just perform in the central areas, but entertained the public throughout the day in different locations of the city. Mária Majtényi was a young, 23-year-old actress in 1919. She would later recall how she and others were taken on a lorry decorated with red flags to Budapest's Népliget (People's Park, southeast of the centre), where on an improvised stage she performed a Russian dance with a colleague from the drama school. She says she then recited Petőfi's *The Whole Sea Has Revolted* and Zseni Várnai's *Don't shoot, my son, for I will be there*.[31] Afterwards she was taken to outlying places such as Kispest and Újpest to give further performances 'to the assembled people, who previously had never had the opportunity to experience such a thing'.[32]

Reaching out

As we have seen, during the time of the Soviet Republic an attempt was made, partly through the new ticket pricing and distribution system, to open up the theatres to a wider audience—putting it simply, to bring theatre culture to the masses. Indeed, there was also a plan to take it physically to them, as revealed in a published interview given by Béla Reinitz, who spoke of ten or fifteen new places for theatre performances to be established outside central Budapest, which would be served by a new collective of actors.

'Let not the tired worker be forced to come [into the centre] for the theatre,' he declared. 'The theatre must go out to him, so that he can leave work, go home and there find entertainment.'[33]

---

30. Hay (1974), pp. 70–1.
31. The second reference is actually the last line of each verse of Várnai's *To My Soldier Son*.
32. Kron Jenőné (Mária Majtényi)—reminiscences; manuscript in the PTI Archives, PIL 867.f. K-23, pp. 1, 4.
33. 'Budapest új színházai' (Budapest's New Theatres), *Fáklya*, 27 April, p. 7.

Groups of actors also went to the front to entertain the troops of the Red Army. Elemér Baló, the personal secretary of National Theatre director Zoltán Ambrus, would later recall how:

> members of the Red Front Theatre would travel in small groups to visit military barracks and camps and give inspiring, educational and entertaining performances. They hardly got any pay … the actors weren't performing for money … They were loyal sons of the Soviet Republic. There was such a group in [the town of] Gödöllő. They lived permanently among the fighters.[34]

There were also special events for soldiers in Budapest. For example, a 'Day of the Red Soldier' was organised for 5 April, when eminent performers such as Gizi Bajor, Sári Fedák and Aranka Váradi put in an appearance.[35] The successful 'day' was repeated on other occasions, as were 'revolutionary red matinees' for workers. One for Sunday 20 April was advertised three days beforehand in *Pesti Hírlap* (Pest News), which announced that the popular stage performer Mari Jászai would be among those appearing.

The policy of 'opening up to the people' had the result that many theatre auditoriums quite suddenly became packed with a new type of audience, as was noted with enthusiasm by a number of observers, including the renowned writer Zsigmond Móricz. In an article entitled 'New Public', published in *Az Ember* (Man) just ten days after the Soviet Republic had been declared, Móricz wrote about a visit he had paid to the National Theatre to see a production of Herman Heijermans' *The Good Hope*, a social realist drama about the exploitation of sea fishermen.[36]

'I was impressed and enthralled,' he writes, 'when I saw three tobacco factory girls and an old woman with a black headscarf in Count Béla Széchenyi's theatre box.' In fact, he thought the entire auditorium, which was full, had a proletarian feeling about it. Moreover, he says he detected a sparkle in people's eyes, a pure and open appreciation, and looks of innocence and sincerity.

'As if in a room's summer darkness the curtain had been taken down from the window and all at once rich sunlight had streamed in: the great heat of the heart and the light of understanding is now ablaze in proletarian eyes.'

---

34. Elemér Baló—reminiscences; manuscript in the PTI Archives, PIL 867.f. B-24, p. 6.
35. *Színházi élet a forradalmak idején* (Theatre life during the period of revolutions), http://mek.oszk.hu/02000/02065/html/2kotet/154.html (accessed 4 July 2017).
36. Written in 1901, *The Good Hope* was performed ten times at the National Theatre during the Soviet Republic, nine times in Szeged, five times in Hódmezővásárhely and several times at other provincial theatres. Osváth (1962), p. 96.

And so he continued with superlatives about the new public around him, finally remarking: 'I took on an entirely new life during that evening and some kind of exalted and pure feelings arose within me concerning the task of the arts.'[37]

Another observer was equally enthusiastic even nearly three months later. Under the title 'Workers in the Theatres' a contributor to *Népszava* declared: ' … instead of the taverns, the proletarian is going to the theatre. Instead of soporific alcoholic entertainment, with the presentation of human tragedies and victories, both social and individual, as well as past times, the proletarian is becoming conscious of himself and his class.'

The writer then went on to argue that it was false to assert that working people couldn't understand culture, even if there were difficulties regarding the many nuances. 'The reign of the workers is leading to a new resurrection of the arts,' the author confidently asserted. The tone was perhaps predictable, given where it was published, though little concrete evidence was provided.[38]

Nevertheless, the idea that there was a new audience for theatre was quite common. Even the then 68-year-old, renowned actress Lujza Blaha, for many years a stalwart of the National Theatre who was known as 'the nation's nightingale', caught the positive mood. In a published interview she declared:

> I am convinced that only a brighter world can result … I never had any great desires and I don't now … but I have one wish: I'd like to perform a few more times, to appear before the new public, which couldn't previously see me playing some of my best roles from the old plays.[39]

Other observers could have a rather different, perhaps not so lofty view of the 'new public'. In his diary notes for 17 April 1919, Imre Gál describes a visit he paid to the Király (King's) Theatre to watch a performance of Robert Planquette's operetta *The Bells of Corneville*. The auditorium was packed, as was common in those days, he remarks, adding 'of course mainly with manual workers who had obtained tickets through the trade unions'. As it happens, Gál—whose work is called *A Bourgeois in the Storm*—had himself got his own ticket from someone who had connections with one of the unions.

The performance began with a rendering of *The Internationale* and, says Gál, its proletarian spirit was present throughout the evening. Sitting next

37. 'Új közönség', *Az Ember*, 1 April 1919, pp. 14–15.
38. Albert Király, 'Munkások a színházakban', *Népszava*, 25 June 1919, pp. 7–8.
39. *Színházi Élet*, 22 June 1919. Quoted in Remete (1956), p. 289.

to him was a Red Army soldier, who throughout the performance was constantly pestering his neighbour to enlist in the army and join a military mounted band. The latter, apparently a member of a factory orchestra, didn't seem to like the idea and tried to get his soldier friend to remain quiet during the performance—but to no avail. So during one of the intervals he changed places with a woman in their group who then throughout the performance munched popcorn and hummed tunes which were unrelated to what the orchestra was playing.

Behind Gál there was an elderly man, apparently not a worker, whose wife was carefully giving an explanation of every scene. 'It was as if the man wasn't in the theatre but sitting at home, while the woman was telling him over the telephone what was happening on the stage.' For Gál the whole performance was spoiled by these experiences and he could hardly wait to get away.[40]

The theatre producer and director Artúr Bárdos also remembered that the theatres were full during the time of the Soviet Republic. 'The people watched everything,' he says. 'You can't say they were choosy. If need be, they'd even go to see Shakespeare and listen to Mozart.' However, in connection with such performances Bárdos recalls a rather cruel joke going the rounds, according to which you were not supposed to applaud in the theatres when there were certain classical productions being performed, 'in order not to wake up the proletariat'.

'It often happened,' he continues:

> that people sat on the edge of a theatre box playing cards in order to lighten the artistic enjoyment, or they found amusement in, for example, throwing a cap from the rear seats towards the front. However, they generally endured things with a good spirit. Nevertheless, their real love clearly remained the music hall, which was strongly criticised by the Soviet [authorities].[41]

Regarding traditional drama performances, Bárdos reckoned that the regular audience mainly comprised white-collar union members, such as office workers and teachers, as well as their families. They truly welcomed the cheap tickets, which enabled them to attend theatre performances.

Not forgetting the children

As with film screenings in cinemas, there was a drive during the Soviet Republic period to provide special performances for children and in

40. Gál (1937), pp. 73–4.
41. Gratz (1921), p. 724.

particular workers' children, who would otherwise never experience the dramatic arts. The newspapers of the time often carried announcements in this connection. On 15 April, for example, *Vörös Újság* published an item under the title 'Opera performances for proletarian children'.

'At the request of the Friends of Proletarian Children Association,' it stated, 'the Revolutionary Governing Council's person in charge of theatre affairs has ordered that at 10 a.m. on [Sunday] 20 April the Opera House will present the musical *Hansel and Gretel* and the ballet *The Fairy Doll* for proletarian children.'

Similarly, two days later *Pesti Hírlap* announced that the Municipal Orfeum (Music Hall) would present performances for workers' children four times a week, on Tuesdays, Thursdays, Saturday afternoons and Sunday mornings. Children would be taken there in groups organised by the Friends of Proletarian Children Association.

On 1 May 1919 the illustrated weekly *Érdekes Újság* (Interesting News) carried a report about one such group of children attending the Municipal Orfeum. Echoing the enthusiasm of Zsigmond Móricz and others, it spoke in raptures about the children filling the auditorium and gazing in wonder at the red stage curtain. The performance, the report claimed, filled the children with joy. 'Can there be a greater happiness than to address this public of tiny proletarians? Could there be a more grateful, more enthusiastic audience?'[42]

Béla Balázs, one of the prominent figures in the Commissariat for Education and Culture, was particularly interested in developing performances for children in a very special way—by using fairy tales. He even established a Fable Department in the Commissariat, appointing as one of its officials the writer, poet and critic Anna Lesznai, the former wife of Oszkár Jászi and a well-known figure in the progressive cultural circles around Balázs and Lukács. Travelling puppet shows were organised for children and the programme included some of Balázs's own puppet plays. 'Afternoons of fables', promoted by Balázs became very popular. Fairy tales were recited to children by a storyteller, while an artist produced drawings to accompany the theme.[43]

Perhaps not surprisingly, critics appeared attacking Balázs from a materialist, orthodox Marxist perspective. Fables made children superstitious, it was argued, and tales of kings, queens and princesses were unrealistic, not educational and a remnant of outdated ideology. Balázs

42. Quoted in Remete (1956), p. 334.

43. Zsuffa (1986), p. 80. For a fascinating account of the importance of fairy tales for Balázs throughout his life, see the introduction by Jack Zipes to *The Cloak of Dreams*, a collection of Chinese fairy tales by Béla Balázs (Princeton University Press, 2010).

responded in an article entitled 'Don't take the fable away from children!' Opening with the words 'The child before everyone!' he argued that fables provide proletarian children with beauty and joy and are anyway much older than capitalism and even feudalism. They also helped children develop an appreciation for literature.

He ended with a warning:

> Watch out, comrades! When we take the fable away from children, we take away the possibility that they will ever find joy in any kind of poetry. We don't want that—do we? Beware, comrades! When we assault children's tales we sever the roots of all poetry—even of all the arts.[44]

44. 'Ne vegyétek el a gyermekektől a mesét', *Fáklya*, 11 May 1919, pp. 3–4.

8

Music for All

'I liked to see the rich cafés filled with workers drinking coffee from beautiful cups and listening to bands from plush armchairs.' Thus commented—perhaps surprisingly—the British baron, colonel and MP, Josiah Clement Wedgwood, having returned from a fact-finding mission to Budapest.[1]

Wedgwood wasn't the only one to be struck by the 'musical' atmosphere of Budapest in 1919. As noted in the Introduction and Preface respectively, both the British journalist H. N. Brailsford and a then young Arthur Koestler were impressed by the music they encountered in public places. The music on the streets was often associated with noisy recruiting drives for the Red Army, as recalled by Lajos Kassák in connection with one occasion in late April.

'Parades were organised with music and drums. In the streets actors and actresses on decorated vehicles gave recitations and sang. Sári Fedák and other operetta stars participated with all their brilliance in the recruitment of Red soldiers.'[2]

Sári Fedák is often mentioned with regard to public propaganda during the Soviet Republic period. In contrast, Jenő Horváth rarely gets a mention. Horváth was a 19-year-old gypsy violinist and communist sympathiser who not only played in Budapest but roamed the countryside recruiting for the Red Army. As well as improvising, he also composed rousing political songs, though as he couldn't read music he himself never committed his works to paper. In the end he took up arms and died in battle.[3]

In addition to recruiting purposes, public music was also associated with celebrations—and not just on May Day. Kassák recalled the time when, in early June, the news came through that the Red Army had retaken Sátoraljaújhely, some 220 kilometres as the crow flies northeast of Budapest.

---

1. Mitchell (1970), p. 223. Perhaps his remark was not so surprising. Formerly a Liberal, in 1919 Wedgwood joined the Independent Labour Party. As Mitchell perceptively notes, the positive reaction of Wedgwood was of the type echoed by George Orwell in 1936 when he first encountered 'proletarian Barcelona' during the Spanish Civil War.
2. Kassák (1983), p. 583.
3. *Egy elfeledett forradalmár* (A Forgotten Revolutionary), a short but fascinating account of Horváth's life written by Géza Szekeres, was published in 1989. See http://mek.oszk.hu/08900/08914/08914.pdf (accessed 4 July 2017).

> In the clear summer morning every military band and workers' orchestra paraded through the streets with a clamorous hubbub, gathering together the awakening workers. The musicians established themselves in the squares and at the major street crossings, clashing their cymbals, banging their drums and sounding their roaring trumpets. Theatre orchestras gave concerts in front of the theatres. It was an intoxicating display.[4]

This kind of public celebration with music had been going on ever since the Council Republic had been proclaimed on 21 March. Ferenc Józsika remembered with enthusiasm playing on the streets soon after the proclamation: 'We travelled around the city on lorries decorated with flags, giving impromptu concerts in the main streets and squares for the people who had gathered there.' There were soldiers' as well as revolutionary songs, with people in the crowd joining in, and there were recitations of *The Whole Sea Has Revolted*, Sándor Petőfi's rousing poem written during the 1848 anti-Habsburg uprising.[5]

There was also a more serious side to the popular use and appreciation of music. As with theatre, the press was keen to present arguments showing that a new world was about to be born in terms of music culture and society.

Just one week after the proclamation of the Soviet Republic, *Vörös Újság* (Red Gazette) weighed in with an article under the title 'The task of our music culture in the communist state'. 'In the cleansing fire of proletarian revolution the arts are being reborn and are waking up to a new life,' it bombastically declared. 'Breaking free from the rotting framework of the old capitalist society, music is starting out with fresh strength on its conquering path.'

The article argued that so far the great mass of people had only enjoyed access to the inferior products of light music. Now the People Commissariat for Education and Culture was going to enrich people's musical culture with regular workers' concerts. 'Freed from the tiresome burden of giving lessons, artists, composers and music historians will work in cooperation in order to provide proletarian society with music culture cleansed of all refuse. Human dignity is a common treasury of the liberated worker and the independent worker—a guarantee of our future musical culture.'[6]

A few days later *Pesti Hírlap* (Pest News) published an article by the viola player, music historian and Academy professor Antal Molnár entitled 'Music in Socialist Society'. In more measured tones than the *Vörös Újság*

4. Kassák (1983) p. 589.
5. Ferenc Józsika—reminiscences; manuscript in the PTI Archives, PIL 867, J-26, p. 3.
6. 'Zenekultúránk föladata a kommunista államban', *Vörös Újság*, 28 March 1919, p. 7.

article, Molnár argued that at the time of every radical transformation in European society the arts had also changed. However, he asserted: 'We cannot content ourselves with the dream that beginning from the first moment of the present transformation the proletarian masses will immediately become a mature art-appreciating public.'

What was needed initially, argued Molnár, was widespread educational work involving free, state-funded courses and concerts and this would entail taking instruments into public ownership. The result would be the releasing of much musical talent among the mass of people. Then would come the bringing to life of a genuine popular culture in which the fate of musicians would be determined by musical talent rather than connections, patronage and wealth.[7]

The so-called workers' concert movement spread widely during the Soviet Republic, initially under the direction of the renowned musician Ernő Dohnányi,[8] who had been appointed to head the Academy of Music in early 1919, during the previous regime of Mihály Károlyi. For example, the *Seventh Workers' Concert* with the participation of Dohnányi was held in the afternoon of Sunday, 6 April, at the Academy. On the programme were works by Beethoven, Mozart, Mendelssohn and Schumann.[9]

The movement involved concerts for workers, often presenting classical music, and took place not only in established venues such as the Academy of Music and the Vigadó Concert Hall, but also in trade union premises and various other locations, sometimes far from the centre of Budapest. For example, on 3 April *Vörös Újság* reported that a concert featuring opera singers and other musicians had taken place the previous Sunday in the massive industrial district of Csepel, not in some cultural centre, but in the local ammunition works. On 20 April *Újpesti Munkás* (Újpest Worker) announced a forthcoming concert at the Munkás Színház (Workers' Theatre) 'for the proletarian people of Újpest'. The programme would include works by Mozart, Leoncavallo and Saint-Saëns and the ticket prices were being kept to a minimum so that, unlike in previous times, as many people as possible could enjoy the 'spiritual treasures of serious, true art'.[10] On 15 June *Népszava* (People's Voice) announced that a series of 'musical matinees' for the 'proletarian patients' of hospitals who 'always felt they were in a veritable prison' was planned to begin the following day with a concert in the garden of the Central Public Hospital (today the St. Roch Hospital on Rákoczi Road). Those who couldn't make it outside, the

7. 'Zeneművészet a szocialista társadalomban', *Pesti Hírlap*, 2 April 1919, pp. 2–3.
8. Flórián & Vajda (1978), p. 73.
9. A poster advertising the event is reproduced in Ujfalussy (1973), p. 171.
10. Ibid., pp. 193–4 for the article and the programme.

report said, would be able to enjoy the beauty of the music through the open windows.[11]

In a similar vein, there were so-called red soldiers' evenings and concerts in acknowledgement of the Red Army and its deeds. 'Red Soldiers' Day', for example, was celebrated on 12 April at the Opera House. The concert, the majority of tickets for which were available through the trade unions, began with *The Internationale* and *La Marseillaise*, which were followed by a recital of Antal Farkas's *Jön az öcsém* (My Brother is Coming) by Géza Abonyi of the National Theatre.[12] The main performances were of Beethoven's *Leonore Overture No. 3* and his *Ninth Symphony*. During the interval preceding the latter an address was given by Zsigmond Kunfi, the People's Commissar for Education and Culture, which was reported in the following day's *Népszava* under the curious title of 'Revolutionary Divine Homage'.[13] His opening words reflected the optimistic goals of the Soviet Republic's cultural policies.

> To free the creative genius from the cage of wealth, power and economy, and to rescue the worker from the prison of poverty, oppression, ignorance and drabness—this is the spiritual and cultural content of the proletarian revolution. When this evening the Hungarian proletariat meets the spirit of Beethoven, when the worker and the most noble art meet half way, that is a symbol of the work creating a new culture, which is one of the most glorious tasks of the workers' revolution.

The odd title of the speech given in *Népszava* was a reference to a comment made by Kunfi in the course of his presentation:

> A true divine homage to the revolution involves being able to devote ourselves to the teachings of science and the joy of art, if we raise our eyes to the summit of justice and we can open up our emotions and imagination before such sources of beauty and lofty inspiration as found in the music of Beethoven.

Béla Bartók

On 12 April 1919 both *Világ* (World) and *Népszava* carried a report announcing that the People's Commissariat for Education and Culture had

11. 'Zenei délutánok a kórházakban' (Musical Matinees in the Hospitals), *Népszava*, 15 June 1919, p. 10.
12. *Jön az öcsém* was the poem which Mihály Kertész (Michael Curtiz) used as the basis for his propaganda film of the same title—see Chapter 6.
13. 'Forradalmi istentisztelet', *Népszava*, 13 April, 1919, pp. 2–3.

entrusted the direction of music matters to Béla Reinitz (whom we met in the previous chapter) and to work alongside him had chosen a so-called Music Directory of three people, one of whom was the renowned composer and musician Béla Bartók. At the same time, the report said, a Council of Musical Arts was to be established as an advisory body, comprising the most outstanding representatives of the different branches of music. The Music Directory would, for the time being, be based at 6 Szemere Street, in the centre of Budapest, on the premises of the Chamber of Commerce and Industry.[14]

Bartók, who at the time had just turned 38 and was well on his way to becoming one of Hungary's most creative and internationally acknowledged geniuses of the twentieth century, accepted membership of the Music Directory, though his participation in one of the main artistic bodies of the Hungarian Soviet Republic at first glance may seem surprising. He is not known as someone who had pronounced socialist, let alone communist views, and in his personal habits and professional life he was rather withdrawn and inward looking, with an almost puritanical dedication to his work.[15]

On the other hand, he regarded himself as an outsider and a critic of Hungary's conservative music establishment, many of whose members, in turn, had no great admiration for him. The reasons are complex, but can perhaps partly be explained by the fact that although Bartók was a proud Hungarian and set out to do the best for his country, his research into the folk music of the Carpathian Basin led him to believe that what was valuable and pure could not be restricted to national categories, and sometimes at best even reflected a mixture of musical cultures. This hybrid approach—which might today be called fusion or crossover—didn't go down too well with Hungary's nationalist-minded elite.[16] Nor did Bartók's

---

14. In 1969 the Budapest Municipal Council placed a plaque on the wall of the building in Szemere Street recalling that this was where the Music Directory was based in 1919. Bartók and others were named. At the time of writing (August 2017) the plaque was still there, which was very unusual, given that in the years following the 1989–90 political changes virtually all public statues and plaques in Budapest with a 1919 theme were systematically removed.

15. Bartók's participation might not be so surprising were it not for the fact that it is often overlooked. For example, when checked by the author there seemed to be no mention of his activities during the 1919 Soviet Republic in either the Hungarian or English versions of the overview of his life given in the web pages of the specialist Bartók Archives of the Hungarian Academy of Sciences Institute for Musicology—www.zti.hu/bartok/ (accessed 25 May 2016). Similarly, there was no such mention on the wall featuring a chronological account of the main events of his life in the Béla Bartók Memorial House in Budapest—at least not when the author last visited the place.

16. Bartók himself once referred to the folk music of different peoples as '… a continuous give and take of melodies, a constant crossing and recrossing …' From 'Race Purity

strong criticism of the type of 'folk music' favoured by the urban establishment, which he regarded as shallow and inauthentic.

Hence there was a certain rebelliousness in Bartók's views and this was sometimes reflected even in his lifestyle. One of his biographers, Tibor Tallián, records that over ten years before the 1919 events Bartók 'gradually changed his way of life, separating himself from the orderly bourgeois world. He grew a beard, wore a straw hat, exchanged his Hungarian-style national costume—a braided military tunic worn proudly for years—for a Tolstoy shirt and sandals.' Tallián quotes Bartók himself asserting that he had 'a taste for dissonance' and that he sometimes wore his rough and ready clothing 'just to shock' people. His friends, claims Tallián, 'called him an anarchist'.[17]

Anarchist or not, he also developed views about the world around him. 'Is it not then a fine thing, to join with the oppressed,' he wrote to his wife, Márta Ziegler, in December 1916. 'If I, let's say, were a Russian count and found myself in Finland, I'd surely help the Finns against the Russians. This is the explanation for my Slovak and Romanian sympathies; they are the oppressed.'[18]

By 1911 Bartók had moved to Rákoskeresztúr, which was at the time just beyond the official Budapest city limit, practically in the countryside, though at the same time it could be called a garden suburb of the capital. He travelled to the city centre as little as he could—primarily to teach three days a week at the Academy of Music, where he had been appointed a professor of the piano faculty in 1907.

When the First World War broke out Bartók remained untouched by nationalism, which also put him at odds with much of Hungarian society. His sympathies remained with what he termed the 'peasant class ... the lowest stratum of the people, that community which earns its livelihood by soil cultivation or some other similar manual labour ...'[19]

Thus perhaps it is not surprising that Bartók was willing to get involved in 1919, and although there are indications that later he became disillusioned (see the Postscript), it seems that initially he welcomed the changes brought about on 21 March that year. Two weeks after the proclamation of the Soviet Republic, for example, he wrote to his sister Elza:

> Let me begin by saying that now the most important thing is patience. We must wait with confidence until the new chaos transforms into a

---

in Music', in: Suchoff (1992), p. 30. Bartók believed that 'The "racial impurity" finally attained is definitely beneficial'. Ibid., p. 31.

17. Tallián (1981), p. 57.
18. Bartók (1981—letters), p. 248.
19. Tallián (1981), p. 93.

> new order, because this new order will be better than the old for every working man. We must calmly endure all the greater or lesser troubles, possibly injustices, of the temporary and initial state of affairs, in the knowledge that the ultimate purpose of it all is an enormous general turn for the better ...[20]

No doubt there were also other reasons why Bartók was willing to be part of the Music Directory, reasons more closely related to his passion for music. In 1910, Bartók had played a central role in the founding of UZME (Új Magyar Zenei Egyesület—New Hungarian Musical Society), a body promoting avant-garde music. A manifesto was issued and a programme of education was envisaged, but the ministry of culture was reluctant to support what were considered to be extremist trends. With the 'revolutionary changes' heralded by the proclamation of the Council Republic on 21 March 1919 it must have seemed that space might open up for such 'extremism'.

Indeed, just two days after the proclamation, well before the Music Directory was established, an interview with Bartók appeared in *Színházi Élet* (Theatre Life) in which he called for a reform of music teaching. 'In elementary schools there ought to be three years of compulsory singing lessons, including sight reading and notation of simple tunes,' he said. 'Naturally, this would require top-quality teaching staff who would have to be trained for this quite special task.'[21]

Years later Hungary would become internationally famous for its music teaching and emphasis on singing in schools, but given that the Soviet Republic lasted just over four months, as with other grand schemes, in 1919 there was no time to implement Bartók's bold idea.

So much for plans. What of Bartók's activity at the time? In 1969 György Lukács, who 50 years previously had been a People's Commissar for Education and Culture, would recall: '... as a people's commissar, when it came to music I was just a yes-man. I did nothing other, meaning with the help of the apparatus I did nothing other than what the Music Directory wanted—putting it more precisely, what Bartók wanted.'[22] That is presumably a not-uncharacteristic exaggeration on the part of Lukács, who goes on to say, somewhat qualifying his comment, that the Music Directory in essence was in tune with Bartók's ideas.

---

20. Bartók (1981—letters), p. 292.
21. Quoted in Remete (1956), p. 235.
22. Ujfalussy (1976), pp. 210–11. Lukács reiterated the idea in a television interview broadcast in early 1976, in which he asserted: 'What Bartók proposed, we in the cultural commissariat implemented.' See Borus (1978), pp. 179–80.

Bartók himself, in a letter written to his mother on 9 June 1919, stressed that he, Zoltán Kodály and Ernő Dohnányi—his colleagues in the Directory—were there as advisers, 'of course, not as political, but music specialists'. He then says, without going into details, that the work involved a lot of friction and at one point they had wanted to resign. '... great music reforms are being prepared, but the political climate is too unsettled, such that you can't work well or thoroughly enough.'[23]

For a few weeks his appointment as director of the Opera was considered and there were plans for the establishment of a 'music museum', but that idea was changed to setting up an independent department of musical folklore within the National Museum, and Bartók was scheduled to work there.[24]

As indicated above, during the period of the Council Republic Bartók was living in Rákoskeresztúr, beyond the boundary of Budapest, far from all the political noise and agitation he encountered whenever he visited the city centre. He was glad to get away from it all.

As early as 5 April he wrote to his sister: 'I'm happy when I'm again at home and I don't hear all the stuff and nonsense.'[25] Because of the curfew and the many identity checks in the city, he asked for some ID and had got one from Kunfi's Commissariat for Education and Culture on 25 March saying he was an official of the commissariat, which wasn't actually true.[26] Later Reinitz supplied him with an officially stamped document from the commissariat dated 22 May 1919 and signed by himself stating that 'Comrade Béla Bartók, ... on the basis of the decree of 22 April issued by the supreme command of the Budapest Red Guard' was entitled to be out on streets after 11 p.m. At the bottom it was stated that the pass was valid for 30 days.[27] No doubt the necessity of such bureaucratic niceties was troublesome to Bartók, who simply wanted to concentrate on his music.

It was during the Hungarian Soviet Republic, on 21 April 1919, that a special Béla Bartók evening was organised at the Academy of Music. It was special in that this was Bartók's first major public performance for nine years and involved a selection of his works, both old and new. Zoltán Kodály wrote about the evening in the following day's *Pesti Napló* (Pest Diary). He defended Bartók against his former critics and declared that his works were helping a new spirit to blossom.[28]

---

23. Bartók (1981—letters), p. 299.
24. Tallián (1981), p. 117.
25. Bartók (1981—letters), p. 293.
26. Bartók (1981—chronology), p. 170.
27. For a copy of the document, see Bónis (2006), p. 190.
28. *Pesti Napló*, 22 April 1919, p. 7.

In early June Bartók was writing to his mother complaining that Reinitz had been away in Vienna for about three weeks. That was a problem since Reinitz was 'one of the few who could deal with the illegitimate and untalented people who were still pushing themselves forward'.[29] According to the chronology of Bartók's life compiled by his son, it was around this time that he withdrew from public life. However, he didn't 'disappear' entirely.

During the early period of the Soviet Republic Bartók had completed a piano draft of what was to become one of his most internationally renowned compositions, *The Miraculous Mandarin*, though it wasn't something inspired by the new political developments, nor was it commissioned by the new authorities—Bartók had agreed to orchestrate Menyhért Lengyel's libretto in June 1918.

In early July 1919, a private performance of the work was given by Bartók before a small audience gathered in the home of István Thomán, Bartók's former piano teacher at the Academy. *Színházi Élet*, which carried a report of the event titled simply 'The Miraculous Mandarin', described Bartók as 'one of the greatest prides of Hungarian musical arts' and declared: 'He doesn't speak, doesn't announce his plans or "make statements". He aims not to be heard about, rather he comes forward with ready works.' The report indicated that the fully orchestrated *Miraculous Mandarin* would be premiered at the Opera House the following January, predicting that it would be one of the most interesting works of the forthcoming season.[30]

It was not to be. The fall of the Council Republic and with it Bartók's return to a 'state of disgrace', partly because of his involvement in it, put paid to any such plans. In fact, *The Miraculous Mandarin* would never be performed in Hungary throughout Béla Bartók's entire lifetime.[31]

Zoltán Kodály

By 1919 Zoltán Kodály, one of Bartók's colleagues in the Music Directory, was also on his way to becoming an internationally acclaimed figure as a composer, musicologist and music educator. During the Soviet Republic Kodály was deputy director of the Academy of Music and in the absences of its director, Ernő Dohnányi, he took over the leading position. In these roles the two of them were not 'products' of the new Soviet authorities, they had been in place since mid February, having been appointed during the previous Károlyi regime.

29. Bartók (1981—letters), p. 299.
30. 'A csodálatos mandarin', *Színházi Élet*, 13 July 1919, pp. 7–8.
31. See the Postscript.

Probably it was because of Kodály's prominent role at the Academy that, unlike Bartók, he was among those subjected to a quasi-legal investigative process launched towards the end of 1919, a few months after the fall of the Council Republic. A commission of inquiry was established under the chairmanship of Baron Gyula Wlassics, a ministerial adviser in the now reinstated Ministry of Religion and Education. In late September Wlassics had been appointed the Academy's government commissioner.

The hearings, which took place at one of the ministry's premises in Hold Street, dragged on until the end of April 1920 with the 'star' accused being Zoltán Kodály, such that the process is sometimes known as 'the Kodály trial'. That isn't quite accurate and, indeed, Kodály made clever use of arguments about the actual legal status of the commission's work.

Kodály was indicted on a number of counts, the main charges being the following: 1. He had been a member of the Music Directory; 2. He had had *The Internationale* orchestrated by teachers at the Academy; 3. He had allowed Academy premises to be used for recruiting to the Red Army; 4. After the collapse of the Soviet Republic he had been slow in putting out the national flag on the Academy building. Other charges involved alleged administrative errors during the period when he was de facto the head of the institute, such as issuing permits to singing teachers without reference to the committee of management, endorsing documents with a stamp instead of his own hand, and generally behaving in a manner not appropriate for his position. The main charges were clearly political and Kodály in his defence addressed them directly. His responses throw some light on the political conditions existing during the Commune.[32]

Responding to the 'accusation' that he had been a member of the Music Directory, Kodály did not dispute the fact, declaring: 'Regarding the group of which I was a member, I believe that every Hungarian musician would be flattered to be together with Dohnányi and Bartók.' He pointed out that he was the only member of the Directory being charged, but if there was something to complain about its workings then charges should be brought against the entire body. 'As for myself, I am not authorised to speak on behalf of the whole Directory.'

In fact, on 3 February 1920, Bartók wrote to Gyula Wlassics highlighting that he, too, had been a member of the Directory and protesting against Kodály alone being held responsible for whatever that body might have done. It seems to have had no effect on the proceedings and Bartók wasn't even called as a witness.

---

32. Details about and quotations from the 'trial' are taken from the minutes of the proceedings, which are published in full in Ujfalussy (1973), pp. 499–599.

However, Dohnányi, the third member of the Directory, did give evidence. He argued that a distinction should be made between the Music Directory and other, political directories. Downplaying its role, he argued that the body comprising himself, Kodály and Bartók had really little influence on anything and no means to achieve much. 'We were given no state assets and we ourselves received no benefits,' he said. Nothing was done which harmed the interests of the Academy. He admitted only that the Directory had an 'ominous' title, but indicated that such names were commonplace at the time.

As for being involved with the orchestration of *The Internationale*, Kodály said he was basically acting on orders from above, which had been passed on to him by Béla Reinitz. He recalled that it was a Monday when he got an urgent order to the effect that within 24 hours *The Internationale* should be arranged in a manner suitable for playing in every theatre and music hall. His response was to say that was physically impossible and, indeed, the task took six days to be resolved.[33]

Although there was no written order, Kodály told the commission that he understood from Reinitz's manner that there could be no hesitation and that he himself had received the order from the Revolutionary Governing Council. Kodály believed that it was a job he had to organise, like any other, so he distributed the work among teachers who were available and capable. 'In the early days of the dictatorship,' he said, 'when no open opposition was witnessed in any kind of public office, to refuse would have been explicit rebellion.' Kodály also asserted that Reinitz had indicated it wouldn't be wise to refuse the task, since the Academy was already regarded by some as a counter-revolutionary nest and that refusal would only intensify animosity against the institute.

It seems the 'new' *Internationale* was ready by 30 March. An item in that day's *Magyarország* (Hungary) announced that in the evening the public would be able to hear the rearranged version of the 'communist anthem' played at the Opera House.

Coming to the accusation that the Academy had allowed recruiting for the Red Army to take place, Kodály stressed that what had happened was in reality not recruiting, but actually an attempt to save many people from being called up. 'The whole matter can be called a real endeavour against the Red Army,' he declared.

---

33. *The Internationale* was written in 1871 by Eugène Pottier, who had been involved in the Paris Commune, and was set to music seven years later by Pierre de Geyter. It became widely accepted as a left-wing anthem and has been translated into many languages. An early Hungarian version appeared in 1904, after which there were many variations, though its use in Hungary was not widespread until 1919 and the Soviet Republic—the urgency of its introduction then presumably being a desire to emulate Soviet Russian practice.

Giving his evidence, Dohnányi also claimed that the aim was for as few people as possible to be recruited, even calling it a 'counter-revolutionary action'.[34] A doctor had been found who had managed to get 99 per cent exempted, he said, adding that 'the whole recruiting was a pure operetta comedy'.

As for not flying the national flag following the collapse of the Soviet Republic, Kodály related how on 2 August—the day after the collapse—he set off from home not knowing what was happening and that he learnt of the changes from a poster. He maintained he saw no national flags on any public buildings and there was even a red flag flying in Hold Street, where the hearings were taking place. He decided to have the red flag removed from the Academy building, but not yet to replace it with the national flag since he wanted to avoid any potential political attack or the danger the flag might be insulted.

Dohnányi said he suspected the charge involved some malicious defamation, and Kodály himself spoke out against the implication that he was unpatriotic. 'Let he who has done more for Hungary than I come forward to lecture me,' he declared, adding that he had nothing to do with the dictatorship, under which he didn't change from serving the goals he had served throughout his life.

He returned to the theme in a later session, pointing out that all his work had been accomplished without any financial aid from the state but with his own money.

> Where have I obtained the energy for all this? Doubtless from that 'anti-patriotic disposition' of which people are so keen to find me guilty. I have never concerned myself with everyday politics. But, so to say, every bar of music and every folk song I have recorded has been a political act. In my opinion, that is true patriotism—a patriotism of actual deeds, not simply phrase-mongering. And it is for this I am being persecuted.

The end result of the process was that Kodály was dismissed from his position as deputy director of the Academy of Music though, interestingly, in its formal submission the commission of inquiry concluded that Kodály's 'disciplinary offence' related more to his administrative behaviour as a deputy director rather than to any of the more political charges.

As implied by testimonies given during the hearings, the Music Directory may well have been virtually a shell organisation, with no real function.

34. In Hungary's post-1919 era of 'anti-communism', in official parlance the term 'counter-revolutionary' was accepted and used, being regarded as signifying something positive.

After all, Dohnányi was away much of the time, Kodály had his duties at the Academy and Bartók, who lived far from the centre of Budapest, was essentially concerned with pursuing his music work in peace and quiet. Nevertheless, the body which Béla Reinitz headed did have its own offices and its own staff, though as Lajos Kassák noted in connection with the theatre socialisation committee, not everything on the ground functioned smoothly, as witnessed by Irén Gál who began working with Béla Reinitz in the department for music and theatre affairs of the People's Commissariat for Education and Culture in early April 1919.

Irén Gál was the wife of Béla Kun, and no doubt many people would have seen her involvement as a case of political placement. While there might have been an element of that, it is true that she had received a music education and had worked as a piano teacher. Either way, her memoirs record some experiences, which are both amusing and revealing of how things operated at the time.[35]

She turned up for work, found the desk she had been allocated and waited—there was nothing for her to do. 'There's no point in trying to rush things,' she was told by her colleagues. 'The work is complicated, but matters will be sorted out in time.'

However, when the news got round that the wife of the acknowledged leader of the Soviet Republic was working at the department, she had a stream of visitors with requests for 'Comrade Mr. Béla Kun', since 'only he could sort out their problems'.

'You are mistaken,' she replied. 'I'm not working with Béla Kun, but with Béla Reinitz.' And they looked at her in surprise. 'They weren't prepared to accept my response.' The majority of supplicants had nothing to do with music or the theatre, she recalls, but they thought it would be easier to reach her in the Szemere Street office than at the strongly guarded Hungária Hotel, known as the Soviet House, where Béla Kun had his office and the Kuns resided.

One woman—who actually was an actress—complained that she was living with her twelve-year-old daughter in two rooms, which opened onto each other. She wanted a separate room for her daughter, asking 'How can I receive male guests?' Another woman requested that Béla Kun return her jewellery since 'a society lady, whatever the system, cannot go around without jewellery'.

The themes were manifold—transferring money abroad, the release of prisoners, employment matters, shifting belongings, passport problems. She was bombarded by the discontented and the hopeful until one day Reinitz discovered what was going on. He excluded everyone and set someone on

35. Kun (1969), pp. 208–11.

guard to ensure that only people with issues concerning music would be allowed in. It worked. The invasion ceased.

As a postscript to the story, Irén Gál remarks: 'Later I learnt that the majority of those who had come with requests had gone to other offices and were able, with the help of old and—unfortunately—new functionaries, to have their unjustified requests granted in full.'

9

The Pen goes to Battle

On 21 March 1919 the critic Andor Halasi was in the premises of the Otthon Circle, a club for writers and journalists. He would recall the atmosphere there on that day, the expectation, the uncertainty, the different degrees of tension:

> The main hall was packed with members. We knew that something had happened, but no one knew exactly what. Quite contrasting pieces of news were circulating among the assembled crowd. Weeks, months of intense anxiety and ripples of events congealed in our nerves. Our tension was ready to explode.

All of a sudden a strange figure appeared in the doorway:

> a lanky, hump-backed young man, skinny with a starved look, wearing shabby clothes, a dirty white kerchief tied round his neck. With a hoarse voice he shouted into the hall: 'The proletarian dictatorship has been established!' Then he turned around and ran down the stairs ... For a moment the buzzing fell silent. Then there were resounding shouts of 'Bravo!' And then, as if a single sigh of relief had filled the huge hall: 'At last!'[1]

Then followed a feverish exchange of ideas about what kind of fate and what kind of role would be in store for writers and journalists.

With a view to having a say in that, over the following two days the writers met and elected a Writers' Council consisting of 15 prominent people, but how many of them were present at the meeting or knew of their election is open to question. A few days later, Lajos Kassák, for example, issued a statement confirming his speedy resignation from the Council, saying he had had no idea of his election.[2]

---

1. Halasi (1959), pp. 13–14.
2. *Világ* (World), 26 March 1919, p. 7. Kassák said he resigned 'for reasons of principle', but doesn't explain exactly what they were, other than indicating his dissatisfaction over being elected behind his back.

There were a number of reports about the founding meeting of the Writers' Council. One appeared in *Vörös Lobogó* (Red Flag), a weekly close to the communist viewpoint. It began enthusiastically, highlighting that the Writers' Council was the first 'soviet' to be established in the 'Hungarian soviet state'.[3] However, overall the report was very critical, even scathing about many of the participants, describing them as representatives of the previous two decades' dying literature, not fit for purpose, so to say, in the new society. Of the elected committee members, the article claimed that only a couple or so were combative, promising and brave, as opposed to the majority who were resplendent in freshly painted, sparklingly brand-new convictions.

'In the communist state,' the article asserted, 'we want clean, regenerated, honest literature.'[4] It indicated that harsh means should be employed against those compromising the new, required developments.

The author of the article in *Vörös Lobogó* was given as Sándor Márai, which is quite surprising, considering his later reputation as an anti-communist writer with strong 'conservative bourgeois' views.

Nevertheless, Sándor Márai was a fairly regular contributor to *Vörös Lobogó*, both before and after 21 March 1919, the day the Council Republic was proclaimed. Péter Kakuszi's 2006 collection of Márai's early writings includes 14 articles he wrote for it, nine prior to that date and five after.[5] He not only wrote for *Vörös Lobogó* in 1919, but also for other publications, such as *Magyarország* (Hungary). All in all, Kakuszi reproduces 17 articles by Márai published during the period of the Commune. Some of them are reviews. Others are atmospheric accounts of what he encountered in various parts of the country. He also wrote pieces containing quite explicit political comments.

In one entitled 'Referendum', published in early May 1919, Márai fervently sings the praises of the many workers who had decided to heed the call of the Budapest Workers' Council and the Revolutionary Governing Council and volunteer to take up arms as part of a massive recruiting drive for the Red Army. He writes that the struggle against what he calls 'the armed hordes of capital' threatening the country's integrity is no longer a strategic problem and a matter of military tasks, since 'the Hungarian proletarian revolution succeeded at that moment when the factory workers

3. 'Írók tanácsa' (Writers' Council), *Vörös Lobogó*, 28 March 1919. In: Kakuszi (2006), pp. 44–6. In the Hungarian text the term 'szovjet' (soviet) is used, rather than 'tanács' (council). In fact, although they may not have called themselves a soviet or council, a similar, large meeting of people involved in the cinema industry took place on the same day as the writers' gathering began (see the start of Chapter 6).

4. Ibid. p. 46.

5. Kakuszi (2006).

laid down their tools in order to pick up arms'. The struggle is not for towns and counties, he wrote, but 'for the oppressed proletariat of the entire world'. What has taken place recently in the factories of Pest and in the barracks, says Márai, is already part of world history, and he ends with an exhortation: 'Go to the barracks and see this triumphant multitude! Budapest is voting again for the proletarian revolution.'[6]

In 1942, Márai apparently claimed that the explanation for his involvement with the Commune was because, with the workers and the military joining forces, he saw the possibility that the territories being occupied by foreign troops could be regained.[7] That could have been concocted years later, when a nationalistic explanation might have been somewhat 'appealing'. Nevertheless, there is evidence of a certain nationalistic feeling in some of the pieces Márai wrote in 1919.

In a strongly worded article published the very day after his aforementioned 'Referendum' appeared, Márai rails against harsh ceasefire conditions proposed by the Romanians. Although the text is shrouded in the political terminology of how the Romanians were reflecting the dictates of the 'bourgeoisie of capitalist Europe', he also has some rather patronising words about the 'immiserated Romanian peasantry, which, dressed in military uniform is turning their whips against us—this primitive, illiterate people, sunk in backwardness, which has still not realised how to recognise its own class interests'.[8]

Andor Halasi says that soon after its foundation the Writers' Council appointed a committee of three, which was tasked with meeting the People's Commissar for Education and Culture to announce the existence of the Council and learn about what was in store for writers. Thus they met Zsigmond Kunfi and his then deputy, György Lukács. Kunfi wanted to know whether the writers would engage in agit-prop activities. Their response was positive and so a couple of days later another committee was set up to organise propaganda lectures by writers.[9] Many writers gave presentations about politics and the arts, which were often delivered in theatres during intervals between acts.

In addition to the Writers' Council, other, arguably more powerful bodies were established in 1919 to manage the affairs of writers. In the main,

---

6. 'Népszavazás' (Referendum), *Magyarország*, 7 May 1919. In: Kakuszi (2006), pp. 71–2.
7. See: https://pim.hu/hu/marai-sandor/az-akademikus-marai-sandor (accessed 4 July 2017).
8. 'Ökölcsapás' (A Blow with the Fist), *Magyarország*, 8 May 1919. In: Kakuszi (2006), pp. 72–4.
9. Halasi (1959), p. 15.

these were established from above, by the Commissariat for Education and Culture, and as in other sectors of the arts, they often overlapped, particularly in their personnel, creating a complex, rather bureaucratic structure. There was a Writers' Directory, consisting initially of eleven members, and there was a steering committee or board of nearly 30, whose members were charged with overseeing particular tasks.

Another committee was established to draw up a writers' registry, on the basis of which a writers' trade union was also set up, and there was the intriguingly named National Council for Intellectual Production, a kind of licensing body, giving (or withholding) permission for publication. It also had a hand in the matter of allocation of paper for printing, which was a potentially contentious issue, since the shortage of paper was sometimes given as the reason for suspending or restricting the printing of various publications (although the political sympathies of their editors and writers clearly also played a major role in such judgements). Yet another body which appeared was the Socialist Literary, Artistic and Scholarly Society. Behind, or rather above all these stood the People's Commissariat for Education and Culture, with Zsigmond Kunfi and György Lukács at its head, and which itself had its own department for literary and artistic affairs, headed by Béla Balázs.

The activities of the committee drawing up the writers' registry generated a lot of attention, unsurprisingly since getting on the registry meant being entitled to some income. Lajos Kassák, who played a key role in the committee, recalls being bombarded by all sorts of people pleading in the hope that they would be included in the list. His attitude seems to have been fairly broad-minded and he had to tell many applicants that they need not have bothered pestering him, since they were already registered.[10]

Kassák could often be extremely critical of any writer who was not part of his *MA* circle or a close sympathiser, but in this case he was arguably simply implementing the official policy, rather than following his own prejudices. That policy was indicated by a statement published on 25 April in *Fáklya* (Torch), the official mouthpiece of the cultural commissariat. The statement noted that the writers' registry committee had begun its work of examining the applications submitted to it by those who wished to be registered as writers. It asserted that the sole task of the committee was to establish whether or not the applicant truly was a writer.

'Quality, political orientation or world view are not taken into consideration,' the announcement, perhaps surprisingly, declared. 'The registry committee is not functioning as a body for criticism. Its work only involves distinguishing dilettantes from professional writers.' It also promised that

10. Kassák (1983), pp. 364–5.

there would be some kind of appeal process, should anyone feel they had been unfairly excluded from the official list of writers.[11]

This didn't stop a multitude of people approaching the committee, pleading to be included. There were so many that the issue became the subject for a number of humorous writings. For example, an article called 'Who is a Writer?' appeared in the old-established satirical magazine *Borsszem Jankó* (Tom Thumb). It included ten points for helping to identify a true writer. Number five suggested a compulsory annual medical examination for all adults to determine whether what might be moving inside them was genius or worms. The tenth point, noting that it often turned out only after a writer's death whether he or she was great, suggested waiting for a writer to die in order to discover that he or she was actually pretty mediocre.[12]

Sándor Márai also tried his hand at the genre. 'Everyone came, the elderly and the very young,' he wrote in one piece. 'Only the lame, the talented and those suffering from some other physical disability stayed at home.'[13]

Nevertheless, in the early weeks of the Council Republic period there was a great deal of genuine optimism among writers. Lajos Nagy expressed it on behalf of many—albeit with a degree of exaggeration and hyperbole.

'The grim times are over,' he began an article entitled 'How capitalist society paid its writers'.

> Gone are the publishers, their editors and copy editors. It was well known how these gentlemen treated the writers. Everyone has heard about what a ridiculous amount they paid writers for each piece or book. They only accepted and published the works of those writers who were dear to them, who served the ideology of capital and thus satisfied the demands of a bourgeois readership … Writers were slaves working for a pittance.

Nagy then lists a string of publications and the typical rates they used to pay. He ends with a rousing statement:

> All thanks to the revolution of the organised workers which, by bringing down the rule of capital and smashing the entire accursed machinery of

---

11. 'Az írók elhelyezkedése az új rendben' (The Employment of Writers in the New System), *Fáklya*, 25 April 1919, p. 8.
12. Jenő Molnár, 'Ki az író?', *Borsszem Jankó*, 13 April 1919, p. 6. In: József (1967), p. 963.
13. Sándor Márai, 'Szervezkednek az írók' (The Writers are Getting Organised), *Április*, 17 April 1919. In: József (1967), p. 196.

> the capitalist state, has also liberated the artist! There is no longer any capitalist publisher, and there never will be. Let the species be damned![14]

In reality, matters were not so simple, as was recognised by a statement published in the official organ of the cultural commissariat a few days after Nagy's rather bombastic outburst had appeared. It acknowledged that the collapse of the capitalist system of production had produced a 'temporary' situation, which had seriously affected the livelihood of many writers. The number of accepted writings had fallen and with the nationalisation of book publishing the purchase of book manuscripts had ceased 'for the time being'. Without being very specific, the statement declared that the commissariat was going to address the problem with a view to ensuring that writers could continue to make a living.[15]

Hence the importance of the so-called registration committee, the body deciding who could be officially recognised as a writer and thus be entitled to some form of assistance in terms of cash and possibly also bread coupons.

Andor Halasi says that the committee initially comprised six members: Mihály Babits, Lajos Barta, Lajos Fülep, Lajos Kassák, Ernő Osvát and himself. It was agreed that all who could provide evidence of being a writer should be accepted. However, Osvát was in favour of dividing the thus acknowledged writers into three categories, who would receive different levels of support depending on their quality, which led to a major dispute.

The results of the registration committee's work were announced in *Fáklya* on 9 May. Of the 957 applications for 'writer status', it was reported that 550 had been accepted. Well over half of the remainder were mainly young, relatively inexperienced writers who had, for the most part, not appeared in print, or they were unknown to the committee. Thus more information was requested of them. Others were directed to alternative organisations, deemed more appropriate. All in all, the report claimed, only 34 applications had been rejected outright.

The following day *Fáklya* published the full list of registered writers. However, there seems to have been some kind of error, since its next issue contained a list of 18 names, which it said should be added. They included prominent figures such as Mihály Babits and Lajos Hatvany, whose absence from the original list seems odd. Another additional name was that of Jenő Rákosi, who had been a leading figure in the world of journalism and who was known as a staunch opponent of progressive literary circles, as well as for his outspoken conservative political opinions. Also registered officially was the equally conservative writer Ferenc Herczeg.

---

14. 'Hogyan fizette a tőkés társadalom az íróit', *Vörös Lobogó*, 17 April 1919, pp. 31–2.
15. 'Munkát kapnak az írók' (Writers Getting Work), *Fáklya*, 25 April 1919, p. 8.

It might have seemed a little surprising to such people that they had been officially registered. After all, about three weeks previously, on Easter Sunday, Herczeg had been aroused from his sleep in the middle of the night and taken to Budapest's Markó Street courthouse gaol where he found himself in the company of 'politicians, aristocrats, university teachers, commercial wholesalers and top bankers'. The following day he was taken with other prisoners by tram to the transit prison on the far eastern side of the Kőbánya industrial district. Herczeg doesn't indicate what he was charged with, if anything, but presumably he had been taken into custody entirely for political reasons.

In the prison he found himself in solitary confinement, but perhaps he wasn't locked up all the time since, as he remembered: 'I seemed to have a certain special popularity—the prison library contained a number of my books.' On the Wednesday he was woken up in the night and informed he was going to be released. 'I would have liked to remain until morning,' he thought. 'What can you do in Kőbánya in the middle of the night?' He was told that he was being released thanks to the intervention of Zsigmond Kunfi, the People's Commissar for Education and Culture. While receiving his release papers, a line of new prisoners appeared in one of the corridors. Among them he saw Jenő Rákosi.[16]

The registered writers now formed the basis of the writers' trade union, which met for the first time on 11 May, reportedly with 300 people in attendance. On the same day *Pesti Hírlap* (Pest News) published an accolade to those forming the union penned by the noted writer Zsigmond Móricz. Entitled simply 'Five Hundred and Fifty Hungarian Writers', it sang the praises—in rather over-stated language, to say the least—of the gathered writers and their qualities, at least in terms of how Móricz saw them.

> I have been touched to read today a long list of names. Writers, Hungarian writers, five hundred and fifty of them, at the ready, living for the pen and living by the pen; five hundred and fifty writers, specialists in their craft, gathering together in the trade union ... How many I know among them ... Lines by them are ringing in my ears. I feel the colour and fragrance of ideas, and, as if on a fairground ride, I circle round in a daze in the meadow of names ... Five hundred and fifty Hungarian writers, entirely equal. If there is one among them who thinks himself greater than the others, he is lying ... As much as they are individual,

16. *Herczeg Ferenc emlékezései 1919-ről* (Ferenc Herczeg's Memories of 1919), http://mek.oszk.hu/10000/10056/10056.htm#51 (accessed 4 July 2017). The text also appears in Sipos & Donáth (1999), pp. 284–91.

> they are independent and unique wonders: they are bound together in communism; every writer in this world is at the same time is a fighter for the liberation of spirits.[17]

On the same day that the trade union met, the composition of the Writers' Directory, arguably the most important body (in theory, if not in practice), was publicly announced. Its members were: Mihály Babits, Béla Balázs, Lajos Barta, Lajos Bíró, Lajos Kassák, Aladár Komját, Zsigmond Móricz, Ernő Osvát, Béla Révész and Gyula Szini. People's Commissar György Lukács was an ex officio member. The members of the larger steering committee were announced at the same time. The two lists contained the names of many of Hungary's most noted twentieth-century writers.

Establishment of the hugely important National Council for Intellectual Production was announced in *Fáklya* on 27 April, several days before the other, above-mentioned organisations had fully appeared on the scene. Its significance is reflected in the title given to the lengthy *Fáklya* report: 'The Centralisation of Intellectual Production'.[18]

That rather ominous title suggests it all. The National Council was authorised to supervise the publication, production and distribution of books, newspapers, music scores and all other types of printed material. It was closely involved with the work of the Office for Paper and Printing Materials, which itself supervised the resources necessary for publishing anything.

The journalist, writer and translator Sándor Szabados was appointed to head the National Council. A former left-wing Social Democrat, he had subsequently joined the Communist Party after its formation in Hungary. Following his appointment, Szabados occupied one of the most powerful positions in the cultural world of the Council Republic. Indeed, although he was in a sense operating 'behind the scenes' and was not as 'public' as People's Commissar György Lukács, the pair of them together have been called the 'directors of the Soviet Republic's cultural policy'.[19]

The Socialist Literary, Artistic and Scholarly Society had held its founding meeting much earlier, on 23 March. As its name suggests, its aim was to promote specifically socialist literature and arts, and to spread the

---

17. 'Ötszázötven magyar író', *Pesti Hírlap*, 11 May 1919, p. 2.
18. 'A szellemi termelés központosítása', *Fáklya*, 27 April 1919, p. 3.
19. Csaplár (1987), p. 150. Nevertheless, Szabados is by no means as well known as Lukács. After the fall of the Council Republic he was among those sentenced to life imprisonment following a trial of Council Republic commissars in mid 1920, but was included in a Soviet-Hungarian exchange involving repatriated Hungarian prisoners of war. He went to the Soviet Union where he eventually fell victim to Stalin's purges of the 1930s, unlike Lukács, who managed to survive the Great Terror there.

message among workers as widely and cheaply as possible. Lajos Kassák was at the meeting and he would recall his surprise at the numbers, particularly as most of the participants were unknown to him. 'Probably these are the great figures of secret literary, artistic and scholarly life,' he ironically mused to himself as he looked around suspiciously, detecting an atmosphere of 'foul, pernicious opportunism'.

It reminded him of the great surge of people towards the Social Democratic Party and the trade unions, which had begun several months previously. 'Everybody became a socialist and simultaneously the socialist movement lost its character. The same is happening today.'[20]

Kassák didn't remain silent. Criticising those who had spoken and objecting to the lack of genuine writers and artists in the room, he announced that he didn't want to be a member of a body which, in his opinion, would prove to be an empty shell, without any justification for its existence. The indignation was palpable, but with that he left the meeting.

Perhaps the rush among writers of all sorts to join the new organisations, which Kassák observed, was fuelled by a fear that remaining a member of older bodies might count against them. There was some justification for that, considering the fate of the Kisfaludy Literary Society, which traced its roots back to the 1830s. On 30 March György Lukács, as Deputy People's Commissar for Education and Culture, had signed a decree prohibiting its meetings. The move was undoubtedly made for political reasons. Only the day before *Vörös Újság* (Red Gazette) had described the organisation in an article as 'the most reactionary Hungarian literary society'.[21]

A new direction?

So much for organisations, but what of the policies of the new regime regarding writers and literature? In the weeks following 21 March several articles touching on the issue appeared in the press. Common themes were that a new world was opening up for writers, who would no longer be bound by capitalist practices driven by financial imperatives. Quality would now be important, not making money, satisfying bourgeois tastes or submitting to the requirements of the implicit censorship of traditional publishing.

At the same time, it was stressed that art for art's sake was not a legitimate basis for producing literature. A new worldview and a new content were required, which would match the changing times. However, any explanation

20. Kassák (1983), pp. 538–9.
21. For the *Vörös Újság* article and the decree, see József (1967), pp. 42 and 709.

of how the new content should be categorised was often vague, though it was also often noted that there would be no 'official line' vis-à-vis literature and that progressive developments should be assessed on the basis of free discussion.

These last two points were highlighted by Béla Balázs in a speech he delivered in April outlining the standpoint of the cultural commissariat. Nevertheless, other parts of his speech seemed to contradict them. After referring to György Lukács's pronouncements regarding not favouring any particular tendencies (see Chapter 5), he continued by defending the need for what he implied would be the temporary centralisation of literary life, for which he gave three reasons. Printing and publishing had been centralised, for economic considerations. The new government had to exercise political supervision. It also had to intervene positively to ensure that good literature was directed towards the masses.

Without pulling any punches, he also admitted that censorship was unavoidable, saying that it would be exercised by the state. Then, somewhat contradictorily, though perhaps as a 'sweetener on the pill', he indicated that the censors would come from the writers' own ranks—although they would be complemented by the government's own people. The latter were necessary in view of the danger of conservatism arising and to ensure that 'in literature the door would remain open towards the left'.[22]

The issue of censorship was addressed equally bluntly, albeit also ambiguously and in a contradictory manner, by Béla Kun in a response he gave to a question put to him by the American reporter Crystal Eastman, who asked him whether he 'found necessary a complete suppression of free speech and press'.

'We do not practise general suppression of free speech and free press at all,' replied Kun:

> Workmen's papers are published without the intervention of any censorship. Among working men there is perfect freedom of speech and of holding meetings; this freedom is enjoyed not only by the workmen who share our views but also by those whose views are different. The anarchists, for instance, publish a paper and other printed matter. There are also citizen's papers, for instance, *XX. Század* (Twentieth Century), a periodical published by the society for sociology, without any control or restriction being exercised upon it. We only suppress bourgeois papers having decidedly counter-revolutionary intentions.

---

22. For a report of the speech, see 'A közoktatási Népbiztosság irodalmi programja' (The Plan for Literature of the People's Commissariat for Education and Culture), *Magyarország*, 19 April 1919. In: József (1967), pp. 199–201.

> We are doing this not because we are afraid of them, but because we want in this way to obviate the necessity of suppressing counter-revolution by force of arms.[23]

Regarding the popularisation of culture in general and literature in particular, Lajos Magyar had written an article for *Az Ember* (Man) prior to Balázs's speech with the title 'Literature in the Council Republic', in which he asserted that the new state welcomed literature and the arts with an open heart, without wanting uniformity and without tampering with artistic creativity. 'The Council Republic is naturally putting an end to the unhealthy situation whereby beauty and the arts are the prerogative of the capitalist classes.' People's libraries and reading rooms were opening, and cultural education was being put within reach of all.[24]

Helping to put that idea into practice, in the middle of May the weekly *Nőmunkás* (Woman Worker) announced it would soon start to publish a column about literature, saying: 'Literature is an outstandingly helpful partner of socialism. But only *real* literature.' Several lines later, that was clarified—sort of: 'Since real literature is also socialist literature.'[25]

Earlier in May, *Vörös Újság* had run an article under the title 'Books Belong to the Working People!' which proclaimed it was the duty of the government to make cultural and scientific books available to as many people as possible, which, it asserted, necessitated the nationalisation of all kinds of libraries, as well as publishing and distribution enterprises. In addition, the article highlighted the urgent need to translate as many important foreign works as possible. The author of the anonymous piece, which appeared in the paper's regular 'Communist Culture' section, seems to have had in mind works by Marx, Engels and others of a Marxist orientation.[26]

A Marx Translation Committee was established. Translating Marx's *Capital* was regarded as a priority project and attempts were made to involve a wide circle of people. There is a letter by the writer Dezső Kosztolányi, himself an experienced translator, in which he says he had been invited to, and participated in a meeting at the commissariat to discuss with others the translation of *Capital*.[27]

---

23. Eastman (1919), p. 6.
24. 'Az irodalom a Tanácsköztársaságban', *Az Ember*, 1 April 1919. In: József (1967), pp. 71–2.
25. *Nőmunkás*, 17 May 1919, pp. 3–4.
26. 'A könyv a dolgozó népé', *Vörös Újság*, 7 May 1919, pp. 7–8.
27. The (undated) letter is reproduced in József (1967), pp. 774–5. In a footnote (pp. 1144–5), József quotes a source indicating that up to 50 writers and specialist translators had been called on to work with the Marx Translation Committee, which began its work at the end of May.

The People's Commissariat of Culture was of the view that not just Marxist texts but also quality works of foreign literature should also be translated into Hungarian and circulated widely, and with this in mind a Translator's Bureau was established. As reported in *Vörös Újság*, its task was to ensure the translation of valuable old works, as well as standard works of modern and modernist literature.

'It is almost natural that the first project will be the translation of Dostoyevsky's complete works,' the report declared.[28] Translations were also planned of works by Gogol, Tolstoy, Ibsen, Goethe and Shakespeare, and the names of Balzac, Meredith and others were also mentioned.

It was clearly an ambitious project, but perhaps it is not surprising that the results achieved appear to have been limited. After all, translating literature requires time and within just one month after the appearance of the *Vörös Újság* report, the Hungarian Soviet Republic had ceased to exist.

Making their point

What were writers actually writing during the Council Republic? Mention has already been made of Sándor Márai, but the others? They were also writing—quite a lot—not so much books as short stories, essays, poems, reviews, sketches and reports, often published in newspapers. A comprehensive overview is beyond the scope of this book, but what follows is a brief indication of the kinds of texts produced by a number of writers, in particular some of the more prominent and well-known ones.

In the immediate wake of the proclamation of the Soviet Republic on 21 March—obviously before it became clear how developments would actually turn out—many writers, like others, were swept along in a wave of enthusiasm, and this was reflected in what some of them wrote.

The 34-year-old poet, sketch writer and dramatist Ernő Szép, for example, wrote an enthusiastic account of a mass rally in front of parliament, which took place on Sunday, 23 March, to celebrate the proclamation of the Council Republic two days earlier. Entitled simply 'Sunday', it records his experiences of joining the throng in the company of bakery workers marching towards parliament—the atmosphere, the flags and banner, the humorous banter, the music and singing, the crowds on rooftops and lampposts, a demobilised youth selling cigarettes, the rousing speakers' words.[29]

28. 'A világirodalom a kultúra szolgálatában' (World Literature in the Service of Culture), *Vörös Újság*, 2 July 1919, p. 7. In: József (1967), p. 573.

29. 'Vasárnap', *Pesti Futár* (Pest Courier), 28 March 1919, pp. 3–9.

A similar, arguably even greater, initial enthusiasm was expressed by Árpád Tóth in his poem 'The New God', which was published on 1 April. Opening with the words 'People! A new God is speaking to you!' it talks of a figure born in blood … a large blood-coloured, naked figure, which crosses countries, reverberating on the Earth with an earth-shaking voice, from the 'red East to the pallid West', crying: 'I have come! The Red God has arrived!'[30]

A few days after the Council Republic had been proclaimed, Zsigmond Móricz was writing about what he saw as a 'new public' turning up for theatre performances[31] and, as noted above, in early May he was again enthusing, this time about the 550 writers who formed the writers' trade union. In the intervening period, Móricz was very active in support of the Commune, particularly by means of his writings. In early April, for example, he wrote a short propaganda piece called 'Capital', in which the capitalist tells his son to accumulate capital, because money means everything and replaces reason, strength and work.

The communist, writes Móricz, also tells his son to accumulate capital, but his type of capital is different. If you live in close association with your fellow humans, then you are liberated and you can happily realise the inner content of your own humanity. Be an artist without vanity. Be a scholar or be a worker—there is no need to be part of a machine of exploitation. Gather the real treasures; accumulate the most precious values of your calling. Be a human being, urges Móricz, just and without anger.[32]

In April Zsigmond Móricz travelled to western Hungary, to Somogy County. Always interested in the fate of Hungary's peasantry, he was keen to experience at first hand the developments underway in that area of rural Hungary. Móricz was duly impressed by what he saw, which resulted in a number of enthusiastic journalistic reports.

What particularly impressed him were the many large estates, which had been taken over and transformed into jointly owned agricultural cooperatives. This, it seemed to Móricz was the way forward. 'You couldn't ask for anything more ideal, more social,' he wrote.[33]

Another article, under the bold heading 'In Hungary Nobody Starves to Death', he contested the view that the changing agricultural system would lead to shortages of food and other goods. After detailing what he had seen in terms of production and distribution, he added that Communism,

---

30. 'Az új Isten', *Nyugat*, 1919, No. 7. http://epa.oszk.hu/00000/00022/00265/07835.htm (accessed 4 July 2017).
31. See Chapter 7.
32. 'Tőke', *Pesti Futár*, 4 April 1919, pp. 4–5.
33. 'Magyarország a béke útján' (Hungary on the Road of Peace), *Pesti Hírlap*, 15 April 1919, p. 2.

which many had feared would mean regimentation, was going to usher in a wonderful era, where the individual could blossom. In Hungary, not only was no one dying of hunger, but a happy human life was beginning.[34]

It may well be that Zsigmond Móricz was excessively influenced by the circumstances of his visit to western Hungary, rather like the later 'fellow travellers' who were taken in by their officially organised visits to the Soviet Union. After all, Móricz travelled with Jenő Hamburger, the People's Commissar for Agriculture, and was being shown around with a group which included foreign journalists.

Be that as it may, another passionate article by Móricz followed a visit to a school in the village of Szentjakab. It made him ponder about the necessity for good education for all, not just for the children of the wealthy, as well as the importance of learning.[35]

Two writings by Móricz on other themes appeared in early May: 'Here only Goodness Helps' and 'I Want to See the Poor Hungarian People Happy'.[36] The former in particular, a short story in the form of reportage, reflected a Tolstoyan approach, which might appear odd, but in fact there was a trend at the time, even among some communists, to adopt a Tolstoyan and utopistic, almost religious way of thinking.[37]

When the Hungarian Soviet Republic was proclaimed on 21 March 1919, the poet and writer Gyula Juhász, who was approaching his 36th birthday, was living in his birthplace, Szeged in the southern part of Hungary. Within days, he would become one of the first figures of Hungarian literature to publicly come out in favour of the new regime.

On 25 March, the front page of *Délmagyarország* (Southern Hungary), a local publication of which Juhász was a leading contributor, was taken up by his 'Concise Revolutionary Catechism', comprising 15 simple questions about the meaning, essence and nature of proletarian dictatorship and why there was one in Hungary; about the significance of the Russian Revolution and its lessons for Hungary; about the nature of a communist system, its

34. 'Magyarországon nem hal éhen senki', *Pesti Hírlap*, 17 April 1919, pp. 2–3.
35. 'A szentjakabi iskola' (The Szentjakab School), *Somogyi Vörös Újság*, 15 April 1919.
36. 'Itt csak a jóság segít', *Fáklya*, 1 May 1919, pp. 3–4; 'Boldognak akarom látni a szegény magyar népet', *Pesti Hírlap*, 4 May 1919, pp. 2–3.
37. One of those who was drawn to concepts of what might be called revolutionary Christianity was Ervin Sinkó. He was part of a discussion group, which used to meet regularly at the Soviet House (the requisitioned Hungária Hotel in Budapest) to debate ideas. Years later in Moscow, Béla Kun told Sinkó: 'I didn't know that right in the midst of the dictatorship, there in the Hungária, a couple of doors away from my room, every night a whole group were making Marxist theology out of Marxism and turning theological problems into Marxist problems.' (Sinkó, 1988, p. 139.)

beliefs and when it could be achieved; and about the forerunners of the Hungarian revolution.

The answers were equally simple. For example: Proletarian dictatorship meant the transition from the bankrupt capitalist system of production to the communist world system of production and the communist world system 'will be a society of working people, in which everyone will live from work in a human commonwealth aiming at the happiness of all, without war, and realising the real earthly possibilities of beauty, goodness and justice.'[38]

Thereafter, along with the writer Ferenc Móra, Juhász was active in Szeged, organising special theatre performances, concerts and lectures for workers. However, the town had been in the control of French forces since late 1918 and never really came under the influence of the Revolutionary Governing Council in Budapest. Thus the local revolutionary 'directory' was only short lived, meaning that quite soon Juhász was forced out of his position of, in effect, being the director of the local theatre. In addition, due to the local political circumstances, Szeged became a centre of Hungarian counter-revolutionary plotters, anti-communist officers and others, who formed a series of so-called counter-revolutionary governments there. Hence it was not a good time to be in Szeged if, like Gyula Juhász, you had left-wing leanings and were publicly active.

Nevertheless, he continued to write and his poems were published fairly frequently in *Délmagyarország* up to the end of July and the collapse of the Soviet Republic in Hungary.

One of Juhász's verses, *Tercets for Ferenc Móra*, was penned in solidarity with his friend and colleague Ferenc Móra, who had been pressurised to resign his editorship of *Szegedi Napló* (Szeged Diary).[39]

Móra was a novelist, journalist and museologist. He had been director of the Szeged library and museum since 1917 and editor-in-chief of *Szegedi Napló* since 1913. A few days after the proclamation of the Soviet Republic, a leading article he wrote, 'Memento', was published on the front page of the newspaper and, not surprisingly given its opening words, it caused quite a stir.

'The first week of proletarian dictatorship has passed. Perhaps never before in history has there been a dictatorship so uncompromisingly

38. 'Forradalmi Kis Káté', *Délmagyarország*, 25 March 1919, p. 1. For a reproduction of the front page, see: www.sk-szeged.hu/statikus_html/kiallitas/juhaszgy/kiskate.html (accessed 4 July 2017).
39. 'Terzinák Móra Ferencnek', *Szegedi Napló*, 13 May 1919.

resolute and yet so divinely humane. So far in history there have only been bloody dictatorships.'[40]

Facing criticism, Móra didn't withdraw completely from public life, even though, as indicated above, the 'official' political atmosphere in Szeged, for Juhász and himself, was not friendly. Nevertheless, even on the very eve of the collapse of the Commune, on 31 July, Móra turned up at the local Workers' Centre and gave a recitation of his recently composed verse, *Petőfi a mienk* (Petőfi is Ours).[41]

Sándor Bródy, one of the most noted Hungarian writers and dramatists of the turn of the century, was 55 years of age when the Council Republic was proclaimed. Although not taking a particularly active part in the activities of the Commune, he nevertheless contributed with a number of writings. For example, a couple of weeks after the Soviet Republic had been formed, a statement he wrote was published under the title 'A Suitable Time for Drama'.

'Now we can really start to write plays,' he proclaimed.

> This is the right time for me and the right time for drama, since there's no better theme in the world than the sharp and harsh truth. I have to acknowledge that for a long time I was kept back from the stage because actually you had to write for the bourgeoisie, otherwise a play would be a failure well in advance.[42]

Bródy wrote a new, one-act play especially for the 1 May celebrations. According to *Fáklya*, the committee organising the celebrations commissioned a number of well-known playwrights, including Ferenc Molnár, to produce a play for May Day, but only Bródy's *Orgonavirág* (Lilac) was ready on time.[43]

No doubt the future internationally-known dramatist Gyula Háy would have been happy to be commissioned to write a play for May Day, but at the time he was approaching his 19th birthday and hadn't yet made a name for himself. However, he was out on the streets of Budapest on 1 May, with what must have seemed like most of the city's population, observing what was in effect a massive, open-air theatrical performance. As he would later

---

40. 'Memento', *Szegedi Napló*, 1 April 1919. In: Remete (1956), pp. 190–2.
41. The radical poet Sándor Petőfi was one of the youthful leaders of the 1848 anti-Habsburg revolution in Pest. He lost his life during the subsequent War of Independence. Petőfi was one of the figures mentioned by Juhász in his 'Catechism' in answer to the question about the forerunners of the revolution.
42. 'A drámának való idő', *Színházi Élet*, 6–12 April 1919. In: József (1967), pp. 97–8.
43. 'Vörös Május' (Red May), *Fáklya*, 29 April 1919, pp. 4–5.

recall: 'Earnest-looking gentlemen—the greatest poets and writers in the land—waited on the lorries for their turn to read aloud from their works.'

'What did it matter,' he adds, 'whether anybody understood them?'[44]

Háy himself was an enthusiastic, youthful supporter of the Soviet Republic and very early on he went to the cultural commissariat's office in Budapest's Hold Street looking for a job. He found one as a propagandist for young workers. It was his first permanent employment. Háy set up a club in central Budapest as a centre for promoting Marxist ideology. He tried some Freud, too, but his lecture about the great psychoanalyst produced only laughter and two of the older girls, presumably embarrassed, stopped coming.[45]

The writer and dramatist Ferenc Molnár was much older and more experienced as a writer than Gyula Háy by the time the Soviet Republic was proclaimed. His play *Liliom*, later adapted for the Rodgers and Hammerstein musical *Carousel*, and his equally internationally renowned novel *The Paul Street Boys*, had both been written before the First World War. Molnár might not have produced a play for May Day in 1919, despite the commission, but maybe that is not surprising, since he appears not to have been among the writers who were prominent during the Council Republic period or particularly sympathetic to its politics, though one source indicates he was among those writers who gave 'educational' presentations for workers during the intervals in theatre performances.[46]

Like Ferenc Molnár, Gyula Krúdy was born in 1878 and by 1919 he, too, was a popular, well-established writer and journalist. Krúdy, however, was very supportive of the Council Republic, at least in its early period, even though he was by no means a communist in the party sense of the term.

Within just a few days of the proclamation of the Soviet Republic, Krúdy was writing an article entitled 'Old and New Fictional Heroes', in which he asked where all the new writers were who could record the revolution. He wanted to see libraries filled with books about the birth of the new world, so that in the future people would understand what had happened in Hungary.[47]

Later in 'New History has to be Written', he was asserting that the new history was a work of exposure. Writers had to turn away from the

---

44. Hay (1974), p. 71.
45. Ibid., p. 58.
46. 'Haladó írók a Tanácsköztársaság szolgálatában' (Progressive Writers in the Service of the Council Republic), http://mek.oszk.hu/02200/02228/html/05/299.html (accessed 31 January 2017), part of *A magyar irodalom története 1905-től 1919-ig* (The History of Hungarian Literature, 1905–1919). Budapest, Akadémiai Kiadó, 1965.
47. 'Régi és új regényhősök', *Magyarország*, 25 March 1919.

traditional fine lies. Monuments of monarchs should be pulled down in order to expose how much sawdust they contained. Krúdy advocated summoning the spirit of *György Dózsa* 'There's no need to fear the new history, the new Hungary,' he proclaimed. 'Let the old world perish and fall to pieces.'[48]

Like Zsigmond Móricz, Gyula Krúdy travelled around the country and produced a series of reports about what he had witnessed. Also like Móricz, he seems to have been suitably impressed. In 'What Kind of Hungary', for example, he appears to have welcomed the disappearance of the gentry.[49]

His experiences were compiled into a pamphlet published by the cultural commissariat, which dealt with the agricultural cooperatives in Fejér County. The text, says Béla Katona in his 1969 study, was simultaneously a mixture of report and social documentary, as well as an explanation of decrees and a work of propaganda at the same time. But what was striking was the 'convincing passion, with which he castigated the crimes of the old world, and attentively noted the manifestations of the developing new life ... With pleasure he stated that at last the land belonged to the people.'[50]

The title of one of Krúdy's 1919 newspaper articles, 'Poor Children on the Island', was a reference to Budapest's Margaret Island. As noted previously, for many years Margaret Island had been an exclusive playground of the well-to-do and a fee had to be paid as an entrance charge. The entrance fee was abolished in April 1919 and thus the island became open to all. Krúdy happily sings the praises of the resulting transformation.

'Young girls stand in a circle, singing like flowers in the gardens. The boys run in all directions like spring rainwater. The sound of poor children fills the island like a May breeze brings colour and fragrance to the world.'[51]

Appropriately, the article was published on 1 May, when as part of the massive 1919 May Day celebrations, Margaret Island was turned into a children's paradise (see Chapter 2).

The Hungarian Soviet Republic was proclaimed on 21 March 1919, eight days before Dezső Kosztolányi's 34th birthday. Although some years younger than Ferenc Molnár and Gyula Krúdy, the writer, poet, critic and

---

48. Új történelmet kell írni', *Magyarország*, 16 April 1919. György Dózsa was the leader of a peasants' revolt in 1514. Although the revolt was defeated and Dózsa was himself captured and executed, his name has gone down in history as being associated with populist movements of rebellion and has been invoked many times during different periods of upheaval and revolutionary change, as well as in literature and poetry.
49. 'Milyen Magyarország', *Pesti Futár*, 16 May 1919, pp. 3–4.
50. See Katona (1969) in the bibliography.
51. 'Szegény gyerekek a szigeten', *Érdekes Újság*, 1 May 1919. In: Remete (1956), pp. 335–7.

journalist Kosztolányi was, like them, part of the generation of literary figures who had made a name for themselves prior to the First World War. In the light of his post-1919 views of the Commune (see the Postscript) it is perhaps surprising to learn that he, too, expressed certain ideas supportive of the new regime.

On 30 March, a hard-hitting article by Kosztolányi entitled 'The New Theatre' was published in *Színházi Élet* (Theatre Life), in which he castigated the theatre of old as being corrupted by capital. Sometimes society had a bad conscience, he says, which it tried to alleviate by covering wounds and blemishes with beauty spots. Kosztolányi asks if we should regret the passing of this art and such theatres. He gives a resounding 'no', welcoming what he calls the 'Bolshevik theatre' and concluding by asserting that the theatre will not be a place of amusement, rather a 'temple of devotion for free, moral people'.[52]

Kosztolányi wrote a number of articles during the Soviet Republic, often on theatre themes, but they were not quite as politically loaded as 'The New Theatre'. One piece, however, on a rather different subject, was fairly sentimental and fitted neatly in the contemporary political atmosphere, almost in the manner of propaganda.

In 'Unsightly Mariska ... Beautiful Mariska ...', published on 11 May, Kosztolányi describes how two months previously he had visited a children's hospital, where he encountered a sad child lying in a bed. Her name was Mariska, a worker's daughter, and she was seriously ill, having drunk some liquid containing caustic soda at home. He thought she was two years old, but it turned out she was over six. Nevertheless, at the same time she had the appearance of a dispirited, withered old woman. She had been lying in hospital for ten months, had lost all sense of taste, and had to be fed through a tube. She was entirely uncommunicative and only if she was addressed as 'beautiful Mariska' could a faint smile be raised.

Kosztolányi now begs the 'sanctimonious reader' not to take out a handkerchief and shed some tears. He describes how in working-class families, where the father is at the factory and the mother is standing in a queue for coal, a hungry child, not being under the watchful eye of a guardian, Fraulein or 'miss', might well seek out food and drink and inadvertently swallow something dangerous, as Mariska had done. Such occurrences were not uncommon, he wants to tell the reader.

However, he also has a more cheerful tale to relate. He recalls how recently he happened to be passing a day nursery for proletarian children on Andrássy Avenue. He saw happy children sitting on the steps of the

52. 'Az új színház', *Színházi Élet*, 30 March 1919.

mansion, dressed in red, and others throwing a red ball into the May air. The state was providing soap, combs and brushes for proletarian children, so all the young ones he saw looked clean, neat and tidy.

For a long time he marvelled at them flitting around in the garden in a carefree manner. He thought of unsightly Mariska who could no longer taste sugar or know the pleasure of a smile, and he thought of these children who are no longer swallowing caustic soda and will remain beautiful forever. 'Beautiful Mariskas,' he writes, 'all of you, throw up the red balls in jubilation—all the way to the sky!'[53]

While many well-established writers were enthusiastic about the Soviet Republic, particularly in its early phases, their degree of sympathy and involvement could vary greatly. The writer and poet Frigyes Karinthy, for example, who had been strongly anti-war and had welcomed Hungary's immediate post-war changes, was a member of the Writers' Directory steering committee, announced in early May 1919, but he seems to have essentially remained in the background during the period of the Commune. An adaptation of his poem *Vérmező* (Field of Blood) was staged on 1 May at Budapest's Madách Theatre as part of its May Day celebratory programme, but it was a modified version of something he had written many years before.[54] The staged poetic drama was about the French Revolution and the so-called Hungarian Jacobins who were executed in 1795 in the place subsequently known as Vérmező. As noted in Chapter 2, in 1919 the location was one of the focal points of the May Day demonstrations in Budapest.

Mihály Babits was a member of the Writers' Directory and also a member of its all-important registration committee. In addition, he was appointed a university professor by the cultural commissariat—a post he accepted. However, even though he had warmly welcomed the Chrysanthemum Revolution in 1918 and the changes it brought about, during the time of the Commune he essentially concentrated on his teaching and educational activities and wasn't at the forefront of those writers singing its praises.

Furthermore, he doesn't seem to have thought highly of what was produced by others. As he wrote in the November issue of *Nyugat* after the fall of the Council Republic: 'The months of the proletarian dictatorship

53. 'Csúnya Mariska ... szép Mariska ...', *Pesti Napló*, 11 May 1919. In: Remete (1956), pp. 342–3.

54. Boldizsár Vörös, 'Forradalom a műalkotásban—műalkotás a forradalomban. Karinthy Frigyes: Vérmező' (Revolution in a Work of Art—A Work of Art in the Revolution. Frigyes Karinthy: Vérmező), *Budapesti Negyed*, No. 65, Autumn 2009, pp. 313–38.

were the months of silence in literature.'[55] And in a letter he admitted: 'During the proletarian dictatorship my own outlook shifted completely in a conservative direction.'[56] However he adds a remark indicating that 'conservatism' could have different meanings for different people.

55. Quoted by Tamás Ungvári in his study of Babits in 1918–19. See Ungvári (1959), p. 247.
56. Ibid., p. 248.

10
Why?

In a text published in 1959, 40 years after the Hungarian Soviet Republic had fallen, the painter Bertalan Pór, who was 79 years old at the time, reflected on why he had become a keen supporter of the Commune.

'It's no wonder that I myself became an active militant of the proletarian dictatorship—life nurtured me for that,' he recalled.

> Already in my youth I was discontented with the existing social system. My life was full of hardship and up and downs. That is why ever since I was young there was a longing in my heart for a better, more beautiful life, and I realised relatively quickly that a new life could only be created on the basis of a different, socialist social structure. My dissatisfaction also found expression in my works. Fraternising and talking with Russian soldiers in the autumn of 1917 also helped to ripen my revolutionary ideas, and when the [Communist] Party was founded, I felt that a new life was beginning for me, too.[1]

The details of Pór's trajectory—from dissatisfied youth to socialist, to revolutionary, to activist of the Soviet Republic—were not necessarily typical, but the longing for a 'better, more beautiful life' was a common sentiment behind much of the support for the Commune in its early days.

In an interview published in 1978, the dancer, teacher and choreographer, Valéria Dienes, 99 years of age at the time of publication, was asked how she came to hear of the 1919 Soviet Republic. She replied that one evening her husband came home and said he had joined the Communist Party.

> I thought to myself, this was a good thing, since surely there would be some kind of new world. All of us had waited for years for something to change around us and we rejoiced when the news came. Pál said to me that the world was being renewed and now we were going to do something different from previous people. I was very happy and all this got me in the struggle.[2]

---

1. Gábor (1959), p. 8.
2. Borus (1978), p. 41.

As it happened, she couldn't do too much herself since she was pregnant with her third child, although apparently she did prepare a proposal for the reform of women's sports for the leaders of the Soviet Republic.[3]

Without a doubt, there was widespread enthusiasm when the Council Republic was born. In the early evening of 21 March, the young poet József Nádass, who had been severely injured during the Great War and who had joined the Communist Party in 1918, was attending a packed meeting in the former chamber of Parliament's Lower House in what is today Bródy Sándor Street next to the National Museum. The crowd was listening to a presentation by György Lukács on 'Old Culture and New Culture', when all of a sudden Tibor Szamuely burst into the hall, mounted the platform and announced that the revolution had been victorious and that the Hungarian Soviet Republic had been declared.

'It's impossible to describe in words the feeling, the excitement of all of us,' Nádass would recall.

> Certainly the majority of those present were not Communist Party members. Indeed, it's likely there were many there who were still not favourable to the idea of the proletarian dictatorship, but the rapturous enthusiasm swept away everyone. They rejoiced, cried out, roared and shouted hurrah! I don't know how many times, three times or four times, over and over again we sang *The Internationale.*

Then, forgetting all about Lukács and his theories of culture, those assembled streamed out of the building and joined the crowds outside, demonstrating and celebrating in the streets of central Budapest.[4]

Even far from the capital, when news about the Soviet Republic broke it could generate a similar level of enthusiasm. In Balmazújváros, in eastern Hungary, the future writer Péter Veres was a 22-year-old, well-read socialist, active in the recently formed local branch of the agricultural labourers' trade union. He had also been involved in the village committee set up during the Károlyi regime to distribute land. On hearing the news on 22 March

3. *Encyclopaedia Britannica.* See: www.britannica.com/biography/Valeria-Dienes (accessed 4 July 2017).

4. Nádass (1959), p. 196. If the majority at the meeting were not Communist Party members, it is perhaps surprising that they were familiar with the words of *The Internationale.* Maybe they just mumbled along, or maybe it was only a minority who sang. Lajos Kassák, who was also there, makes no mention of any singing, though in other respects his account is similar to that of Nádass. See Kassák (1983), pp. 487–9. Lukács was able to deliver his interrupted lecture later, in June, at the new Marx-Engels Workers' University.

about events in Budapest he rushed off to meet other activists and discuss the situation.

> In the village [I and other radicals] were considered the 'real communists', so now we had to step forward. I hurried to the village hall and of course I was full of excitement—our time has come, this will be the whole thing, the real revolution ... There's no time for brooding, what's needed is action ... the power has to be seized—that's the first step.

Naive maybe, but certainly not lacking in enthusiasm![5]

Ninety years after the Soviet Republic had fallen, art historian Éva Forgács wrote: 'Shaken by World War I and the ensuing October 1918 revolution, the inadequacy of Count Mihály Károlyi's coalition government that emerged out of that revolution, and driven by a desire for social justice, almost the entire Hungarian intelligentsia participated in some way in the Commune.'[6]

Writing much earlier, soon after the events, Oszkár Jászi, who was certainly no supporter of the Commune, expressed a somewhat similar opinion: 'In its first weeks the proletarian dictatorship was thoroughly popular, strange to say, among the middle class and the petty bourgeoisie.'[7]

According to Jászi, the 'most attractive aspect' of the new regime, which generated 'a new spirit in the community', involved an 'apostolic fanaticism for a new religion, the first concern of which was for the spread of education and art'.[8]

'Under the direction of George Lukács,' says Jászi, 'the policy of the dictators in regard to education and art was certainly distinguished by many great ideals.' Though he does add that 'they were hardly more than experiments *in vacuo*'.[9]

Regarding journalists and their support for the new regime, Jászi asserts:

> It must not be supposed that the Hungarian Press was merely performing forced labour for the dictatorship, at all events in the first [period]. I make bold to maintain that on the contrary the great majority of the journalists were at first serving the Commune with enthusiasm.

5. Veres (1959), pp. 251–2. In later years Péter Veres would become nationally known. See the Postscript.
6. Forgács (2009), p. 109.
7. Jászi (1924), p. 115.
8. Ibid., p. 146.
9. Ibid., p. 146.

Though, again, he adds a modifying rider:

> Hysterical by nature, the Hungarian journalists hastened to prostrate themselves before the new rulers; prostitute by habit, they served now as in the past the interests of the men who paid them. And not only the journalists. Nearly the whole of the Hungarian intellectual middle class ... served the dictatorship as they had before served capitalism [10]

Apart from journalists, as we have seen in previous chapters it was also painters, film-makers, musicians, theatre professionals and writers who enthusiastically gave their support when the Council Republic was declared on 21 March, and, indeed, for some time after. So where did all the enthusiasm originate? Why did so many people in the arts world get involved, willingly supporting with their talents the new regime? Very few of them could be described as communists or communist sympathisers, in the manner of Bertalan Pór, so what was the reason—or to put it more realistically, what were the reasons?

At its simplest, it could be said there was a type of 'bandwagon' or 'herd' effect in operation. People were swept along and got caught up in the general enthusiasm for a new beginning and a different kind of world. 'Something was in the air', so to say. Yet this 'something' wasn't unique to Hungary. It is easy to forget that in the wake of the First World War there was an upsurge of radicalism not only in Hungary or even just Europe, but also worldwide, from Canada to India, from the USA to South Africa. Without denying the Hungarian specifics, there are many examples of post-1918 radicalism which indicate that Hungary's upheaval in 1919 was not an entirely isolated phenomenon, requiring extra-special explanation.

Worldwide upheavals

> We are standing on the threshold of a new age. We are entering a period of the emancipation of labour from the thraldom of wage slavery. It is the time of which poets have dreamed, the time for which in every country men and women have striven, have gone to prison, have sacrificed their lives. Thrones are tumbling like skittles. Revolution like a cleansing gale sweeps through Europe.

These words are from a Bolshevik leaflet distributed among Allied troops in Russia in 1919.[11] In their romanticism, they capture a mood which was

10. Ibid., pp. 115–16.

11. Quoted in Mitchell (1970), p. 11. David Mitchell's *1919: Red Mirage* is a racy, atmospheric account, quite gripping in its style, of the many political and labour

not exclusive to Russia. Elsewhere, too, it must have seemed that the world was being turned upside down. What follows are a number of examples briefly illustrating that.[12]

Early January 1919 saw the Spartacist Revolt in Berlin. The revolt was crushed and its charismatic leaders Karl Liebknecht and Rosa Luxemburg were killed on 15 January while under arrest. On 18 January the Versailles Peace Conference formally opened in Paris. Although it embodied a certain new idealism in relation to world affairs, unlike earlier international peace conferences, the defeated parties were excluded from the deliberations until the terms of the treaty were ready for submission. It did not bode well for Hungary, one of those excluded.

On 21 January in Ireland, Sinn Fein decided not to attend Parliament in Westminster after winning a landslide victory in the previous month's elections. Instead they organised a parliament in Dublin (the Dail Eireann) and declared Irish independence from Britain. The last day of the month saw the so-called Battle of George Square in Glasgow. The city had a history of radicalism, and World War I turned it into a centre for organised protest against poor working conditions. The Liberal government feared the mass rally was the beginning of a working class revolution along the lines of the Russian Revolution. The rally was broken up by police, and troops and tanks were deployed on Clydeside.

The Seattle General Strike of 1919 in early February was a five-day general work stoppage by more than 60,000 people. Workers in several unions struck to gain higher wages after two years of World War I wage controls. Although the strike was non-violent and lasted less than a week, government officials, the press, and much of the public viewed the strike as a radical attempt to subvert US institutions. It was an early example of America's 'Red Scare' of 1919 and 1920.

Spain was that rare country where the labour movement was very strongly influenced, even dominated, by anarchist and anarcho-syndicalist rather than socialist or Marxist ideas. The Spanish *Confederación Nacional del Trabajo* (CNT—National Confederation of Labour), in its libertarian fear of permanent bureaucracy, in principle objected to paid officials and large standing funds, other than prisoner support funds. In February 1919,

---

movement upheavals which spread across the world after the end of the First World War. In contrast with many works of history, it is not only international in scope, it also contains a large amount of 'history from below', as opposed to focussing on events primarily at the political, diplomatic and state level.

12. The details which follow are compiled primarily from: Mitchell (1970); Chronology 1919—Indiana University Bloomington (www.indiana.edu/~league/1919.htm); and BBC—History, British History Timeline (www.bbc.co.uk/history/british/timeline/worldwars_timeline_noflash.shtml), both accessed 5 July 2017.

all 100,000 CNT workers in Barcelona went on strike. Factories ground to a halt. There was little violence, though thousands were arrested. The strike lasted a month and ended with a truce. But the revolt spread south, resulting in large-scale strikes in Seville and Granada. A surge of militancy spread among peasants in Andalusia, many of whom had joined the CNT. Terrified landowners, fearing 'Bolshevism' fled to the towns.

The Third International was established on 2 March. Although it would become under the thumb of Moscow, it set out to support and coordinate the wave of labour revolts around the world. But not all the new movements were of the left. On 23 March Benito Mussolini, who had been a radical socialist, formed the first Fascio di Combattimento in Italy, which marked the initial step towards the establishment of the Fascist Party. He became a nationalist, calling for a stronger Italy.

On 18 March the Rowlatt Act extended the wartime suspension of civil liberties in India. In protest, Gandhi called for the use of non-violent civil disobedience, and for non-cooperation with the British government. On 10 April a large crowd attending a Sikh religious festival in defiance of British martial law was fired on without warning. More than 300 people were killed. The 'Amritsar Massacre' crystallised growing Indian discontent with British rule and the movement for India's independence became even stronger.

April was a particularly 'hot' month. Italy was in turmoil, with serious tension between the left and the right. The month witnessed the Fascists burning down the Milan offices of *Avanti*, the socialist daily of which Mussolini had once been editor. In Bavaria, not far from Hungary, the Munich Soviet was declared on the lines of a regional workers' council. Its leading figures were a mixture of radical socialists, anarchists and romantics. In South Africa workers in Johannesburg took over the town hall and prepared to administer the city. In Australia a massive strike of miners and seamen in New South Wales turned into a trial of strength with the government, courts and reformist trade unions.

In Canada, in mid May a ballot of workers in Winnipeg overwhelmingly voted for a general strike in solidarity with metal workers struggling for better conditions. A seemingly revolutionary situation developed and the term 'Winnipeg Soviet' was employed. The previous year, even before the war was over, on 2 August 1918 Canada had witnessed the country's first general strike, which took place in Vancouver as a political protest against the killing under suspicious circumstances of draft evader and labour activist Albert Goodwin.

And so it continued. Later in the year there was even a police strike in London and Liverpool for recognition of the National Union of Police and Prison Officers. Over 2000 strikers were dismissed.

All the movements had their popular romantics. On the right in Italy, there was Gabriele D'Annunzio, the literary figure turned national war hero who set up the short-lived Regency of Carnaro in Fiume, installing himself as its leader. On the left in Ukraine, there was Nestor Makhno, who led what was in effect an independent anarchist peasant army, which opposed both the Reds and the Whites.

The Russian effect

It cannot be argued that the above events had any direct influence on developments in Hungary. Many of them—perhaps even most of them—would have happened without being noticed in Hungary. Yet they simply show that Hungary wasn't unique.

The effects of the developments in Russia, however, were different, and not only due to their scale. Many of the supporters of the new regime in Hungary had been prisoners of war in Russia, where they had been radicalised by Bolshevik propaganda. But there were others, too, who derived great inspiration from the Russian Revolution and the idea of 'communism'. To many people today this might seem strange, but it should be noted that at the time Russian society and politics was still volatile, not yet having fully gone down the road of totalitarianism. The suppression of the Kronstadt revolt in 1921, which arguably marked the end of the Russian revolutionary process, was still two years away and there was not yet such a phenomenon as 'Stalinism' to smear the image of 'communism'.[13]

True, astute observers, well informed about the Russian scene, might have noted the signs already indicating Bolshevik authoritarian practices—for example, the erosion of worker's power, as exercised in the form of factory committees, in favour of centralised control exercised by the ruling party—but such observers were few and far between in Hungary. Nor did Hungary have any strong traditions of libertarian socialism, anarchism, anarcho-syndicalism or council-communism, which had in their ideas, implicitly or explicitly, an in-built, radical left-wing critique of Bolshevik

---

13. Kronstadt is the name of the city and fortress at the eastern end of Kotlin Island, which lies in the Gulf of Finland, about 30km from St Petersburg. In 1905 and again throughout 1917 the sailors of Kronstadt were at the forefront of revolutionary activity, being involved in almost every turn of events in St Petersburg. In March 1921, a revolt occurred on the island, which threatened Bolshevik power. The rebels, who included many communists, adopted a 15-point statement in favour of more democracy and freedom. They were brutally crushed. The Kronstadt uprising was a classic, spontaneous, left-wing revolt from below. Its inspiration was anarcho-populist, in favour of direct democracy, against Bolshevik dictatorship, but also against any restoration of the pre-1917 order.

ideas and practices. Oszkár Jászi had some insight into such matters, but he was not typical of Hungarian intellectuals in general.

However, Hungary's draw towards Bolshevik Russia was not just a matter of political ideas, it also involved considerations of international *realpolitik*, as explained by the Social Democrat Vilmos Böhm to the British writer Ellis Ashmead-Bartlett when the latter was in Budapest during the period of the Commune.

'You cannot blame us for becoming Bolshevists,' Böhm asserted. 'The Entente took absolutely no notice of us at all until we formed a Soviet. Whilst we were endeavouring to establish a Constitutional Government, they merely bullied and insulted us.'

Ashmead-Bartlett, who generally had no sympathy at all for Hungary's Soviet Republic, simply adds: 'How could I deny the truth of Böhm's words!'[14]

Similar sentiments had been expressed by Sándor Garbai, a former stonemason and long-standing Social Democratic Party leader, who filled the post of president of the Revolutionary Governing Council throughout the entire period of the Commune. Addressing a meeting of the Budapest Workers' Council in the early evening of 21 March, he told the assembled crowd: 'The imperialists of the Entente took democracy and national self-determination as their slogans, but since victory they have acted differently. Our hope for peace was destroyed by the ukase from Colonel Vyx. There is no longer any doubt that those gentlemen in Paris wish to give us an imperialist peace ... From now on we must look to the east for justice, as it has been denied to us in the west.'[15]

In the end, what came from the east was verbal solidarity and encouragement, but not much more. The Hungarians were left on their own to deal with the Entente powers and to physically stem the advances of Romanian and Czech forces. As will be seen in the next chapter, in the end the endeavours failed, but until the turning point came on the battlefield, the new regime in Hungary gained support not only from those who sympathised with its socialism, but also from many people who took a stance essentially on nationalist grounds, namely instead of an 'anti-imperialist' struggle, they saw a fight to defend the homeland.

We have seen in Chapter 3 how many of the dramatic posters produced in 1919 were on the theme of recruiting for the Red Army. The posters were rather unclear as to whether the Red Army was fighting primarily

---

14. Ashmead-Bartlett (1923), p. 139. Initially invited to write for *The Daily Telegraph*, Ashmead-Bartlett was in Budapest twice in the spring of 1919. On his second visit he was accompanied by C. A. Macartney, who was reporting for *The Times*.
15. Pastor (1976), p. 142.

against imperialism or for patriotic and even nationalistic reasons, though in the early period perhaps it didn't matter. On the other hand, in Oszkár Jászi's view, one of the reasons for the popular acceptance of the Council Republic lay precisely in the 'demagogic, unprincipled way it played upon the popular chauvinism, and awakened in the masses, after their national humiliation, a belief that the Soviet Republic would enter into hostilities against the new and imperialistic neighbouring states and would quickly reconquer the lost territories ... the great successes of the Red Army were attributable at least as much to nationalist as to Socialist feeling among the soldiery.'[16]

Whether or not the regime did indeed appeal to popular chauvinism in an unprincipled way, years later György Lukács, who himself served for a while as a front-line commissar, also acknowledged that there were large swathes of peasant soldiers who were fighting for essentially nationalist reasons. When asked in an interview about the peasants in the Red Army, he replied: 'The national element played a huge role ... the army was essentially a Hungarian army, putting up a defence against foreign attacks.'[17]

Ervin Sinkó indicates that the Red Army was essentially a peasant army, although he regards that from a different perspective. 'The industrial workers in the provincial areas did not want to be soldiers. After four and a half years of war they were not willing to risk their lives for any kind of fine words.' It was mainly peasants who were recruited, he claims, and that was for the pay. Skilled workers were unmoved and those who did join up he describes as 'rather a proletarian mob'.[18]

On the domestic front

Needless to say, apart from matters relating to Hungary's perceived rightful place in the new post-war central European order, there were also reasons connected to Hungary's internal or domestic developments which partly explain the widespread support for the Council Republic.

One was that the transfer of power on 21 March 1919 took place smoothly and without bloodshed, indeed it might have seemed to have taken place almost naturally. The fact that Zsigmond Kunfi was appointed People's Commissar for Education and Culture in the new Revolutionary Governing Council would have calmed the potential fears of many people in the arts world. The Social Democrat Kunfi, relatively speaking a moderate among the new commissars, had held the same position, albeit

16. Jászi (1924), p. 117.
17. Borus (1978), p. 189.
18. Sinkó (1990), p. 85.

under a different name, during the Károlyi regime, so his appointment seemed to signal a continuation of the liberal policies towards the arts of the previous months.

Even his deputy, György Lukács, a member of the Communist Party, was an intellectual involved with culture, fairly well known for his writings about literature and literary theory. As recently as December 1918, after the formation of the Communist Party, Lukács's critical essay 'Bolshevism as a Moral Problem' had appeared, in which he concluded that 'Bolshevism rests on the metaphysical assumption that the bad can engender the good ... This author is unable to share this belief.'[19] True, in the same month Lukács joined the Communist Party, but it could well have appeared to many people in the arts world, even three months later, that they had little to fear from him.

In addition, the statements issued by the new cultural commissariat expressing openness and tolerance towards different artistic and cultural trends can also account for the enthusiasm among intellectuals, as can the widespread participation of well-known, established figures in the various arts directories set up under the new regime.

Even the communist Béla Kun, acknowledged as the main leader of the Council Republic, might not have aroused widespread alarm among intellectuals. It will be remembered from Chapter 1 that there was a lot of sympathy for Kun due to the brutal treatment he received in prison following his arrest, and that of other communists, in the early hours of 21 February. But apart from that, those who knew Kun or were familiar with his background would have known that, if not as a literary person himself, he was someone with a keen interest in literature dating back to his early years.

When he was a boy, Béla Kun attended a Calvinist school in Zilah, Transylvania (today Zalău in Romania). He found himself being tutored by the school's star pupil of the time, the future noted poet and polemicist Endre Ady. Later Kun was a regular at the Café New York in Kolozsvár (Cluj-Napolca, Romania), mixing with poets, artists and actors. His first piece to appear in *Népszava* was actually a review of a book about Hungarian drama. Kun was one of the founders of the literary Bólyai Circle, where he again met Ady, and he would also renew contact with Ady later, in Budapest.[20]

---

19. Lukács (1918). The quote here comes from the 1977 translation, p. 424—see bibliography.

20. Borsányi (1993), pp. 3, 23–4, 27. Borsányi says that years later, when Kun was in emigration in Moscow, literature remained his first love. He would dot his conversation with literary quotes, including lines from Ady. He was informed about German literature and French art, and spoke French with Malraux. 'He was far more tolerant in literary matters than in politics,' Borsányi writes. 'Perhaps it was due to the sacred respect for writing which he had entertained since childhood and which was char-

In addition, despite the utter condemnation of Kun—at the time and in subsequent decades—as a ruthless communist dictator, in political terms he was actually more or less a 'centrist' in terms of the Communist Party, and someone who would sometimes intervene to prevent violent excesses. In a work published in the US in 1971, history professor Peter Kenez asserted that 'Kun had the reputation of being a kind-hearted man, and people persecuted by the regime frequently turned to him for mercy rather than the socialists'.[21]

Furthermore, in the new Revolutionary Governing Council, formed following the declaration of the Council Republic, among the twelve people's commissars Kun was the only communist, and among their 21 deputies, only seven were communist. True, after a month, the formal distinction between commissars and deputy commissars disappeared, but nevertheless the imbalance between leaders who were members of the Social Democratic Party and those who were members of the Communist Party is quite striking and raises the question: to what extent were the communists actually in control? If the more moderate social democrats were, or were at the time perceived to be playing a major role in the direction of developments, then this, too, might help to explain the perhaps otherwise surprising widespread support for the Commune.

Kenez suggests that in Hungary in 1919 there was no sharp line between communists and socialists, and he questions the usefulness of such labels for the period. He believes that history has been distorted, which happened 'because historians and memoirists portrayed communism in 1919 not as it was but as it would become, and projected a later ideological split into a period when it did not yet exist.'[22]

As for the relation of forces in the coalition, Kenez asserts it is not helpful to compare the role of the two parties, because old party labels

---

acteristic of his whole generation.' Ibid., pp. 388, 417. Borsányi's assessment of Kun is in stark contrast with something Dezső Kosztolányi's wife once wrote. She relates an incident, which apparently took place after the Chrysanthemum Revolution, but before the Soviet Republic was proclaimed. She says Kosztolányi went to see Béla Kun, whom he had previously known as a journalist, to ask what would happen to him and other writers. Kun allegedly responded: 'There's no need for you in the proletarian state. Poetry is not required. You will learn some trade. If you are obstinate, we will execute you.' (Kosztolányi, 1990, p. 193.) However, perhaps it is relevant that her book is subtitled 'A Biographical Novel'.

21. Kenez (1971), p. 76. The following story was related to the author by Alex Bandy, for many years head of the Budapest bureau of Associated Press. In 1919 Bandy's grandfather, Imre Szűtsy, was a captain in the national gendarmerie. At one point, he and several fellow officers were detained and sentenced to be hung. This was in or around Salgótarján. Kun came by on an inspection tour and, recognising one of the men as a former classmate, chatted with him, and then ordered all of them released.

22. Ibid., p. 63.

had lost most of their meaning. More meaningful would be to look at the influence of leaders or groups. 'But if one must designate the senior party of the two participating parties,' he concludes, 'it seems preferable to name the Socialists.'[23]

That is perhaps a surprising notion, contrary to what many observers have asserted. Part of his argument is based on evidence highlighted by Rudolph Tőkés which indicates that in 1919 the Hungarian communists were not as all-powerful as often assumed.

In the opinion of Tőkés, from the third week on it was the socialists who prevailed in the field of domestic politics. As evidence, he points to the composition of the three Revolutionary Governing Council committees. The political committee was chaired by Sándor Garbai, a socialist, and comprised three socialists and two communists; the economic committee was also chaired by Garbai and had five socialists and just two communists; the military committee was chaired by Böhm, also a socialist, but in this case three out of five members were communists.[24]

Tőkés also highlights the nature of the Commissariat for Education and Culture's important Department of State Propaganda for Socialism, in which the communists were outnumbered six to one. The only communist section head, Béla Fogarasi, had a staff of six to attend to the affairs of establishing workers' universities, while his six socialist colleagues, helped by 358 staff members, 'were busy writing scientific, popular, military, rural and youth propaganda pamphlets, leaflets and posters'.[25]

'It appears that the communist drive for control of the united party was doomed to failure from the very beginning,' says Tőkés. 'The dichotomy between the power presumed to be wielded by the considerable communist contingent at the summit of the party structure and the actual extent of communist control exercised over the agitation, propaganda, educational and organizational aspects of the apparatus was a most conclusive indication of their inferior position in the [united] Hungarian Socialist Party.'[26]

Further evidence is that delegates to the Budapest Council of Workers' and Soldiers' Deputies, elected in early April, were predominantly socialists. Its five-man presidium included only one communist. However, perhaps most telling of all is that at the first congress of the united party, which began on 12 June, when it came to the election of a party executive, with the exception of Béla Kun, the communists failed to receive enough votes

23. Ibid., p. 83.
24. Tőkés (1967), p. 158, n. 48. Tőkés quotes the minutes of the Governing Council.
25. Ibid., p. 167. In a footnote, Tőkés says that over a period of four months the department produced an astounding number of 334 pamphlets in nearly 24 million copies and 84 posters in nearly half a million copies.
26. Ibid., p. 167.

to qualify them as members! The communists then announced they would abandon the party unless the election was reheld. Tőkés says that, perhaps to maintain working-class unity or to keep the communists on board, a new slate including some communists 'was elected by acclamation by a most reluctant party congress'.[27]

Nevertheless, Rudolph Tőkés acknowledges that with the attempted counter-revolutionary putsch of 24 June and its aftermath (see next chapter) many of the moderate socialists, believing that a negative turning-point had been reached, withdrew from their leading roles, leaving power more or less in the hands of the communists. But this is a far cry from the often-repeated assertion that the whole experience of the 1919 Hungarian Soviet Republic was one simply and entirely of hard-line communist dictatorship.

Interestingly, confirmation of the relative weakness of the Communist Party comes from none other than one of its leading figures, György Lukács, who asserted in an interview broadcast in 1976 that 'before the dictatorship [as he put it] the Communist Party unfortunately was not a seriously organised party'. At the time of unity, he said, there were individual communists here and there, and small communist groups, but essentially the party was fragmented. 'The consequence which followed was that every Communist people's commissar, wherever he was ... how can I put it ... organised his activity in his own way.'[28]

Not only the arts

Perhaps somewhat more relevant for providing answers as to why many people in the arts world regarded the Council Republic in a favourable light was what might be called the general progressive intellectual context in which they found themselves. This book concentrates on artists, film-makers, theatre people, musicians and writers, and the relations between them and the new regime, but there were plenty of developments initiated in other fields, which could only have added to the belief that some kind of new, positive order was being created. It is beyond the scope of this book to cover all those fields, so what follows simply touches on a couple of themes, namely education and young people, in order to illustrate this assertion.

Serious thought was given to transforming and modernising the academic world and there were some interesting 'firsts' during the Council Republic. For example, Irén Götz was appointed a professor of chemistry, thus

27. Ibid., p. 184.
28. Borus (1978), p. 178.

becoming the first woman in Hungary to occupy such a post. What by international comparison was even more groundbreaking was that the world's first academic department of psychoanalysis was established in Budapest in 1919 under the direction of Freud's Hungarian disciple, Sándor Ferenczi, the key figure of the so-called Budapest School of Psychoanalysis. Other people active during the Commune who later became nationally and/or internationally renowned included the sociologist Karl Mannheim, the art historian Arnold Hauser, who in 1919 worked on reforming the art education system, the literary historian Marcell Benedek and György Hevesi, who in 1943 (then known as George de Hevesi) would be awarded a Nobel Prize for chemistry. After the fall of the commune Hevesi was dismissed from his position and barred from teaching at the university. He left Hungary in March 1920. Exile was also the fate which befell Karl Mannheim. As with so many others who were forced or felt obliged to leave, Hungary's loss would be other countries' gain.

As for schools and schooling, the new regime devoted a great deal of attention to the issue. Very early on all non-state schools and training institutes were nationalised. Education was centralised with a view to the better distribution of available resources. According to Frank Eckelt, whose essay on the domestic policies of the Commune was published in America in 1971, one of the first successes of the programme was the elimination in villages and small towns of so-called gradeless schools, where there was one teacher for pupils of ages differing by up to six years in one room. Schools were consolidated for the better utilisation of teachers and combinations of classes were developed depending on age distribution. The need was asserted for a reduction of class sizes, coeducation and the common use of facilities such as gyms and play areas by all schools in the same area.

Curriculum was also a prime target. 'Mathematics and physics studies were to be left unchanged,' says Eckelt,

> but the instruction of Latin and Greek was to cease, to be replaced by an expanded study of the Hungarian language and world literature. Special emphasis was placed on the reading of good books without hair-splitting debates as to their literary merit preceding the reading. Courses in composition, modern languages, the natural sciences, as well as physical exercise were to be enlarged.[29]

History was to be the only subject radically changed, in order that pupils would grow up better prepared for the new society. The idea was that the

29. Eckelt (1971), p. 66.

Marxist interpretation of history would provide the basis for the new teaching, but there was an obvious lack of teachers who had any notion about such concepts as wage labour, capitalist production and class law in a bourgeois society.

According to Eckelt, despite preferential treatment, including relatively high salaries, most teachers were either hostile or remained passive to the new order. One problem was that they could not cope with the numerous orders coming from above, and the demands for cultural reorientation, particularly as the end of the school year approached. The same problem affected the changes envisioned for the library service, the idea being that books should be made more accessible for the mass of the population. Hand in hand with that was the drive initiated to eradicate illiteracy, which was still widespread, particularly in the countryside.

Overall, due to the shortage of time and resources, the plans for massive changes and modernisation in the field of public education were never fully realised. However, it is easy to appreciate that the plans and proposals themselves would have appealed to many people concerned with the development and spread of culture.

Linked to the above was something which, according to Frank Eckelt, was never the subject of any major criticism, namely the Council Republic's overall policy in relation to children. A genuine attempt was made to improve the lives of the many deprived children of proletarian families. Apart from trying to reform the schooling system, feeding centres for children were established. The legal stigma of illegitimacy was abolished, the relevant decree of the Revolutionary Governing Council boldly beginning with the words 'Hungary's Council Republic does not recognise the status of illegitimate children'.[30] Compulsory, free, medical examinations were ordered for all children between six and fourteen years of age. Dentists were paid to give two hours a day free care to school children recommended to them. Public spas and baths were nationalised and formerly fashionable resorts by Lake Balaton were commandeered to give urban children the chance to have at least one holiday.

Kindergartens were renamed 'play schools' and poems glorifying war were to be eliminated in favour of texts asserting peace, brotherly love and equality.[31] As seen in earlier chapters, there were theatre performances for children and five cinemas in Budapest were allocated especially for the screening of films for children.

---

30. Pongrácz (1919), p. 17. The decree was issued on 25 March, just four days after the declaration of the Soviet Republic.
31. Ibid., pp. 64–5.

Professional and other concerns

Apart from being attracted by grand schemes and progressive ideas, there were, of course, other reasons for people to willingly support the Council Republic as active participants. Sometimes the reasons were based on professional concerns. Writing in 1920, Béla Bartók reflected on why, the previous year, he and his fellow musicians, Zoltán Kodály and Ernő Dohnányi, had agreed to participate in the Music Directory. His reasoning was both pragmatic and idealistic.

> The artists ... although not avowed communists, accepted this mission for several reasons: on the one hand they hoped for an improvement in general conditions and, on the other, were desirous of preventing any acts of force that might endanger music life and of cutting the ground from under the feet of ungifted musical parvenus.[32]

There were also much more mundane reasons for getting involved with the new structures of the Commune. The need to get on a payroll was one obvious motivation. We have seen that for writers getting onto the official registry was essential for being in a position to have work published and for receiving some kind of income.

Soon after the Council Republic was established, the young Gyula Háy visited the Education Commissariat in Budapest's Hold Street looking for a job. He found a large crowd there with the same intention. His later reflection on the encounter indicates some of the mixed motives which were prevalent at the time.

'People wanted to be on the payroll of the new state and to be issued with ration cards,' Háy recalled, 'and it was not only because one had somehow to live, but also because it was proof that one belonged, that one was accepted by the new order as being a useful person.'[33]

It is not easy to unravel to what extent such motives were genuine and deep-seated in a positive sense and to what extent they reflected the bandwagon effect alluded to earlier in this chapter. Either way, there were also clearly less agreeable—in the self-centred sense—motives at play. Oszkár Jászi would recall the following piercing observation about how some people behaved after the Soviet Republic had been established:

---

32. Tallián (1981), p. 118. As will be seen in the next chapter, Bartók's hopes turned out to be not so realistic and perhaps too optimistic.
33. Hay (1974), p. 58.

> The usual Hungarian chase for government posts began, and of course the most reactionary and clerical and militarist elements became the loudest shouters, and the most merciless and uncompromising executioners for the Communist system; while persons who for decades had been selflessly serving the cause of social progress, were pushed everywhere into the background by these greedy bands of placemen.[34]

Jászi had seen it all before, following the Chrysanthemum Revolution in 1918. As he remembered:

> When the [October] revolution had succeeded, there streamed into its camp those elements who support whatever government comes to the surface, and others who had past sins to cover up by the loud profession of new loyalties ... The truth was that there was an uninterrupted stream of truckling deputations, crowding forward to swear allegiance at any price to the National Council.[35]

However, such behaviour wasn't the only phenomenon where a parallel could be drawn between the Károlyi period and what happened in the weeks and months following 21 March 1919. Indeed, it is quite relevant to question the degree to which the activities of artists, film-makers, theatre people, musicians and writers during the period of the Council Republic signalled something new, a break with the immediate past, or whether they were activities which in many respects were actually a continuation of what had already been happening before the Commune was established. If the latter is true, or even partly true, it might also help to explain some of the enthusiasm for the new Soviet Republic.

Change or continuity?

'We who lived through 31 October 1918,' the critic Andor Halasi would recall,

> cannot forget that liberating storm the event stirred up in our souls. The revolution has broken out! The legal system handcuffing us to Austria was shattered. The monarchical form of state had disappeared into thin air. The structure of the old society was tottering. Its rotten supporting

34. Jászi (1924), p. 116.
35. Ibid., pp. 36–7.

pillars were falling down. The dispossessed could have their voice heard. The street was now theirs.[36]

Although Halasi and others might gradually become disillusioned with the results of the Chrysanthemum Revolution, there is no doubt that joy over the collapse of the Austro-Hungarian Dual Monarchy was widespread and enthusiasm for a new beginning was extensive. You can see this in the many photographs taken at the time showing the celebrating crowds thronging the streets of Budapest and the soldiers with white chrysanthemums in their caps hanging onto vehicles as they passed through the city.

Within a few days of the victory, an impassioned proclamation appeared with the title *To the Hungarian Intelligentsia!* which was signed by nearly 100 well-known figures, mostly in the arts world.

What seems remarkable is not only the number of signatures gathered, but the fact that the proclamation, which was published in *Világ* (World) on 3 November, was not directly concerned with arts policy. It had a broader, political scope. It was, in essence, a declaration of support for recognising the freedom and autonomy of non-Hungarian nations in a new federation, very much in tune with the ideas of Oszkár Jászi, the minister responsible for nationalities in the new government. Without naming any particular groups, it implicitly called for solidarity with those Slovaks, Serbs, Romanians and others who had taken advantage of the collapse of the old system to free themselves of strict control from Budapest. In that sense it was very radical and in contrast with more conservative opinion. The declaration ended by proclaiming that while patriotism was a duty, at the same time being human was more important: 'Because while the motherland is sacred, humanity is even more sacred!'[37]

As was seen in Chapter 1, it soon became clear that the idea of autonomy within Hungary was not welcomed by the non-Hungarian nationalities, but that didn't dampen the general enthusiasm for change in other fields on the part of many of the signatories. Writers were among those at the forefront.

Soon after the October 1918 Revolution, 75 Hungarian writers were among the contributors to a publication entitled *A diadalmas forradalom könyve* (Book of the Victorious Revolution). Edited by the poet Oszkár Gellért, it was a collection of testimonies which, as the title suggests, was in effect a panegyric on the events which had taken place. Endre Ady

36. Halasi (1959), p. 9.
37. *Világ*, 3 November 1918, p. 12. The text and list of signatories can also be found in Babus (2002).

contributed a poem, as did Mihály Babits. Dezső Kosztolányi also had a poem published in the volume, plus a short piece of prose under the heading 'The Red Panorama'. Zsigmond Móricz had a contribution simply entitled 'Revolution'. Other contributors included Gyula Krúdy, Ferenc Molnár and Ernő Szép.

Although not for the collection, Babits wrote 'Long Live the Republic!' a declaration which began with the words: 'Brothers and sisters! The Hungarian people have achieved freedom. It wasn't received from the king—the people themselves attained it.'[38] However, it seems that this short but rousing text was not published at the time, though Babits was certainly a strong supporter of the new republic, as indicated by other pieces which did appear in print, such as his *Az Első pillanatban* (In the First Instant), in which he asserted: 'With regard to simply a human point of view, the Hungarian revolution was a veritable wonder.'[39]

Among the many writers supporting the new regime, Zsigmond Móricz was one of the most active. In December he travelled to the Alföld, the Great Hungarian Plain to the east of the Danube. He produced articles for newspapers about the conditions he encountered in the countryside. He painted a picture of peasant life and agricultural conditions—his favourite themes—urging land reform. Móricz personally attended and then wrote about the early ceremonies of land distribution, including one at Kerepes on 20 February 1919 and at Kápolna three days later, where the president, Mihály Károlyi symbolically divided up one of his own estates.

As regards organisational matters, on 1 December 1918 a meeting of writers formally launched the Vörösmarty Academy, a body set up as an alternative to older, more conservative, well-established literary associations. A preparatory meeting had taken place four days previously and selected Endre Ady as president, with Mihály Babits and Zsigmond Móricz as his deputies. Ady attended the meeting but was already seriously ill. What he actually said, or was able to say, and at what point in the meeting has been recalled in different ways, but it seems that this was Ady's last public appearance.[40] A couple of days later invitations were sent out for the formal founding meeting, scheduled to take place at the Academy of Sciences on 1 December, appropriately enough the date of birth in 1800 of Mihály Vörösmarty, the prominent Hungarian poet, dramatist and political activist, who was an MP during the 1848-49 War of Independence against Habsburg rule.

38. 'Éljen a köztársaság!' In: Remete (1956), pp. 113–14.
39. Ungvári (1959), p. 238.
40. For this meeting and the subsequent activities of the Vörösmarty Academy, see Németh (2012).

The founding meeting was attended by many well-known literary figures, including Mihály Babits, Milán Füst, Frigyes Karinthy, Lajos Kassák, Dezső Kosztolányi, Ferenc Molnár, Zsigmond Móricz, Aladár Schöpflin and Árpád Tóth. Due to his illness, Endre Ady could not attend, so his place in the chair was taken by Zsigmond Móricz.

In his speech Móricz stressed the notion of preserving a unified national culture, while acknowledging European values. Unity would prevent the break-up of the country. It was perhaps sadly ironic that on the very same day in Gyulafehérvár (then in Hungary, today Alba Iulia in Romania) representatives of Hungary's ethnic Romanians declared for the unification with Romania of areas in Hungary largely populated by Romanians.

The tasks proposed for the new organisation were quite ambitious and included taking a stance on the major issues arising in literary life, organising celebratory meetings, initiating book publishing and issuing a magazine, necessitating perhaps a permanent editorial committee, as well as making awards. It seems that the participants had in mind something on the lines of France's Goncourt Academy.

The burial of the writer Margit Kaffka, one of the many thousands who fell victim to the major epidemic of Spanish flu, which had been sweeping through Hungary, took place on 4 December. Zsigmond Móricz, already representing the Vörösmarty Academy, was one of the speakers at the funeral ceremony. Then, towards the end of the following month it wasn't only the literary world which was shocked to learn about the death of another writer, the great poet Endre Ady. The death notice was issued by the Vörösmarty Academy, which also undertook the arrangements for the funeral, scheduled to take place on 29 January.

On the appointed day the coffin was set up in the large vestibule of the National Museum. The speakers included Zsigmond Móricz and Mihály Babits. So many people tried to attend the ceremony that in the crush, chaos erupted. When the police arrived, they could not fully control the situation. Eventually the coffin was brought out, taken down the steps and placed in a large, solemnly decorated, horse-drawn hearse. From the museum it was taken to the Kerepesi Cemetery, where many of the noted figures of Hungarian history lay buried. One of the speakers there was the painter Károly Kernstok, who, as we have seen, was to head an artists' free school during the Council Republic period.

Among the many wreaths at Ady's funeral there was one from the government. The text on the ribbon read: 'For the poet of the new Hungary—the government of the Hungarian People's Republic.'[41] The

---

41. Boldizsár Vörös, 'Két rendszer, két halott, két temetés' (Two Systems, Two Deceased, Two Funerals), *Médiakutató*, 2004 autumn. www.mediakutato.hu/cikk/2004_03_osz/08_ket_rendszer (accessed 5 July 2017).

new authorities had already signalled their view of Ady. On 17 November 1918, the day after the People's Republic was declared, a delegation of government and National Council representatives visited Ady in his central Budapest flat to greet him as the poet of the revolution. It was a far cry from the reaction Ady had received from official circles in earlier years, which had not been entirely surprising given his extremely critical views of Hungarian society and politics.

Apart from writers, large numbers of artists, film-makers, musicians and theatre professionals also welcomed the Chrysanthemum Revolution. What is presented below is a brief indication of some of the other developments which prefigured what happened in the arts world during the period of the Soviet Republic.

The striking poster art of the Commune has deservedly been highlighted, but it wasn't something entirely new. The radical political poster was already playing a role in earlier months. Eye-catching colourful images celebrating the end of monarchy and the rise of republican democracy were produced by Mihály Bíró, Marcell Vértes and other artists, and plastered across the walls of Budapest. Bíró, for example, created a memorable image depicting a strong-muscled proletarian towering over the Hungarian parliament. A paintbrush in hand, he is slapping red paint on the building. The slogan on the poster—produced in anticipation of elections scheduled for 13 April 1919, but which never took place—proclaimed: 'A Red Parliament! Vote Social Democrat!'

Even free schools in the arts promoting new approaches were not unknown before the Commune. On 23 February 1919, *Világ* reported that Róbert Berényi had opened a painting school in the Városmajor area of Buda. The report noted: 'After the revolution the reign of the old clique in the fine arts is also collapsing and hopefully the new, free way forward of the progressive arts is opening up.'[42] And as noted in Chapter 5, the efforts of Lajos Kassák and the *MA* circle in promoting avant-garde ideas in the arts were well underway and even predated October 1918.

The painter Károly Kernstok, a good friend of Oszkár Jászi, was appointed a government commissioner in the Ministry of Religion and Public Education, as the cultural ministry was then called.

Film director Sándor (Alexander) Korda was also quite active during the period of the Council Republic, but he was already 'politically involved' to an extent earlier. A comment of his published in *Mozihét* (Cinema Weekly) in December 1918 has often been highlighted: 'Those who still represent the ruling classes would do well to examine themselves and desist

42. Quoted in Szíj (1963), p. 121.

from defending their precarious positions so desperately ... No one should struggle against socialism.'[43]

The 'socialism' is likely a reference to the liberal socialism of Mihály Károlyi, with whom Korda was friendly. Nevertheless, it seems that Korda and others looked forward to the nationalisation of the film industry, if only as a means of countering the perceived stranglehold of distributors and exhibitors to the detriment of producers and directors. Be that as it may, at the close of 1918 the Károlyi government appointed Korda commissioner of film production with authorisation to organise, as István Nemeskürty puts it, 'progressive bourgeois film production'.[44]

Around the same time, and also prefiguring developments at the start of the Commune, a Film Council was established, involving representatives of all branches of the film industry, as was a federation representing its technical, professional and artistic workers. Cinema actors and actresses also began to organise on a fresh basis, forming a special section of the Budapest Actors' Federation.[45]

In music modernists and others more open to modern trends were given greater acknowledgement. Béla Bartók, Ernő Dohnányi, Zoltán Kodály and Béla Reinitz, who had put Ady's poems to music, were invited to join the Specialist Arts Committee of the National Council. All four would later be involved with the Music Directory during the Soviet Republic period. Ödön Mihalovich, who for years had directed the Academy of Music was pensioned off and replaced by Dohnányi, though according to Tibor Hajdu, his deputy Kodály was the real moving force at the Academy.[46]

Music on the streets as part of political demonstrations was not unknown before the Council republic. An often reproduced photograph shows a gypsy band playing amidst the huge crowd assembled in front of parliament on 16 November 1918, the day the new republic was proclaimed. Workers' concerts, sometimes free, were introduced with the idea of spreading music appreciation more widely. According to one source, on the very afternoon of 21 March 1919, just prior to the declaration of the Soviet Republic, a special performance for proletarian children was being held in the Opera House.[47]

We have seen in an earlier chapter that much thought was given during the Council Republic to creating a 'new' theatre for a 'new' audience. Similar efforts were underway in the preceding period, following the

43. Quoted in Nemeskürty (1974), p. 41.
44. Ibid., p. 42.
45. Reports in *Színházi Élet* (Theatre Life) reproduced in: Garai (1969), pp. 38–41.
46. Hajdu (1968), p. 292.
47. Bart (2007), p. 446.

Chrysanthemum Revolution. Already in mid November 1918, Lajos Nagy was writing in *Figáró* a piece entitled 'How should a revolutionary play be written'.[48] There were also special productions aimed at the 'new public', prefiguring those of later months. There were ideas for a new workers' theatre, the Soldiers' Council organised theatre performances in the barracks, and the main theatres aimed to update their programmes. The actor and future Dracula, Béla Lugosi, was prominent in the reorganisation of a new trade union for actors and used the pages of *Népszava* to advocate the nationalisation of theatres.[49]

As happened under the Commune later, the cultural policies implemented and the new ideas floated in the wake of the October Revolution barely had time to take root and flourish. It is often noted that the Hungarian Soviet Republic lasted just over four months—133 days is the usual formulation. Yet it should not be forgotten that the preceding period, from the Chrysanthemum Revolution of late October 1918 to the formation of the Council Republic on 21 March 1919, also lasted for less than five months. In both cases there was a shortage of time for the realisation of new, sometimes quite grandiose schemes.

Comparing what happened on the cultural front in the Károlyi period and during the Council Republic, Tibor Hajdu asserts: 'In this field there was the smallest difference between the two revolutions.'[50] No wonder that many people in the arts world were happy, at least initially, to support the new Soviet Republic, with Zsigmond Kunfi and György Lukács at the head of its cultural commissariat. For intellectuals and artists of all kinds, it arguably represented a continuation, rather than a rupture.[51]

---

48. 'Hogyan kell forradalmi színdarabot írni?', *Figáró*, 13 November, 1918. In: Remete (1956), pp. 115–16.
49. Hajdu (1968), pp. 292–3.
50. Ibid., p. 293.
51. It could be further argued that the changes initiated following the 1918 October Revolution were themselves prefigured by earlier progressive and radical activities and trends witnessed in Hungary before and during the First World War. An account of those is beyond the scope of this book, but interested readers might turn with profit to, among others, the following works: Mario D. Fenyo, *Literature and Political Change: Budapest, 1908–1918* (Philadelphia, American Philosophical Society, 1987); Judit Frigyesi, *Béla Bartók and Turn-of-the-Century Budapest* (Berkeley, University of California Press, 1998), which, in addition to Bartók, includes much on Ady; Mary Gluck, *Georg Lukács and his Generation. 1900–1918* (Cambridge, Massachusetts, Harvard University Press, 1985); and David Kettler's study 'Culture and Revolution: Lukács in the Hungarian Revolutions of 1918–19' (see bibliography), which—despite its title—includes a large section about Lukács and others in the pre-1918 period.

11
What Went Wrong?

A variety of signs indicate that enthusiasm for the Soviet Republic among people in the arts world and Hungarian intellectuals generally tended to diminish as time went by. Why was that? What went wrong?

The simple answer is that what went wrong was inextricably linked to the underlying instability of the regime and that it gradually became clear that the Council Republic was doomed to a short life. Indeed, on 1 August 1919, after not much more than four months, it ceased to exist. Nothing succeeds like success in attracting support, and lack of success, or the prospect of such, tends to turn people away—a reverse 'bandwagon effect', like the one touched on in the previous chapter, though in an opposite direction.

The Hungarian Soviet Republic collapsed relatively quickly for a number of reasons. The most obvious was the successful military intervention on the part of external forces. Dramatically, by late July Romanian troops were approaching Budapest and very soon were in control of most of the country east of the Danube, while Czechoslovak forces held the territory of what is today Slovakia, which had been part of Hungary up to the First World War. However, apart from the all-too-obvious external pressures, there were also internal conflicts and contradictions, which undermined the Soviet Republic, hastening its demise.

These various factors, external and internal, will be discussed briefly in turn. Needless to say, the impact of many, if not most of these factors affected people in all walks of life, not just those involved in the arts world, but there were some issues, notably those relating to intellectual freedom in general and censorship in particular, which directly concerned those in the 'creative professions'.

Military intervention[1]

The Hungarian Soviet Republic was established at a perilous time, when the country was facing a severe threat of further foreign intervention if the demands expressed in the notorious 'Vix note' were not met.

1. The details given below about military intervention and the Hungarian responses are mainly based on the chronology of events in Vincze et al. (1979), pp. 529–82.

It is not surprising, therefore, that recruiting to a new 'Red Army' began very soon after the change of regime on 21 March 1919. Arguably what is surprising is that the new Soviet Republic was more or less 'left in peace' for a few weeks, albeit that the threat of further intervention was constant. Those weeks, from 21 March up to the middle of April, and then those following up to the May Day celebrations and even somewhat beyond, witnessed what might be called the 'heroic' period of the Soviet Republic, when many of the developments in the arts world described in earlier chapters took place.

In fact there was a point in early April when an agreement might have been reached with the Western powers represented at the Paris Peace Conference, which just possibly might have extended the relatively peaceful period by a significant amount. The point in question concerned the curious episode of the visit paid to Budapest by General Smuts.

Jan Christian Smuts was the head of a mission sent to the Hungarian capital by the Peace Conference in order to examine the possibilities of an agreed armistice line between the Hungarians and the Romanians, as well as to assess the new regime in Budapest. 'A curious business,' wrote Field-Marshal Sir Henry Wilson in his diary, 'that a Welshman is sending a Dutchman to tell a Hungarian not to fight a Romanian.'[2]

The special train carrying Smuts and his entourage arrived at Budapest's Eastern Railway Station early in the morning of 4 April. Although he had been offered accommodation and promised safe conduct, Smuts was reluctant to leave his carriage and so the negotiations took place in a siding of the station. During a break, Harold Nicolson, then a young diplomat accompanying Smuts, walked down the platform with Béla Kun, who, unconventionally in protocol terms, offered the stump of his cigarette to a train driver who had asked for a light. 'Béla Kun darts little pink eyes at me to see whether I am impressed by this proletarian scene,' Nicolson later recalled. 'I maintain an impression of noble impassivity.'[3]

While Smuts seems to have been prepared to approach the Hungarians with a relatively open mind, Nicolson was perhaps a rather curious choice to send on such a delicate mission, particularly in view of his condescending attitude to the defeated nations and their peoples. Of the Hungarians he would write:

---

2. Quoted in Mitchell (1970), p. 171. The Welshman was Lloyd George, UK prime minister and a major figure at the Versailles Peace Conference. Smuts was born in Cape Colony (today part of South Africa). His ancestors were mainly Dutch.
3. Nicolson (1964), p. 299.

> I confess that I regarded, and still regard, that Turanian tribe with acute distaste. Like their cousins the Turks, they had destroyed much and created nothing. Buda Pest was a false city devoid of any autochthonous reality. For centuries the Magyars had oppressed their subject nationalities. The hour of liberation and of retribution was at hand.[4]

As it happened, there was little progress. Kun insisted that the armistice agreement of the previous November should be adhered to and the Romanians withdraw, while Smuts tried to achieve a settlement closer to the 'Vix note', albeit promising that any arrangement would not be final regarding the question of borders. Nevertheless, the position of the Hungarians was to reject much of what Smuts was demanding. With that, without allowing time for further negotiations. Smuts packed his bags (though since he had never left the train, probably he had never had to fully unpack them) and ordered the train to leave, which it did, pulling out of the Eastern Railway Station the day after it had arrived.

The Hungarian press triumphally boasted that the imperialists' representative had been rebuffed, signalling a great diplomatic victory for the young Hungarian Soviet Republic. However, the triumphalism soon proved to be unfounded.[5]

Perhaps the Hungarian commissars didn't quite believe their own propaganda and thus they continued to prepare for resistance to further military intervention. On 6 April, the day after Smuts left Budapest, a huge recruiting rally, reportedly attracting several hundred thousand people, took place in front of the Millennium Monument in what is today known as Heroes' Square.[6] In addition, the Revolutionary Governing Council soon decided to call up former officers. Their fears were justified. On 15-16 April the Romanian offensive began. The circumstances were not good from Budapest's perspective. At that time the Red Army was outnumbered two to one on the Romanian front and three to one on the Czechoslovak front.[7] Thus on the surface it seems that the eventual military defeat of the Soviet Republic could perhaps have already been predicted. However,

---

4. Ibid., p. 34. Nicolson, who seems not to have cared about making outrageous comments, would describe Kun as having 'the face of a sulky and uncertain criminal', and someone who was accompanying Kun as 'a little oily Jew'. Ibid. p. 298.
5. A detailed account of the Smuts mission to Budapest, its background and immediate consequences, is given by Zsuzsa L. Nagy in 'The Mission of General Smuts to Budapest, April 1919', published in 1965 in *Acta Historica Academiae Scientiarum Hungaricae*. See bibliography for further details.
6. Vincze et al. (1979), p. 540.
7. Hajdu (1979), p. 94.

the situation was fluid and the Hungarians did manage to achieve some successes, albeit that they were relatively short-lived.

On 18 April the government discussed the military situation. 'Most of the commissars were not aware of its seriousness, but perhaps for that very reason opinion was unanimous in favour of continuing the fight.'[8] The following day the Budapest Workers' Soviet called for the mass mobilisation of the proletariat. Half the workers of the capital, according to Tibor Hajdu, would leave for the front.

On 20 April the Romanians reached Nagyvárad (today Oradea in Romania). Three days later they were at the major town of Debrecen. Within a week, to the north Czechoslovak and Romanian troops had met. By the end of April the Czechoslovaks had taken Sátoraljaújhely and were approaching Miskolc. Meanwhile, the Romanians had reached the River Tisza almost everywhere along its length.

The town of Komárom straddles the Danube to the northwest of Budapest. Czech forces had occupied the northern part of the town in January 1919. During the night of 30 April, Hungarian workers, soldiers and miners, crossing the Danube by Elizabeth Bridge and by ferry, tried to retake that part of the town. The Czechs forced their assailants back onto the bridge. Some managed to flee, but about 200–300 were mercilessly butchered.

Thus as thousands joyfully celebrated the 'first free May Day' in Budapest, the young Council Republic was again in a perilous position. In addition to the disaster at Komárom, the intervention forces were now in control of the whole region to the east of the Tisza, a huge chunk of territory. The same day witnessed the suppression in Munich of the Bavarian Soviet Republic, 'the only western ally of the Hungarian Soviet Republic'.[9] It must have seemed clear to those casting their eyes away from Budapest during the May Day celebrations that the Commune was approaching catastrophe.

Perhaps this explains the mood of Béla Kun, as witnessed in a strange encounter recalled by Mihály Károlyi, who says he visited Kun on 1 May in the 'House of Soviets', the elegant Hotel Hungária on the Pest embankment, now commandeered as the residence and offices of leading commissars.[10]

---

8. Ibid., p. 96.
9. Ibid., p. 105.
10. Hungary's commissars seemed to copy, whether consciously or not, many of the practices of the Bolsheviks in Russia. Use of the Hungária in Budapest echoed the takeover of the posh Hotel Astoria in Petrograd for use by leading comrades. The Astoria was also called the 'House of Soviets' and, as in Budapest, rumours abounded about incredible comfort and alleged orgies. See Serge (2012), pp. 92–3.

'Kun lay stretched out on his couch in a state of complete moral collapse. I could not get a reasonable word out of him, so I visited Sigmund Kunfi next door, who told me that Kun had broken down completely and talked of giving up the fight.'[11]

Kun's depression, if that is what it can be called, was soon over. Four days later he travelled to Komárom to meet Vavro Šrobar, the Czechoslovak minister for Slovak affairs, although nothing tangible resulted from the talks.

By the middle of May, according to Tibor Hajdu, the strength of the Red Army was close to 120,000, including 44,000 who had been called up after 3 May. At the same time, Hajdu notes that:

> A major part of the radical intelligentsia which had, in the beginning, enthusiastically supported the Soviet Republic ... now turned their back on the Red War because of their pacifist feelings. It was not by chance that great writers like Móricz, Babits and Árpád Tóth, who had waxed enthusiastic over the March orders that proclaimed the destruction of capitalism, did not write a single line in support of the Red Army.[12]

The Red Army, its strength having increased, launched a determined counteroffensive in the last third of May and soon liberated Miskolc, along with other places in the northeast. However the big prize was capturing the town of Kassa (today Košice in eastern Slovakia) on 6 June. To celebrate the victory, the following day a big rally was organised in front of the parliament building in Budapest. However, it was on the very same day that the portentous 'Clemenceau note' reached Budapest.

The French prime minister Georges Clemenceau was also the president of the Paris Peace Conference. Speaking on behalf of the latter, he demanded, *inter alia*, that Hungary cease its attacks on Czechoslovak forces and withdraw its troops. He also indicated that the Romanians should withdraw from much of the area east of the Tisza.

A couple of days later Kun responded to Clemenceau with a telegram, in which he reiterated that Hungary was fighting a defensive war because the Belgrade armistice had been broken, but that the fighting could end if the interested states gathered in Vienna to negotiate a cease fire. Meanwhile, Hungarian forces continued to enjoy successes and on 10 June a massive celebratory rally was held in Kassa, where Kun and other leaders from Budapest spoke.

---

11. Károlyi (1956), p. 160.
12. Hajdu (1979), pp. 114–15.

Another note from Clemenceau on 13 June again demanded the withdrawal of Hungarian forces, giving a deadline of 18 June for this to happen. There was a threat that if this didn't happen the Allied powers might take up arms against the Council Republic. There was also a 'promise' that if the Red Army withdrew from Slovak territory, the Romanians would evacuate the territory they had not long before occupied east of the Tisza.

Hungarian commissars and leaders of the ruling party discussed Clemenceau's demand on 15 June. There was a heated debate, with some 'hard liners', including György Lukács and Tibor Szamuely, arguing against withdrawal of the Red Army. However, in the end the meeting accepted in principle that a retreat should be ordered. Although it was only a decision 'in principle', it raised some tricky issues. Why give up the gains made? What had the fighting been all about, anyway?

Such questions uncovered some of the ambiguities in relation to the support given to the Soviet Republic. They particularly concerned those supporting the regime essentially for nationalist reasons, in defence of Hungary's traditional territorial integrity, irrespective of, or despite any socialist ideology. They included many peasant soldiers and members of the officer corps of the old army who had been recruited or had joined, often quite willingly, the Red Army. For them, the idea of withdrawal was a disappointing one, which tended to lessen their support for the regime.

As for left-wingers and dedicated proletarian supporters, although some took the view that the fight against 'the imperialists' and their proxy armies should continue, others could take comfort in the view that real revolution could not, should not, be exported by means of armed force. After all, 'world revolution' was supposed to be around the corner, so as long as the political gains made so far in Hungary were maintained, why shed blood for what could be perceived as 'purely' nationalist reasons? However, in reality the divisions were not so clearcut.

Meanwhile, another danger involving force was looming for the commissars, this time on the home front—counter-revolution. A number of anti-regime manifestations had occurred over a period of several weeks, which appeared to culminate in an attempted armed putsch in Budapest on 24 June. Shots were fired at the 'Soviet House' from gunboats on the Danube. The telephone exchange in the Joseph Town district was occupied, as was the Ludovika military academy. Serious though the situation was, the Soviet authorities quickly suppressed the uprising. Nevertheless, it was an ominous development and served to confirm that the regime was not entirely stable.

According to Rudolf Tőkés, the anti-regime forces attracted groups of former professional officers, disabled war veterans and workers who had deserted from the Red Army. However, 'the majority of the population was by then too exhausted by the multitude of rapid and violent political changes ... to rally around an anti-communist, anti-Semitic, "Christian-National" platform (or any platform, for that matter) ...' and despite the deteriorating internal situation, the government was still strong enough to suppress the poorly organised and ill-coordinated uprising.[13]

Tőkés then highlights the psychological impact of the short-lived insurrection, saying it indicated the government's lack of public support. Soon after the first insurgent gunboat began to fire on the Soviet House, he asserts, national flags appeared at many windows, patrons in coffee houses burst into patriotic songs and churches in working-class districts were filled by women praying for the end of the Commune.[14]

The day after the attempted putsch Kun sent a telegram to Clemenceau asking for assurances that the Romanians would indeed implement a withdrawal. Then at the end of June, without any real guarantees, the Hungarians began evacuating Slovak territory, but on 2 July Romania's prime minister, Ion I. C. Brătianu, informed Clemenceau that his country's troops would leave the area east of the Tisza only after Hungary's Red Army had been demobilised.

Another blow came on 7 July when Czechoslovak forces entered Kassa. It was just one month since the Hungarians had triumphantly captured the town. Three days later, not wanting to stare defeat in the face and believing the situation could still be turned around, the Revolutionary Governing Council decided to liberate the area east of the Tisza, though it took ten days or so for the offensive to get going.

Very briefly, in the new campaign the Red Army enjoyed some successes but on balance the Romanians had the upper hand and quite soon the Hungarian forces were in retreat. As the Romanians were poised to advance towards Budapest, there was a certain surreal atmosphere in the capital. As if nothing was amiss, on 26 July another group of children, 700 in all, set off from Budapest for a holiday at Lake Balaton.[15]

Yet something was, indeed, amiss. On 29 July Romanian troops crossed the Tisza at a couple of places. The Hungarian forces retreated towards Budapest and the Red Army began to disintegrate. The next day in an ultimatum the Entente powers called for the resignation of the Revolutionary Governing Council. Following some bluster and hard talk, the resignation actually took place on 1 August, just a couple of days before Romanian units reached the outskirts of Budapest. Béla Kun, along with many of his leading comrades, boarded a special train and fled to Vienna.

---

13. Tőkés (1967), pp. 193–4.
14. Ibid., p. 194.
15. Vincze et al. (1979), p. 579.

Thus the Hungarian Soviet Republic of 1919, and with it all the attempts at progressive experiments in the arts and other fields came to an abrupt end.[16]

Economic chaos

The first Congress of Young Workers took place in Budapest on 20–22 June. When Béla Kun stood on the platform and addressed the delegates he encountered—according to his biographer, György Borsányi—more unbridled enthusiasm and devotion than he had at any previous forum. The young crowd had no doubts that the slogan adorning the wall of the hall would become reality: 'We will not be exploited proletarians!' When Kun reassured them that they would, indeed, reach the promised land, 'the audience became exultant'.[17] Later in the same day, Kun had to address another assembly, this time of women workers, but his reception there was quite different:

> The mood of the women workers at the MÁV [Hungarian Railways—B.D.] Machine Plant was altogether different from that of the young workers. Here he was not greeted with enthusiastic cheers. On the contrary, he had to answer a long series of embarrassing questions. The husbands were out at the front, the women had to spend hours queuing up to obtain meagre rations of oatmeal or potato (while they heard colourful details about the five-course meals accompanying the alleged orgies in the headquarters of the Soviet government).

Kun had to explain why some were at the front while other healthy men of military age remained calmly behind and had time to provide for their families, even if by peddling goods. 'Kun could hardly have left this assembly with the feeling that he had convinced his audience.'[18]

Perhaps the five-course meals and the orgies were elements of an urban legend of the time,[19] but the key points about shortages and hardship

16. Hungary's Red Army of 1919 might have suffered a crushing defeat, but occasionally the memory of it was revived in the post-1945 era. One Red Army monument, erected in 1959, the 40th anniversary of the Commune, could still be seen in its original location at the time these lines were written. A more than life-size figure, standing on top of a pedestal, is depicted arm raised, brandishing a rifle. Originally, an inscription (now gone) simply said: A Fighter of the Hungarian Red Army'. The work stands in Budapest's Újpest district.
17. Borsányi (1993), p. 187.
18. Ibid., p. 187. Borsányi says that Kun's speech was not reported in *Vörös Újság*.
19. Or maybe not entirely. The British correspondent Ellis Ashmead-Bartlett relates the story of how he and his colleague C. A. Macartney attended a lavish dinner at the

were undoubtedly true, and the women's meeting was just one, relatively open manifestation of the problems the Revolutionary Governing Council faced on the home front, namely economic chaos and its associated dissatisfaction.

The poor economic situation and industrial disorganisation were clearly part of the legacy of the First World War and the break-up of the Habsburg Empire, along with its internal economic ties. Blame could also be justifiably attributed to the continuing blockade against Hungary imposed by the powers which emerged victorious during the 1914–18 war. But there were also domestic circumstances and practices, which proved to be highly unpopular, thus undermining support for the Soviet regime.[20]

Housing was one issue. The government's nationalisation of apartments and buildings caused many problems and much dissatisfaction, as well as corruption as people tried to bend the new rules about requisition and the distribution of rooms and furniture for their own benefit. Yet the housing problem wasn't all of the new government's making. At the outbreak of war in 1914, Budapest had a population of 800,000. By 1919 that figure had grown by more than 100 per cent to reach 1,800,000—a tremendous increase, causing great difficulties in relation to both accommodation and food supply. At one point there was even a proposal drawn up for the Budapest Revolutionary Workers' and Soldiers' Council, which suggested that males over 18 who were not working should be removed from the capital and sent to provincial industrial centres or to the countryside to help with agriculture and food production.[21]

The employment policies of the revolutionary government were, on the surface, positive and appealing. Piecework was abolished and a 48-hour week instituted. Wages and salaries were increased and insurance made compulsory. The government was supposed to ensure full employment. All well and good, except that in the inflationary environment and with the war-disrupted economy, the gains had a tendency to remain gains on paper only, and the lack of increased productivity, or even simply basic production in some areas, made it difficult for the authorities to deliver what their promises implied. At the same time, unnecessary bureaucratic regulations

---

Ritz Hotel, which had been planned in honour of the visit of General Smuts. In the event, Smuts didn't attend but the big dinner went ahead with much drinking of wine and champagne (despite the ban on alcohol). Ashmead-Bartlett says that at 3 a.m. the commissars József Pogány and Vilmos Böhm plus others went to his room to carry on drinking. See: Ashmead-Bartlett (1923), pp. 112, 120–1.

20. The following is only a brief account. For more detail, see Frank Eckelt's study in: Völgyes (1971), pp. 61–88.

21. 'Plan to move part of the Budapest population to the provinces', document reproduced in Sipos & Donáth (1999), pp. 281–3.

were issued about all sorts of minutiae. In the given circumstances, what was the point of passing precise decrees regulating, for example, the price and exact composition of lemonade sold at theatres and cinemas?

One of the biggest problems the leading commissars faced was widespread discontent in the countryside. In a perhaps rare example of *not* following the Russian example, the Revolutionary Governing Council of the Hungarian Soviet Republic chose, as a general approach, not to divide land among those who worked it, parcelling it out among small, individual owners and thus ensuring support of the landless peasant, but to jump that stage, so to say, and go straight for large socialised estates in the form of agricultural cooperatives. Those appointed to manage these enterprises were more often than not former owners or those they had employed as managers, in the belief that they were the people with the best experience. But to the peasant it simply appeared that nothing had changed. The problem was compounded by the type of people sent to the countryside as agitators. They were often city types, ignorant of peasant traditions and practices, and they generated many complaints.

Zsigmond Móricz waxed lyrical in his writings about cooperatives in Somogy County in western Hungary, but they were the exception rather than the rule. Certainly other, essentially urban intellectuals could see that not all was quite right with the government's agricultural policy.

In 1919 the future noted writer Gyula Háy was an enthusiastic youthful supporter of the Commune, but there was something he found disturbing, namely the question of why Béla Kun didn't continue Mihály Károlyi's land distribution.

> The question left me no peace, and at times it positively tormented me. Although not once during those 133 days did it occur to me to doubt that Béla Kun's policy was right and in the people's best interests. I *wanted* to believe that it was so, and I succeeded. At 19 I succeeded easily. In later years, later decades, it became more difficult ... But the failure to understand and the inability to justify—these tormented me already in those early years.[22]

On 16 June 1919 during the first National Congress Of Soviets, Commissar Jenő Varga, an economist and head of the National Economic Council, gave a speech in which he was scathing about the economic situation. He pinpointed the fall in productivity, saying that individual output was 50 per cent below the pre-war level. He complained that the old industrial discipline had disappeared and criticised the abolition of piecework, bemoaning the

22. Hay (1974), p. 65.

fact that men 'have not yet attained the higher type of Socialist mentality which will be the starting point of the coming generation'.[23]

A month later *Népszava* (People's Voice) published a lengthy article by Varga taking up two-thirds of its front page and entitled 'Corruption', in which he pulled no punches as he laid into public apathy and the 'loose moral attitude', which he said could be found in every strata of society.

> The proletariat take as much advantage of their official power as the educated men ... Trustees sent to the rural areas occupy themselves with the hoarding of foodstuffs. The village committees issue orders against food deliveries ... The Red Guards, instead of strictly enforcing all orders, in many places themselves participate in transgressions. The biggest worry of the office workers is how to find a new swindle to get into a higher pay category. ... The food supplies are robbed on their way to the capital. ... This situation is desperate and decent men are unable to produce anything due to the constant fear that no matter whom they entrust with something, the result is always bribery and corruption.[24]

Varga's interventions hardly painted a picture of positive socialist construction. His words, coming as they did from the mouth and pen of a leading comrade, indicate how bad the situation was just three months after the Council Republic had been established.

Linked with perceptions of corruption, there was criticism that old privileges were reappearing. György Lukács himself would remember the accusations. 'Once, when I delivered a lecture in Budapest, someone took the platform after the lecture and said: "Well, it's just like old times. Comrade Lukács came by car and will leave by car, just like the leaders of the old regime."' Lukács claims he retorted by explaining what he had to do the following morning, offering to give up his car and leave on foot if someone else would undertake to handle the tasks. His rather patronising response seems—at least according to his own account—to have worked. 'The workers laughed and said that I was right.'[25]

Dictatorship and terror

If the military setbacks and the economic difficulties weren't enough to make intellectuals in the arts world, not to mention anyone else, lose faith

23. Quoted in Jászi (1924), p. 139. According to Tőkés (1967, p. 196), Varga would launch a 'campaign of "socialist work competition" that called for a seven-day working week without overtime pay!'
24. Jenő Varga, 'Korrupció', *Népszava*, 15 July 1919, p. 1. The extracts quoted are from Eckelt (1971) p. 87.
25. Quoted in Fekete & Karádi (1981), p. 105.

in the Soviet Republic, the perceived increasing dictatorial nature of the regime and, in particular, the use of violence and terror certainly were.

In Hungary during the interwar years, it was commonplace to dismiss the 1919 Soviet Republic as simply nothing other than a totally negative period characterised by violence and dictatorship.[26] It was as if all traces of anything that could even remotely be described as positive in connection with the period had to be erased from historical memory and discourse. Needless to say, this was an over-simplistic and ideologically driven view, and yet it was a view which certainly had a grounding in facts and reality.

That the new Soviet regime wasted no time at all in making its position clear is well shown by the fact that the very first decree issued by the newly formed Revolutionary Governing Council on the day the Council Republic was proclaimed declared that anyone who opposed the commands of the new authorities with arms or incited rebellion against the new regime would receive a death sentence imposed by a revolutionary tribunal. Similarly, anyone engaged in robbery or looting would also be liable to a death sentence.[27]

Within a month of the new regime assuming power, on 19 April the taking of hostages was ordered with a view to stemming what were perceived as counter-revolutionary stirrings. A total of 489 wealthy individuals, well-known politicians and others were arrested and held in prison. In the event, none of those imprisoned were executed and they were all released at the end of May.[28] Nevertheless, the move understandably led to fear and antipathy among many people.

In the wake of the attempted counter-revolutionary putsch in Budapest on 24 June, many people were arrested and among those over a dozen were sentenced to be executed. However, once again the central authorities were—in their own terms—relatively lenient and the death sentences were not carried out.[29]

Such leniency did not fully characterise the Council Republic—far from it. In the provinces in particular, there was a wave of terror and summary executions in response to developments perceived as being counter-revolutionary. Tibor Szamuely and his notorious leather-coated 'Lenin Boys'

26. In fact, it is still fairly commonplace today.

27. For the text of the first decree, see Pongrácz (1919), p. 13. A death sentence for looting wasn't an empty threat. For example, in early May Géza Nemes, a 31-year-old Red Guard, was executed by firing squad in the square in front of parliament. Accused of looting, his plea for clemency was rejected by the Revolutionary Governing Council. See 'Kivégeztek egy fosztogatót az Országház-téren' (Looter Executed in Parliament Square), *Népszava*, 4 May 1919, p. 7.

28. Vincze et al. (1979), p. 545.

29. Ibid., p. 574.

toured the country in a special 'Death Train' in response to reports (true or otherwise) of opposition activity. Summary public hangings of those believed to have been involved took place on the spot and forced requisitions of cattle, corn and other goods were imposed on the locality. Then the train would move on, later to quell yet another 'rebellion' in another area.

Szamuely and his group were not the only people applying terror tactics and committing atrocities. An equally, if not even more notorious group was the gang of enforcers headed by the 27-year-old József Cserny, who had trained as a leather worker and served in the navy during the war. His group based itself in the Batthyány Mansion in central Budapest. They placed an ominous sign above the entrance declaring themselves the 'Terror Group of the Revolutionary Government Council', though unlike Szamuely's 'Lenin Boys', who were officially under the wing of the Military Affairs Commissariat, the Cserny Gang was more or less independent, not being formally subordinate to any official authority. Vilmos Böhm, a leading Social Democrat who at the time was Commander-in-Chief of the Red Army, would later remark that, apart from seizing apartments and property, and arresting many, 'they killed people, including some who had absolutely nothing to do with counter-revolution'. And he adds, perceptively: 'If unconsciously, they were actually allies of the counter-revolutionaries.'[30]

In view of its extreme and violent activities, the government tried to disband the group, which it succeeded in doing at the end of April, but many of its members continued their actions as part of other groups. In the public mind the groups were conflated, perhaps unsurprisingly since their members tended to favour the trademark leather coat or jacket and they were often all simply known as the 'Lenin Boys'.

The justification for terror was usually given as suppressing counter-revolution, particularly if it was seen as containing the seeds of violent opposition. *Vörös Újság* spelt it out quite simply very early on, in a prominent article entitled 'The Dictatorship of the Proletariat', published on 22 March, one day after the new revolutionary government had assumed power. 'Red terror only becomes necessary where there is active White terror,' it proclaimed.[31]

The problem with that was that it left entirely open the question as to who would define what actually constituted 'White terror', thus in practice leaving it to the authorities in power to decide for themselves. The results and consequences have been subject to much debate and are not fully agreed. Estimates of the numbers of people killed by the 'Red Terror' of 1919 vary

30. Böhm (1923), p. 378.
31. 'A proletárság diktaturája', *Vörös Újság*, 22 March 1919, p. 3.

substantially. Historian Péter Konok refers to four different sources, with their numbers ranging from 200 to 600.[32]

Apart from killing, terror could also take the form of strong-arm intimidation tactics. There were reports of drunken bands conducting hanging rehearsals, demanding food and clothing, and generally keeping villages in a state of constant fear. Even in urban areas there were practices which could be called 'soft terror' tactics, as Katinka Károlyi, the wife of Hungary's former president, would recall:

> Arrogant young men entered private houses to take inventories of jam pots and other trifles, and housewives were warned that they must not touch them, as, from now on, they belonged to the State. This put the housewives backs up and made them bitter enemies of the regime.[33]

It should be noted that the authorities did make attempts at curbing excesses, even if they were not always successful. And some of the leaders were less bloodthirsty than others. In one of his speeches to the Workers' Council in early May, Béla Kun, for example, rejected the suggestion that hostages and political prisoners be executed.[34] When the young, 20-year-old Ervin Sinkó was military commander of the town of Kecskemét in May 1919, the participants of a suppressed counter-revolutionary plot were subject to only mild sentencing, involving some 'ideological retraining'. In a tragic twist, after the fall of the Soviet Republic the counter-revolutionary officers whose life Sinkó saved perpetrated one of the worst bloodbaths during the subsequent White Terror in Orgovány, near Kecskemét.[35]

Other leaders in the new political establishment were not as lenient as Sinkó and had no compunction about executing people who were not even counter-revolutionaries. György Lukács, for example, spent some time at the front as a political commissar. He was sent to the town of Tiszafüred in eastern Hungary, where he found the Hungarians on the defensive, since some units of the Red Army had run away without firing a shot. The result was that the Romanians took the town.

'I set about restoring order as energetically as I could,' Lukács would recall. 'That is to say, when we crossed the river to Poroszló, I set up a

32. Konok (2011), p. 50.
33. Károlyi (1966), p. 201.
34. Weltner (1929), p. 179.
35. Neubauer and Török (2009), pp. 25–6. Rudolph Tőkés (1967, p. 153, n. 38) notes a similar occurrence of leniency on the part of Sinkó. He says that after the attempted putsch on 24 June, several military-school cadet participants were arrested, but rather than being executed for treason Sinkó insisted that instead they be obliged to take part in a month-long Marxist seminar, which he personally conducted.

court-martial and had eight men belonging to the battalion that had run away in panic shot in the market-place. By these means I more or less managed to restore order.'[36]

Mihály Czine remarks that as the circumstances changed and the difficulties increased, there was an intensification of the dictatorship, which resulted in writers such as Zsigmond Móricz withdrawing into 'internal exile'. The developments, he argues, surprised writers not schooled in Marxism, writers who had had a naive belief in the wonders the Council Republic would bring, even from day one, but were not prepared for the journey involved. This added, he says, to the complaints individual writers might have had and to the misunderstandings arising from the government's ambiguous arts policy, especially in relation to the 'Party line'.[37]

Meanwhile, concern about the increasingly dictatorial nature of the regime slowly emerged even among members of the Revolutionary Governing Council. The Social Democratic People's Commissar for Education and Culture, Zsigmond Kunfi, for example, was rather disturbed by some of the developments underway, as shown by his article 'The Methods of Dictatorship', published a week before the June national congress of the Socialist Party of Hungary, the name adopted when the Social Democrats and Communists formed a united party in March. Actually, Kunfi defended the existence of the proletarian dictatorship as such. What he was worried about was the lack of moderation and the tendency to equate any form of dissatisfaction as an expression of counter-revolution, and he was particularly concerned about freedom of expression and publication.[38]

He expressed his views more publicly on 12 June, the first day of the Party congress, which took place in the parliament building, where he asserted that 'if we should continue applying the present methods of dictatorship … it will lead to the downfall of the proletariat.'[39] And referring to cultural policy he declared the following.

> I maintain that the development of science, literature and the arts is inconceivable without an atmosphere of freedom. During the ten weeks of proletarian dictatorship we have seen … too many frightened men who should be contributing to literature and the arts … but do not dare, knowing not what the menacing words of dictatorship really mean … I shall not tolerate any policy which goes against the majority of organised workers, even if it is practised under the banner of an active revolutionary

36. Lukács (1983), p. 65.
37. Czine (1959), p. 231.
38. 'A diktatúra módszerei', *Az Ember*, 5 June 1919, pp. 3–5.
39. Quoted by Tőkés (1967), pp. 178–9.

> minority that wishes to create an oligarchy and is designed to push waverers aside and does so under comrade Lenin's name.[40]

Perhaps unsurprisingly, Kunfi withdrew from his position as People's Commissar for Education and Culture. In a reorganisation of the Revolutionary Governing Council, which took place soon after the Party congress, his place was taken by the much more hardline József Pogány. Maybe what was surprising is that Kunfi had ever accepted the role of cultural commissar at all, albeit that it was a continuation of the post he had held (though under a different name) during the Károlyi regime. Indeed, just over three months before the Council Republic was declared, Kunfi had stated: 'As a socialist I appreciate the aims of Bolshevism, but I disapprove of its terroristic, anti-democratic methods.'[41] Perhaps he did not anticipate that Hungary's Bolsheviks would wield so much power as they were actually to have in practice.

One aspect of the slide towards dictatorship and fear-inducing tactics, which deeply offended many people, particularly in the conservative, strongly religious countryside, as well as anyone interested in preserving freedom of thought, was the way in which the authorities dealt with the issue of religion and the churches.

Many ambiguities and contradictions surrounded the matter, since in principle the Soviet Republic proclaimed the freedom of belief, albeit declaring that it was a private matter. Thus the separation of church and state was declared, as was the separation of the churches and education. At the same time, church property was nationalised. On the other hand, as seen above with some of the 'freelance' terror groups and agitators, there were many 'unofficial' atrocities and administrative measures applied against the churches, which seriously undermined the freedom of belief and generated much opposition.

András Koltai, whose work about the Hungarian Piarists and the Council Republic was published in 2013, acknowledges that 'although ideologically the leaders of the proletarian dictatorship were clearly anti-church' there was a conflict between those who took a radical, hard-line position on the

40. Ibid., p. 179. Kunfi's speech at the congress was reported in *Népszava* the following day, 13 June 1919, pp. 4–5.

41. Vermes (1971), p. 50. Vermes attributes the remark to an interview with United Press and provides a footnote with a reference to *Pesti Hírlap* (Pest News), 6 December 1918, p. 2. The present author checked that issue of *Pesti Hírlap*, but was unable to find the remark.

question and those who adopted a more moderate standpoint. 'In the end,' he asserts, 'the latter, more moderate line became characteristic.'[42]

That wasn't how everyone saw it at the time. Mihály Károlyi would remember how the church policy was implemented, though his criticism was expressed rather mildly:

> Although the churches were not closed and no one was actually persecuted for his religion, anti-religious propaganda, for the purpose of 'enlightening' the rural population, was carried out most tactlessly by Jewish youths from Budapest. This tactlessness was exploited by the Catholic Church and by the Counter-Revolution.[43]

Namely, it tended to encourage the latent anti-Semitism directed against the regime, many of whose political leaders were of Jewish descent.

Rudolf Tőkés has described the situation is a much more blunt manner. According to him:

> The government's reckless anti-religious campaign, headed by the defrocked priest Oszkár Fáber ... caused irrevocable damage during the first three months of the revolution. Churches desecrated by the Lenin Boys, priests insulted and harassed by Red Guardsmen, and the removal and burning of crucifixes by zealous local communists were hardly conducive to good will among the people towards the new government of the proletariat.[44]

The press and censorship

In his *Revolution and Counter-Revolution in Hungary*, Oszkár Jászi, minister for nationalities during the Károlyi regime, recounts a revealing story concerning an aspect of publishing policy during the Soviet Republic. He writes that in his last will and testament Ervin Szabó, who died on 30 September 1918, specified that he wanted his friend Oszkár Jászi to revise for publication the manuscript of his work about class struggles during Hungary's 1848–49 Revolution. Szabó was a prominent intellectual associated with the Social Democratic Party, though a dissenter from that

42. Koltai (2013), p. 16.
43. Károlyi (1956), p. 162.
44. Tőkés (1967), p. 193. András Koltai's 2013 work (p. 17) describes Oszkár Fáber as a former Piarist novice and attributes the organisation he headed with the ominous title of Liquidating Office for Religious Affairs.

party's rather dry, orthodox Marxism and a promoter of ideas close to anarcho-syndicalism.

Nevertheless, Szabó was such a well-known, popular figure in the Hungarian labour movement that during the Soviet Republic the communists tried to appropriate him for themselves.[45] Thus it would have been difficult for them to accept that one of his important manuscripts would be edited by someone such as Oszkár Jászi, a radical liberal with socialist sympathies, but someone who was also known as being strongly anti-Bolshevik.

Jászi asserts that Béla Kun sent him a message asking for the manuscript, saying they wanted a trusted communist to edit it for publication. Those now in power, Jászi recalls, 'would regard the compliance with Szabó's last wish as a piece of bourgeois sentimentality!'[46] It seems the new authorities were in favour of freedom of publication, as long as it took place under their control.

Such potentially threatening ambiguities were repeated by György Lukács many years later when he recalled that at one point in 1919 Oszkár Jászi had approached him asking about his critical sociological journal *Huszadik Század* (Twentieth Century). Lukács, then a cultural commissar, says he told Jászi that if he didn't engage in open counter-revolutionary propaganda he would be able to publish the journal without any problem. However, he didn't say what precisely 'counter-revolutionary propaganda' meant and who would have defined it. Lukács then raised the question as to why Jászi left Hungary in 1919. 'He didn't leave because of us,' he asserted. 'He feared the counter-revolution, that's why he left.'[47]

That wasn't quite how Oszkár Jászi himself explained his departure. 'On May 1, 1919, I left Hungary, as I was unable to tolerate the complete denial of freedom of thought and conscience which characterised [the] system.' However, he does add that he also expected the collapse of the Commune 'and its inevitable sequence of White anarchy'.[48]

As for newspapers, Lukács acknowledges the existence of 'a certain open sabotage', but explains this by a decree which prohibited papers from representing the old political line. The result was, he claimed, that leading articles would be published about the weather. Lukács says the editors were called into the commissariat and told they would be given the themes by the People's Commissars and they had to write editorials about them![49]

45. For a little bit more on this theme, see the chapter about May Day and the bust of Ervin Szabó.
46. Jászi (1924), p. 146.
47. Borus (1978), p. 182.
48. Jászi (1924), p. 110.
49. Borus (1978), p. 182.

Dissatisfaction was rife. Towards the end of April Imre Gál was noting in his diary: 'The press is now already completely dominated by the terror of the communists.' He acknowledged that the papers were not officially nationalised, but all editorial offices had to follow directives from above and could only print news which suited the government. Recurring themes included Red Army victories and the coming world revolution. 'The terror of censorship,' he noted, 'is much more vituperative than during the war.'[50]

Gál was by no means a supporter of the Commune, as the title of his work implies,[51] but there were others who were somewhat more sympathetic to the regime who also noted the restrictions on the press. The prominent Social Democrat and long-standing editor of *Népszava*, Jakab Weltner, was one. Weltner had initially been a supporter of the merger between his party and the communists, indeed he had been one of the people who negotiated and signed the unity deal, but he never abandoned his distrust of the communists. Regarding the press, he would later recall:

> The decrees of the Revolutionary Governing Council had to be published entirely without any comments, and it was impossible to refuse the articles of the leading Bolsheviks ... Nothing could be said about opposition or a counter-revolutionary atmosphere, since every publisher knew that the moment a position was taken against the dictatorship, the paper would be banned ... But banning papers was mistaken because it threatened the livelihood of hundreds of journalists. With such methods the dictatorship automatically increased the number of its opponents and generated counter-revolutionary sympathies.[52]

Weltner says that Béla Kun tried to win over the journalists, but was unsuccessful because of the strong influence the people around *Vörös Újság* (Red Gazette) had in the government. As for himself, he says he was always trailed and harassed by two people armed with grenades and revolvers, and that later in Vienna one of the former Lenin Boys told him that in the Batthyányi Mansion—the base of the terrorist Cserny Gang—they often sang a rhyming verse about breaking his neck.

Ferenc Göndör was also a left-wing, albeit critical, journalist. In his memoirs he says that Béla Kun told him he had been appointed (apparently without his knowledge) People's Commissar for Press Matters. He rejected the title, but the media reported his appointment, so he spoke out in denial at the journalist's club. However, when the Press Directory was formed

50. Gál (1937), pp. 98–9.
51. *A polgár a viharban* (A Bourgeois in the Storm).
52. Weltner (1929), pp. 177, 215, 216.

with him nominated as its head, he accepted the (unpaid) post. He also became president of the journalists' trade union.

Göndör claims that the Press Directory, with the support of the printers' union, struggled to stop the banning of publications right from the start, with the result that they prevented the closure of some bourgeois papers early on, but that due to pressure from 'the radical communist wing' in the government, there were several victims in the early days and a number of publications were indeed closed down.[53]

Göndör also asserts that in the period of the Commune journalists could only write what the proletarian dictatorship tolerated. Articles were born, he says, 'under an indisputable terror … the basis of the press system itself was actually simply terror and every publishing house acted as its own censor' in order to ensure that nothing 'anti-communist' appeared.[54] Göndör contrasts this with the period of the Károlyi regime, when there was no censorship.

Like Weltner, Göndör recalls that he, too, felt some intimidation. After the attempted putsch on 24 June, he says some Lenin Boys sought him out at night three times, though as a precaution he was sleeping elsewhere. The visits stopped, he says, after Weltner telephoned Béla Kun and threatened to publish the details.

Why would he have been a target? Göndör recalls a row he had with Kun over positive articles about Mihály Károlyi appearing in *Az Ember* (Man), a weekly journal he had established in 1918. That in itself was probably not enough to provide an explanation. Maybe what was more poignant was a speech he says he made at a meeting of the Budapest Workers' Council in which he strongly criticised Tibor Szamuely, whom he clearly disliked.[55] He says the speech was greeted with much applause, but that no full report of the event was published.

In addition, there was the controversy generated by attacks on the official literary policy, which involved Göndör and *Az Ember*, and which resulted in publication of the journal being suspended for a number of weeks.[56]

The reason given for banning or temporarily suspending other publications was usually the paper shortage, but as with *Az Ember*, in reality it was more a question of political sympathies. And as Göndör indicates, while some such actions might have been prevented, many newspapers and journals were banned from quite early on.

53. Göndör (1922), p. 73.
54. Ibid., p. 76.
55. He claims that on one occasion Szamuely ominously approached him demonstratively showing some jewellery, saying they were the treasures of people who had recently been hung. See Göndör (1922), p. 89.
56. See Chapter 5.

By 25 March, four days after the proclamation of the Council Republic, eleven publications had already been banned.[57] Within two days a further 25 suffered the same fate. On 7 April another 233 were banned and 50 papers were referred to the commissariat for consideration. By 22 May, another 12 publications had been banned. By June there were only a handful of dailies still published in Budapest (plus 25 outside the capital). However, there were still 50 weeklies appearing in Budapest and 58 elsewhere across the country. In addition, there were 60 trade union publications and well-established journals such as *Huszadik Század* and *Nyugat* (Occident), not to mention Kassák's *MA* (Today)—though see the end of Chapter 5 for the difficulties it encountered—as well as publications covering particular themes such as film and theatre.

As Weltner noted, taking drastic action involving stopping the publication of a newspaper or journal created discontent not only among readers but also among journalists and print workers who lost their income—not to mention writers of literature, who often contributed short stories, reports and other commentaries to the newspapers. In order to avoid loss of incomes, sometimes the editor would be replaced by someone believed to be more sympathetic to the regime. In that way, publication would continue but with a political orientation more acceptable to the authorities. Another method was to take over the entire operation and set it on a new course. For example, the editorial and publishing staff, as well as the printers of *Déli Hírlap* (Southern News) were taken over for the publication of *Vörös Katona* (Red Soldier).

As for the journalists, rumblings of discontent came to a head in what would turn out to be the final weeks of the Commune. At a meeting of the journalists' trade union on 8 July, Zoltán Szász made a speech which was extremely critical of the regime. He called for the return of press freedom and the reappearance of banned publications. He also opposed the forced reallocation to other jobs of journalists who had been made redundant due to their publications being suppressed. A majority at the meeting supported his proposal, which led to a split, the pro-regime journalists forming a new body called the Socialist-Communist Press Workers' Revolutionary Organisation, but there was little time left in the life of the Commune for it to have any impact.[58]

---

57. This and subsequent figures for the number of banned and surviving publications derive from Farkas József's 1969 book about the press in 1919.

58. Farkas, József (1969), pp. 74–6. The mention of forced reallocation of journalists could have been a reference to the proposal that journalists made redundant should be sent to the countryside to help, for example, with the campaign to eradicate illiteracy.

Illusions and contradictions

Injuries and deaths experienced as a result of fighting against Romanian and Czechoslovak forces; the loss of immense swathes of territory; economic disruption, food shortages, corruption and bad management; discontent and opposition in the countryside; dictatorship, summary (in) justice, violence, terror tactics, attacks on churches; replacement of editors, censorship, suspension and closure of publications—is it any wonder that enthusiasm for the Soviet Republic died down as the weeks went by?

Some time after 1 May 1919, the writer György Bölöni was travelling on a train in Switzerland, where he had been appointed during the Károlyi regime as a press attaché to the Hungarian diplomatic delegation in Bern. While on the train he read a report which had appeared in *Vörös Újság* about the events in Budapest on the 'first free May Day'. On the train he also met a Swiss worker who, as it happened, had been in Budapest on 1 May. His enthusiastic account of what he had seen and the upbeat newspaper report convinced Bölöni that he should return to Hungary.[59]

When making the journey home, he decided to stop off in Vienna, where he was surprised to encounter several friends and acquaintances, including Oszkár Jászi, whom he regarded as progressives but who had decided to leave Hungary, due to their strong criticism of developments there. Nevertheless, he continued his journey to Budapest, arriving in early June.

It wasn't the most appropriate of times to be enthusiastic. Furthermore, as Romanian forces drew closer to Budapest, he detected a certain anti-communist atmosphere in the air and writers were disappearing from the scene. Dezső Kosztolányi, for example, who was supposed to be editing and contributing to a new journal together with Bölöni, could never be reached on the telephone.

At one point, soon after the attempted counter-revolutionary putsch in Budapest, Bölöni met Zsigmond Móricz, whom he found weary, despondent and out of spirits. 'The events at the front had greatly shaken him. Matters developing in a tragic manner and the signs of counter-revolution in the provinces had broken his faith and confidence.'

Given the devaluation of the currency, writers were no longer attracted by the fees they might be paid. Bölöni and Móricz managed to joke about him being paid for future work in kilos of wheat—not such a fanciful idea, remarked Bölöni, in view of the difficulties in Budapest of obtaining food, and flour in particular.

---

59. For this and what follows, see Bölöni (1959), pp. 39–43.

'At that time all trace of enthusiasm, and sympathy or identification with the communist revolution had disappeared among writers and journalists, and generally among intellectuals,' Bölöni would recall.

Perhaps this wasn't too surprising in the case of Zsigmond Móricz, who had often appeared to be so enthusiastic, he seemed to be suffering from a form of blind optimism. 'In the cooperatives … calm and happy peace rule,' he had written in mid April.[60] Two months later, as Bölöni discovered, his enthusiasm had drained away.

Yet there were others who had had a more sober disposition but who likewise became disillusioned for a variety of reasons. Béla Bartók, for example, had quite willingly participated as a member of the Music Directory, but he also had a change of heart. Writing in 1920, Bartók reflected on his experiences of the previous year. 'In principle, [the new] regime favoured the progressive talent even more than its predecessor,' i.e. the Károlyi regime. But he also says that 'an absolute delirium', which had existed since November 1918,

> to call into being 'monumental' institutions seized certain sections, spreading continuously until it almost took on maniacal proportions, without any reference to the sparse material aid available … Protectionism and bureaucracy flourished as never before. The Council's Government was just as narrow-minded as the former bourgeois administrations had been.[61]

Decades later, Frank Eckelt would summarise in a more general way the inherent deficiencies of the Council Republic's domestic policies:

> Hundreds of years of exploitation, ignorance and superstition could not be cured, even under ideal circumstances … The leaders of the Hungarian Soviet Republic, blinded by Marxist dogma, failed to realise that internalised value systems could not be changed overnight. The humanitarian idealism which permeated so much of their social programmes was doomed to failure due to the lack of funds, the lack of time and errors in execution. Failure of its armed forces, political and economic quarantine by the Western powers and the failure of the Russian Soviet Republic to link forces with its beleaguered ally, all contributed to the internal collapse of the Hungarian soviet government.

With dissolution of the regime obvious by July, no amount of effort on its part could save its domestic programme. Inflation nullified the raises the

60. Hajdu (1979), p. 90.
61. Tallián (1981), pp. 118–19.

> workers and peasants received from the government. The lack of goods and widespread corruption destroyed their morale. The dreams of March ended on 1 August, when the first soviet government outside of Russia collapsed. Its leaders fled into exile and the nation faced a return to the feudal and chauvinistic policies of her nineteenth-century masters.[62]

In political terms, was there something contradictory in the whole Council Republic project, which pointed to major contradictions right from the start, and would generate disillusionment, particularly for those who saw hope in the political ideals proclaimed by the new regime?

Put more concretely, did the events of 21 March 1919 and the proclamation of the Hungarian Council Republic represent, as often claimed at the time and later, a genuine proletarian revolution and the establishment of a proletarian dictatorship acting to liberate the oppressed? Or was it a seizure of power *in the name of the Hungarian proletariat* and the establishment of a regime which ruled *over the proletariat*? There is clearly a difference, though they have often been confused—in relation to Hungary 1919 and elsewhere.

When the leaders of the Social Democratic Party and the Communist Party held negotiations in Budapest's Transit Prison on 21 March and came to an agreement to join forces in a newly named Socialist Party of Hungary, they issued a statement declaring the unity of their two parties and the establishment of a new regime. The short text contains the following very revealing sentence: 'In the name of the proletariat, the party immediately assumes all power.' That is quite clear—it was an assumption of power by the leaders of a newly created party, rather than the conquest of power resulting from some kind of revolution.

The next sentence seems rather contradictory: 'The proletarian dictatorship is exercised by the workers', peasants' and soldiers' councils.'[63] Was it the councils who were supposed to have the power or the party? While it is true that both the Soldiers' Council and the Budapest Workers' Council quickly endorsed the new regime on 21 March and that formally speaking the councils were often regarded as the supreme bodies during the period of the Commune, in practice it was always the Revolutionary Governing Council, i.e. the People's Commissars comprising leading party members, which held the real power, even though they certainly required the support of large sections of the population.

62. Völgyes (1971), p. 88.

63. *Az egyesülési határozat* (The Resolution on Unity). For the full text, see: https://hu.wikisource.org/wiki/Az_egyes%C3%BCl%C3%A9si_hat%C3%A1rozat (accessed 5 July 2017).

This distinction between party and proletariat could have some serious consequences, particularly when there were perceived clashes of interest between the ruling regime and the people in whose name it claimed to be exercising power. At its extreme, there could be a certain intolerant fanaticism, expressed even against the proletariat. For example, in a decree of 6 June 1919, Tibor Szamuely, announced the following:

> Striking, which was always a rightful weapon used in a capitalist state against private capital, now, in the new system of a socialist society, is the most infamous treachery against the interests of the working class. Thus, whoever today advocates a strike against the proletarian state is a counter-revolutionary, whom the proletarian power will deal with as the most dangerous opponent. We will stifle every motion of counter-revolution in its infancy. Whoever participates in counter-revolution or advocates counter-revolution, whether they uphold it or keep quiet, will pay for it with their lives.[64]

Criticism of the fanaticism in regard to strikes and other issues was expressed a couple of weeks later by Zsigmond Kunfi when speaking at the Congress of Soviets. He felt compelled to remark:

> In my view the conception advanced by comrades Pogány and Szamuely of the role and function of the Hungarian proletariat in the international revolution, amounts to this, that they ascribe to the Hungarian proletariat the role of saviour of the world, and that if necessary they will have it bleed to death in performing its part. This conception of Messianic Socialism ... I do not share.[65]

The seemingly contradictory, anti-proletarian attitude on the part of leaders claiming to represent the proletariat was expressed on more than one occasion by Béla Kun. For example, on 22 March, the day after the declaration of the Soviet Republic, Kun was approached by a three-person delegation representing a First World War veterans' association who requested the payment of 5400 crowns for their members. Rudolf Tőkés says the association comprised disabled veterans, to whom the Communist Party, in a pledge made earlier in the heat of the communists' political campaigning, had promised 5400 crowns severance pay.[66] Former soldiers, disabled or otherwise, could be found among the most fervent supporters of

---

64. Quoted by Konok (2011), p. 46.
65. Jászi (1924), p. 121.
66. Tőkés (1967), p. 156.

the new regime, but Kun dismissed them out of hand. Vilmos Böhm, who witnessed the encounter, has recorded Kun's harsh words. 'Let's have an end to these demands for 5400 crowns, otherwise you'll get 5400 machine-gun bullets instead of 5400 crowns!'[67]

And right at the end, on 1 August 1919, the last day of the Hungarian Soviet Republic, when Kun addressed the Budapest Workers Council in the late afternoon, explaining the decision to resign taken earlier in the day by the Revolutionary Governing Council and the party leadership, instead of restricting himself to stating the obvious—namely that, in view of the approaching Romanian forces and the disintegration of the Red Army, the Commune was doomed—what he actually said clearly seemed to put the blame on the Hungarian working class!

'The proletariat of Hungary,' he declared, 'let down not their leaders but themselves ... the dictatorship of the proletariat has failed economically, politically and militarily.'

> It need not have failed if there had been order here. Even if the transition to socialism and communism had been economically and politically impossible ... if there had been class-conscious, revolutionary proletarian masses, then the dictatorship of the proletariat would not have failed in this way.
>
> I would have liked a different ending. I would have liked the proletariat to fight on the barricades ... if it had declared it would rather die than give up its rule. I wondered whether we should man the barricades ourselves without the masses. We would have willingly sacrificed ourselves, but the question is whether the sacrifice would have been worthwhile in terms of the interests of the international world revolution.
>
> The proletariat, which was dissatisfied with our government, and, in spite of every kind of agitation, kept shouting 'down with the dictatorship of the proletariat' in their own factories, will be even more dissatisfied with any future government.
>
> Now I realise that our experiment to educate the proletarian masses of this country into class-conscious revolutionaries has been in vain. This proletariat needs the most ruthless and cruel dictatorship of the bourgeoisie in order to become revolutionary.[68]

---

67. Böhm (1924), p. 269.
68. Ibid., pp. 462–3. Böhm quotes the shorthand notes taken at the session, though in a footnote wrongly gives the date of the session as 2 August. The minuted notes are taken as authentic and are also quoted by both Tőkés (1967) and Borsányi (1993).

Even some dedicated party activists felt let down by Kun and his inner circle, albeit not necessarily because of his speech to the Budapest Workers' Council on 1 August. The labour movement and socialist women's movement activist of many years Mariska Gárdos was one. Escaping from Hungary after the fall of the Commune, she arrived in Vienna, where she heard something that greatly disturbed her, as she would recall years later:

> It came to my attention that with the fall of the Hungarian Soviet Republic several members of the *Vörös Újság* staff were informed that they could flee on the 'safe conduct' special train [to Austria]. On receiving this information, I felt as if someone had struck me a blow. How could it have happened that I was not made aware of this opportunity to escape, when I was the one who for about twenty years more than anyone else on the staff had been causing trouble for the ruling classes and authorities of Hungary? I certainly could not have expected mercy in the event that I should have fallen into their hands. How else could I explain this 'oversight' other than that the Communist Party of Hungary was no longer in need of my work and had demoted me to second-class membership.[69]

The party no longer needing even its experienced supporters? The recognised leader of the self-styled party of the proletariat blaming the proletariat for the defeat of the Commune? What was going on? Could such apparent contradictions be partly explained by the theories expounded by the revolutionary thinker Jan Waclaw Machajski (1866–1926) who argued that workers and peasants should be extremely wary of Bolshevik-type activists and their organisations. For Machajski, Marxism was nothing other than an ideology reflecting the interests of intellectuals, administrators, technical experts and politicians, who hoped to ride to power on the shoulders of the manual workers.[70]

---

69. Gárdos (1964), p. 99.
70. It is beyond the scope of this book to fully investigate Machajsky's concepts, which were similar to some of the ideas of revolutionary syndicalism. They also resurfaced in later debates about 'bureaucratic collectivism' and 'the new class' in relation to state-socialist regimes. For a brief but concise insight, see: Paul Avrich, 'What is Makhaevism?' *Soviet Studies* 17 (July 1965) pp. 66–75. For an internet version, see: https://libcom.org/history/what-makhaevism-paul-avrich And for a history of the Russian Revolution employing an approach somewhat similar to that of Machajsky, dealing with some myths about party and class, see: Maurice Brinton, *The Bolsheviks and Workers Control, 1917–1921. The State and Counter-Revolution,* London, Solidarity, 1970. The text is reproduced in: David Goodway (ed.), *For Workers' Power. The Selected Writings of Maurice Brinton*, Edinburgh, AK Press, 2004, and is available on a number of websites, for example https://www.marxists.org/archive/brinton/1970/workers-control/ (Both websites mentioned here were accessible on 5 July 2017.)

Postscript
What Happened to Them?

After the fall of the Hungarian Soviet Republic, many of those who had been active or who could have been suspected of having had sympathies for the Council Republic were either forced to emigrate or felt they had to leave Hungary, since they feared reprisals under the new regime or simply anticipated a negative situation, either politically or culturally, or maybe both. This applied both to politicians and artists of various sorts, though there were striking differences in the fate of the two groups.

Virtually all the political leaders of the Hungarian Soviet Republic fled the country in the immediate aftermath of its fall. Some remained in Vienna for a while, others moved to Berlin, then by and large those who were Communist Party members or Party sympathisers ended up in Moscow, particularly in view of Hitler's rise to power in Germany. In contrast to what might have been expected, life for Hungarian communists in the so-called workers' paradise was no bed of roses, red or otherwise. It can be strongly argued that, paradoxically, in the 1930s a Hungarian communist was safer in Hungary, where the Party, albeit tiny, was illegal and its members harassed and imprisoned, than in the Soviet Union under Stalin, given that many Hungarian political emigrés in Moscow fell victim to the Stalinist purges of the late 1930s.

Rudolf Tőkés lists 19 former People's Commissars of the Hungarian Soviet Republic who died during or as a consequence of the Great Terror in the Soviet Union. He also notes that untold scores of lesser-known Hungarian communists were killed or placed in prison camps. Among those 19 leaders who 'disappeared' was the man usually regarded as the de facto leader of the Council Republic, Béla Kun, the former People's Commissar for Foreign Affairs. In view of this, while still surprising on the surface, it is perhaps no wonder that it needed developments like the death of Stalin in 1953 and Khrushchev's famous 'secret speech' denouncing Stalin in early 1956 before any amount of positive attention was paid to 1919 in post-1945 Hungary. Previously it would have been rather out of place, to say the least, to sing the praises of earlier Hungarian communists who had fallen victim to Stalin's purges.[1]

---

1. In so far as they can at all be clearly identified, the varied reasons why individual Hungarian communists fell out of favour in Moscow—reasons which are partly

As for artists of all descriptions, art historian Éva Forgács asserts: 'Among the many waves of exile throughout Hungarian history probably the one following the defeat of the Hungarian Soviet Republic in 1919 drained Hungarian art and culture the most.'[2] That is a sweeping statement and arguably contains much truth, but the picture is somewhat more complex.

Like Rudolf Tőkés, Steven Mansbach also has a list, albeit admittedly an incomplete one, in which he identifies 26 specifically avant-garde artists who fled Hungary following the fall of the 1919 Soviet Republic, most of whom did not go to the Soviet Union, preferring to remain in western Europe, in Vienna, Berlin or Paris, but over half of whom returned to Hungary in the inter-war years, eight of those in the period 1925–27. The latter group included Lajos Kassák, Róbert Berény, Gyula Derkovits and Károly Kernstok.[3]

The intriguing question arises as to why such people would return to the ultra conservative and nationalist Hungary of Miklós Horthy, to the type of politics and society in anticipation of which they had fled from not many years before. Although Mansbach thinks the matter 'has yet to be explained convincingly', he offers some reasons for the phenomenon.[4]

Mansbach argues that the emigré Hungarian avant-garde artists were rarely more than superficially integrated into their host countries, where they had received little official welcome in terms of support. In addition, the attempts to establish a spiritual centre between East and West, with Hungarians at the hub was never effectively realised. Non-Hungarians rarely attended events organised by Hungarians, the language difficulty being one of the barriers. (Both Mansbach and Forgács indicate that a key figure such as Kassák, who revived the journal *MA* in Vienna and who clearly aimed to continue—in Berlin as well as Vienna—the artistic and propaganda activities he had been engaged with in Hungary, could speak no foreign language.)[5] Furthermore, the Hungarian artists in emigration were not very successful in that they had few exhibitions and few sponsors. Nor were they able to fully penetrate the more commercial world of adver-

connected to the ambiguous, shifting interpretations of the Hungarian Soviet Republic on the part of the Soviet leadership—are complex and beyond the scope of this book. Tőkés (1967, pp. 218–26) gives an interesting overview of the changing perspectives regarding 1919 in official communist ideology. His list of the 19 Hungarian leaders who died is given in an appendix on p. 261. For a detailed account of how views of 1919 changed within post-1945 Hungary itself, see Apor (2014).

2. The opening lines of Forgács's 'In the Vacuum of Exile: The Hungarian Activists in Vienna 1919–1926', in: Neubauer & Török (2009), pp. 109–21.

3. S.A. Mansbach, 'Revolutionary Engagements: The Hungarian Avant-Garde', in: Mansbach et al., (1991), pp. 46–91. For the list, see p. 75.

4. Ibid., p. 78.

5. Ibid., p. 78 and Forgács (2009), p. 119.

tising. At the same time, they still felt tied to Hungary and as conditions there slowly improved after the post-1919 'White Terror' many took their chances and returned home.

Mansbach doesn't mention one specific factor, which might have played a significant role, namely the prospect, due to an amnesty, of being able, having returned, to avoid arrest and prosecution in connection with being involved in the Soviet Republic.[6]

Those artists who decided to return, while avoiding arrest, found themselves in a difficult situation, due partly to political considerations and suspicions, and partly to changing tastes and styles, since Modernism was now officially out of favour. Nevertheless, some exhibitions were organised which included returned artists and some found employment in publishing, teaching and even, as in the case of Kassák and Berény, in commercial advertising.

As for writers, their post-1919 story is varied. Many did not emigrate. Even Zsigmond Móricz, one of the most prominent writers during the Council Republic period remained in Hungary, though he did suffer somewhat for his activities. Others, such as Mihály Babits and Dezső Kosztolányi very soon began to express criticisms and doubts they had had during the period, thus displaying what could be perceived as a form of repentance, not that it helped Babits very much (see below).

Perhaps the expected loss of a Hungarian-language readership after emigrating induced many writers to remain in the country. After all, in principle a work by a Hungarian painter could be appreciated wherever it was created, but how many non-Hungarians would have been able to read, let alone appreciate Hungarian literature?

In the music world the picture is also mixed. As noted in Chapter 8, Zoltán Kodály was informally tried and in effect punished for his involvement in the Music Directory and at the Academy of Music, but he didn't emigrate. Béla Bartók considered emigration and left Hungary for a short while, but returned.

Among those involved with cinema and the theatre, the film-makers Sándor (Alexander) Korda and Mihály Kertész (Michael Curtiz) and the actor Béla Lugosi were noted examples of those who emigrated and made a name for themselves outside Hungary. They weren't the only ones. In his history of Hungarian cinema, John Cunningham asserts that most of the film-making community fled to avoid retribution. He adds that even some who had not been involved with the Council Republic left, due to the limited opportunities for work. 'The result of this migration,' he says,

---

6. Éva Forgács (p. 109) refers to 'a 1926 general amnesty', which might well explain why a number of emigrés chose to return to Hungary at that time.

'was that the Hungarian film industry was virtually denuded of all its major talent.'[7]

What follows is not a comprehensive, detailed account, but a set of brief indications of the post-1919 fate of a selection of people who feature in this book. The aim is simply to provide an outline of what befell certain individuals, and to show the similarities as well as the differences between the paths they took, or were forced to take.

* * *

Mihály Babits (1883–1941). The poet, writer, editor and translator Babits welcomed the 1918 Chrysanthemum Revolution and was involved to an extent with the Writers' Directory, set up under the Council Republic. However, as noted at the end of Chapter 9, he himself changed his views during the existence of the Commune and not long after its fall he was writing very negatively about it. However, that didn't shield him from criticism and official harassment, or prevent him from being dismissed from the university post he had taken up during the Commune, nor from being expelled from the Petőfi literary association in early 1920. Nevertheless, throughout the 1920s and 1930s Babits was an editor of the *Nyugat* journal and an influential figure in Hungary's literary life.

Béla Balázs (1884–1949). A close friend of György Lukács for a long time, Balázs held a number of cultural posts during the 1919 Soviet Republic when, as noted in Chapter 7, he was an ardent supporter of children's theatre and an advocate of children's fairy tales. After the fall of the Commune, he first went to Vienna and then moved to Berlin. He penned numerous screenplays, including a 1930 adaptation of *The Threepenny Opera*. Balázs joined the Communist Party of Germany in 1931. He accepted a Soviet invitation to make a film about the Hungarian Soviet Republic, though the project was never fully realised. He started working at the Moscow Film Academy and remained in the Soviet Union for 14 years, dealing with scenarios, children's books and plays. Returning to Hungary after the war, he was involved with the Academy of Film Art and was one of the writers for the film *Somewhere in Europe* (1948), which gained international recognition. Balázs is well known for his work on cinema, *Theory of the Film*.

Béla Bartók (1881–1945). Bartók was a member of the Music Directory in 1919. For his activities, he was suspended from his post at the Academy of

7. Cunningham (2004), p. 25.

Music, but unlike Kodály he did not have to face formal disciplinary proceedings. Bartók was greatly disturbed by the conservative reaction which followed the fall of the Council Republic. In an essay entitled 'Hungary in the Throes of Reaction', he wrote:

> At present it is no longer a question of whether a singer, an artist, a savant is of good repute in his especial class of work but whether he is a Jew or a man of liberal tendencies. For these two sections of humanity are to be excluded so far as possible from all public activity.[8]

In early 1920 Bartók went to Berlin, but in mid April returned to Hungary, where he lived for a further two decades, although he undertook a number of tours to different European countries, as well as the US and Soviet Union. His internationalist, or rather non-nationalist approach to music understanding and appreciation did not suit Hungary's official inter-war politics and he tended to remain somewhat on the margins, despite his growing international reputation.

A scandal erupted because of his *Miraculous Mandarin*, a commentary on modern urban life in the form of a mime-play with libretto by Menyhért (Melchior) Lengyel, which involved erotic allusions. A planned Budapest staging in 1931 was cancelled after the dress rehearsal. The premiere had taken place five years earlier, not in Hungary but in Germany, in Cologne, though it was taken off after one performance.

Throughout the 1930s Hungary drifted steadily in the direction of National Socialism, with 1938 seeing the first of a series of anti-Jewish laws. Bartók was among a number of artists and intellectuals who publicly opposed this. The rising danger of Nazi Germany and the stifling atmosphere at home deeply troubled Bartók. His thoughts turned to emigration, and after his mother passed away he chose voluntary exile in the United States, where he lived from late 1940 to his death in 1945. He was buried in New York, but in 1988 his ashes were brought to Hungary and reburied in Budapest's Farkasrét Cemetery.

Róbert Berény (1887–1953). In 1919 Berény headed the painting department of the Arts Directory and is renowned for his striking recruiting poster *Fegyverbe! Fegyverbe!* (To arms! To arms!). Berény was arrested following the fall of the Soviet Republic. He was freed on the initiative of Ödön Márffy, as in the case of Károly Kernstok (see below), but was obliged to leave the country. He lived in Berlin, where he took up music composition. Berény returned to Hungary in 1926. He continued to

8. Quoted in Tallián (1981), p. 119.

paint and also designed commercial posters, including a series for Modiano cigarette papers. From 1934 he worked in Zebegény, a small town by the Danube not far from the Czechoslovak border. He gained some official recognition and in 1936 he was a recipient of the Szinyei Prize. After 1948 he taught at the Budapest Academy of Fine Arts. He was awarded the Munkácsy Prize in 1950 and 1951, and the high-ranking Kossuth Prize in 1951.

Mihály Bíró (1886–1948). As an artist producing political material, Bíró was heavily involved with the labour movement well before, as well as during 1919. It was he who, in 1911, created the famous poster of the red hammer-wielding worker, which became emblematic for the Hungarian labour movement and was produced countless times in 1919. He was one of the key figures involved with the 'red' decoration of Budapest for the May Day festivities. Three months after the fall of the Soviet Republic Bíró crossed the Austrian border, beginning 28 years of emigration. In Vienna he was able to find work as a graphic artist, as well as produce commercial and film posters. Bíró's life as an emigré took him to both Germany and Czechoslovakia. He continued to produce posters for labour organisations, even sending work for publication in Hungary's Social Democratic newspaper, *Népszava*. After Hitler took over the Sudentenland in 1938, Bíró went to Paris, where although ill and sometimes arrested, he survived the war. In 1947 he returned to Hungary, where he was the recipient of official favour, but illness prevented him from taking up a teaching post.

Ernő Dohnányi (1877–1960). The composer, pianist and conductor Dohnányi was a member of the Music Directory in 1919, along with Bartók and Kodály, in addition to being director of the Academy of Music. After the fall of the Commune, he was suspended from his position at the Academy but he remained in Hungary and, despite his involvement in 1919, during the 1920s was able to fulfil a number of prominent posts in the music world. From 1931 he was the director of Hungarian Radio's music department, and from 1934 again the director of the Academy. After the war he was accused of holding anti-Semitic and extreme right-wing views, charges which were never proven and have been hotly contested. In 1948 he went to Argentina and the following year moved to Florida, where in the last decade of his life he was a professor of piano and music composition.

Sári Fedák (1879–1955). A renowned and very popular operetta singer and actress, in 1919 Fedák was prominent in public propaganda and recruiting drives for the Red Army. Due to such activities, in 1920–21 she was able to perform only in Vienna. In later years she was by no means alone in reorienting her political sympathies. By the time of the Second World War she was promoting irredentist and nationalist ideas. Due to her views and her radio broadcasts during the war, she was subsequently sentenced to one year in prison, after which she lived a much more withdrawn life.

Mariska Gárdos (1885–1973) features several times in the chapter about the May Day celebrations in Budapest, during which she darted around the city giving a number of speeches. A long-standing activist in the Social Democratic labour and women's movements, in 1919 she was on the staff of *Vörös Újság*. She subsequently lived mainly in Vienna and was active in emigré politics. Unlike many other political activists of 1919, Gárdos did not go to the Soviet Union. The fact that her sister, Frida, died in a Soviet prison around 1926 may explain that. However, accepting the risks, she returned to Hungary in 1932 and continued to be politically involved. In 1935 she was sentenced to one year in prison for incitement. During the Second World War she was under police supervision and interned for a while. After the war she was one of the leading figures in the (now 'official') political women's movement. From the end of the 1940s she withdrew from much activity, though she continued to make speeches and to write her memoirs. There used to be a street and a school named after Mariska Gárdos in the Óbuda district of Budapest.

Oszkár Jászi (1875–1957) was minister with responsibilities for nationalities and a key figure in the Károlyi regime. He played no role during the subsequent Soviet Republic, of which he was highly critical, but his perceptive observations about it have often been mentioned in this book. He left Hungary in early May 1919, going first to Vienna, where he was to be active in emigré politics, striving from afar to oppose Hungary's post-1919 Horthy regime and generate support for his longed-for regional, democratic Danube Federation. He undertook a lecture tour in the United States in 1923–4, after which he accepted an invitation from Oberlin College, Ohio, where he was a professor of political science from 1925 until his retirement in 1942. During World War II he was president of the American Federation of Democratic Hungarians. In 1947 he visited Austria, Czechoslovakia and Hungary, coming away with pessimistic views about the future of the region. He died in 1957 in Oberlin. In 1991 Jászi's ashes were brought to Hungary and buried in Budapest's Farkasrét Cemetery.

Gyula Juhász (1883–1937). The poet Juhász was politically active in Szeged both before and during the Council Republic. After 1919 he managed to scrape a living from his articles and verses, though sometimes he was censored. For example, an article entitled 'Our Celebration', which he wrote for *Munka* (Labour), a Szeged Social Democratic daily, to mark May Day in 1921, was published on the front page, but with a white space where part of the article had been censored.[9] In the mid 1920s he visited Vienna for a while, where he met Lajos Kassák and others, though he didn't emigrate as such. His cause of death in 1937 was suicide.

Mihály Károlyi (1875–1955) was a key figure in the period of the Chrysanthemum Revolution and its aftermath. In the months immediately following the end of the First World War, he was initially Hungary's prime minister and later its president, a position he held up to the declaration of the Soviet Republic. He left Hungary in July 1919, living abroad in Austria, Czechoslovakia and Yugoslavia. Later he was in France and, during the war, in London. He was not forgotten at home, though for many he was remembered in a very negative sense. Landowners had not appreciated the example he had set in early 1919 when he voluntarily divided up part of his own estates. Furthermore, the authorities denounced him as a traitor for his radical sympathies and because they believed his weakness had paved the way for both the Soviet Republic and for the dismemberment of Hungary after the Great War. In 1923 he was tried in absentia, accused of treason and treachery. Found guilty, his property was sequestrated.

During his years in exile Károlyi was an active organiser of the anti-fascist and democratic Hungarian forces abroad. He returned to Hungary after World War II, and in 1947–49 was Hungarian ambassador in Paris. However, disaffection over the show trial and execution of the prominent communist László Rajk and other illegalities led to a second exile. He died in France in 1955. Originally buried on the Isle of Wight, his body was finally moved to Budapest and reburied in the Kerepesi Cemetery in 1962.

In 1975 a statue of Károlyi was unveiled in Budapest near the north side of parliament. It was removed prior to the 2014 refashioning of Kossuth Square, which surrounds parliament on three sides, and eventually replaced by a huge monument in memory of István Tisza, Hungary's prime minister throughout most of the First World War and one of Károlyi's prime targets of criticism. The Tisza monument had originally appeared in the same place in 1934 but was pulled down after the Second World War.

Lajos Kassák (1887–1967). After the dissolution of the Council Republic, Kassák spent some time in prison and then left for Vienna, where he re-continued the publication of *MA*. Among his works of this period was

9. For the front page, see: www.sk-szeged.hu/statikus_html/kiallitas/juhaszgy/munka.html (accessed 6 July 2017).

a joint production with László Moholy-Nagy (of Weimar Bauhaus fame) of *Buch neuer Künstler* (Book of New Artists), which appeared in 1922 (republished in English in 1992).

Kassák returned to Hungary in 1926 and continued his publishing activities. His output in this period included *Angyalföld*, the novel's title referring to the name of a working-class district in Budapest. What many regard as his major work is his *Egy ember élete* (One Man's Life), a work of biographical literature which appeared in several volumes in the late 1920s and 1930s. In the same period he was involved in a leftist political-cultural journal and movement called *Munka* (Work), which was concerned with the cultural and political education of young workers and students. Kassák's attitude was critical of both orthodox communism and social democracy, but from a left-wing perspective.

For a while in the post-1945 period Kassák occupied a prominent post, being appointed vice-president of the Hungarian Arts Council. After 1949 and the rise of local Stalinism, his anti-authoritarian unorthodoxy inevitably led to a period of 'internal exile', during which it was difficult for him to get published. Unlike some of his colleagues, however, he never renounced the radical Constructivism of his earlier period, and in the post-1956 era of 'reconciliation' he even received a certain amount of official recognition, being the recipient of the state Kossuth Prize in 1965.

Lajos Kassák died in 1967, aged 80. He is buried in the 'resting place of writers', the large Farkasrét Cemetery in Buda. In 1973 a street in Budapest's Angyalföld district was named after Kassák. At the time of writing, it still bears his name. A small museum in Budapest is devoted to Kassák's life and work.

Károly Kernstok (1873–1940) was a noted artist and head of the artists' free school in Nyergesújfalu established after the formation of the Council Republic (see Chapter 4). Kernstok was arrested very soon after the fall of the Soviet Republic. It went against him that visitors to the free school had included Tibor Szamuely and Béla Kun. The new authorities also disliked him for what was perceived as his radical ideas, his involvement with the local workers' council and his association with radical intellectuals, as well as his earlier activities during the period of the Károlyi regime—he had been a member of the National Council and for a while a state secretary for culture. In the event, he was released fairly quickly, partly due to pressure brought to bear by Ödön Márffy and other artists who sought help from one of the public prosecutors known to be an art lover.[10] Kernstok was

10. Márffy recalled his involvement in the affair in an interview he gave 40 years later, a report of which appeared in *Élet és Irodalom* (Life and Literature) on 23 October 1959.

obliged to leave Hungary, which he did in the autumn of 1919. He lived in Berlin before returning to Hungary in 1926, after which he continued to paint, living much of the time in Nyergesújfalu.

Mihály Kertész (Michael Curtiz, 1886–1962). During the Council Republic period Kertész directed the propaganda film *Jön az öcsém* (My Brother is Coming), for the details of which, see Chapter 6. He left Hungary before the fall of the Soviet Republic, going first to Vienna and later to the United States where he was known as Michael Curtiz. His long, distinguished Hollywood career included directing credits on over 100 films, one of the most famous being the cinema classic *Casablanca* (1942), starring Humphrey Bogart and Ingrid Bergman.

Zoltán Kodály (1882–1967). Like his fellow musicians Béla Bartók and Ernő Dohnányi, in 1919 Kodály was a member of the Music Directory. As detailed in Chapter 8, not long after the fall of the Council Republic, he was the subject of a quasi-legal investigative process in connection with his prominent role in the Academy of Music during the 'revolutionary' period. As a result, Kodály was dismissed from his post as Deputy Director of the Academy and was not allowed to teach there for two years. However, he did not emigrate and relatively soon, in 1923, he had a major public success with the first performance of his *Psalmus Hungaricus*, written to celebrate the 50th anniversary of the union of Buda, Óbuda and Pest. Another great success, written nearly 40 years later, was his *Symphony in C Major*. Between the two, Kodály became renowned internationally, not only for his writings on folk music and music education, but also for the many compositions produced during his long career.

The so-called 'Kodály method', which places great emphasis on choral singing and the enjoyment of song, the linking of song with movement, the appreciation of the musical mother tongue, sight singing and notation, improvisatory ability and the ending of musical illiteracy as the basis of cultural education in general, has been applauded and applied worldwide.

Given his desire to bring (or rather give back) musical culture to the broad mass of people, it is understandable how Kodály could survive and even be promoted in Hungary's difficult post-1945 Stalinist era, since at that time there was, on the surface at least, the goal of at last making culture available to all.

Kodály's political views could dovetail into that, but they were not simply 'for the moment'. Well before that era, he had criticised what he saw as a wide gap, including from a musical point of view, between the handful of elite people and the vast majority of the nation. Be that as it may, in the 1950s, Kodály, using his relatively secure position, was able to protect or help a number of musicians who found themselves, for whatever reason, at odds with the politico-cultural establishment.

It was arguably a remarkable achievement that in the decades following 1919 Zoltán Kodály survived and even thrived during quite different political periods—the inter-war, ultra-conservative Horthy era, the post-1945 Stalinist period and the post-1956 Kádár era. He died of a heart attack on 6 March 1967, aged 84. In the decades following Hungary's political changes of 1989–90, he continued to be admired and appreciated, both in his own country and abroad.

Sándor (Alexander) Korda (1893–1956). Already a noted film director in Hungary before 1919, Korda continued making films during the Council Republic. What happened to him in the immediate aftermath of the fall of the revolutionary regime is briefly described in Chapter 6. Having left Hungary in late 1919, Korda made films in a number of countries, working in Vienna, Berlin, Hollywood and London, eventually becoming a leading figure in the British film industry. During the Second World War he spent a few years in America, but returned to the UK in 1942. Of the films he directed, *The Private Life of Henry VIII* (1933) was internationally popular, while *The Third Man* (1949) was among his company's renowned productions. He was the first film producer in Britain to receive a knighthood. One can only speculate what impact he might have had on the Hungarian cinema industry, had he not left Hungary when he did.

Dezső Kosztolányi (1885–1936). In 1919 the writer Kosztolányi adopted what could be interpreted as a moderately supportive position vis-à-vis the Commune, at least for a while. However, soon after the fall of the Council Republic he became associated with the right-wing publication *Új Nemzedék* (New Generation), contributing to its perhaps revealingly-named column 'Pardon', which was highly critical of the Soviet Republic and its leaders. In 1930 Kosztolányi became president of the Hungarian Pen Club, but in the following years he suffered from cancer and had a number of operations. He died in early November 1936. The following month the 'progressive' literary journal *Nyugat* devoted a special issue to him. One of Kosztolányi's well-known novels, *Anna Édes*, written in 1926, details the trials and tribulations of a long-suffering maid and is set in the aftermath of the 1919 events. A film version, directed by the noted Zoltán Fábri, appeared in 1958.

Gyula Krúdy (1878–1933). Soon after the fall of the Soviet Republic, during which he had written a number of enthusiastic articles, Krúdy became the victim of a campaign against him in the press. His financial circumstances deteriorated and his works were published only occasionally. Then, in 1925, which marked the 25th anniversary of his literary activities, he came back into favour to a certain extent. However, he was dogged by health problems and by the early 1930s was living in poor circumstances. Today Krúdy is one of Hungary's most popular, highly regarded writers of the last century.

Béla Kun (1886–1938?). In 1919 Kun was and today still is generally acknowledged as the main political leader of the Hungarian Soviet Republic. On the day of its collapse, he fled on a train with other leading figures to Vienna. He was initially interned in Austria, but after being released he went to Russia. There he was active in the Communist Party and was sent to the Crimean peninsular where the Civil War was still raging. He has often been accused of being involved there with mass arrests, executions and atrocities in his role as President of the Revolutionary Committee of the Crimea, though his biographer György Borsányi questions the reliability of the sources and asserts that the accusations are non-proven. During the 1920s Kun was a leading Comintern operative, serving in Germany, Austria and Czechoslovakia. His most notorious involvement occurred in 1921 when he encouraged the German Communist Party to launch the revolutionary 'March Action', which ended in failure, incurring for Kun in the process Lenin's displeasure. Nevertheless, he continued his activities for the Comintern, though in 1928 he was arrested in Vienna for travelling on a false passport. In Moscow in the 1930s he was involved in much feuding with other Hungarian communist emigrés, though he also devoted energy to helping Hungarian writers. In the late 1930s Kun was caught up in the Great Terror, being arrested and eventually executed. He was 'rehabilitated' a few years after Stalin's death in 1953.

As late as 1986 a large statue composition created by Imre Varga with his characteristic use of metal, depicting Kun exhorting a crowd in the process of rushing forward, was erected in a prominent spot in Budapest. 1986 was the centenary year of Kun's birth and the sculpture was unveiled on a day marking the anniversary of the foundation by Kun and others in November 1918 of what was to become the Hungarian Communist Party. It didn't stand there for many years. In the early 1990s it was removed to the city's Statue Park, where it can be seen today.

Zsigmond Kunfi (1879–1929) was a People's Commissar for Education and Culture (initially the leading one) during the Soviet Republic, though by June 1919 he had become disillusioned. After the fall of the Commune he went to Vienna. Unlike other emigrants who struggled to earn a living, Kunfi found a good job as a foreign editor of *Arbeiter-Zeitung*, a socialist daily published in the Austrian capital. He was active in emigré politics, opposing both the Hungarian Communist Party and the new leadership of the Social Democrats in Budapest. Some say his suicide was caused by a drug overdose. In Hungary on 20 November 1929, two days after his death, there was a nation-wide work stoppage in his memory. In 1947 Kunfi's ashes were reburied in Budapest.

Béla Lugosi (1882–1956). In 1919 Lugosi was very active in the actors' trade union, due to which he was subsequently proscribed from acting and forced to emigrate. After Vienna and Berlin, he went to the USA, where he worked in theatre and film. He perhaps could have returned to Hungary under a 1926 amnesty, but didn't. Arguably his most famous film success was playing the title role in *Dracula* (1931), with which he was thereafter forever associated.

György Lukács (1885–1971). In 1919 Lukács was a prominent figure in the Commissariat for Education and Culture and in the arts world in general. Soon after the fall of the Council Republic he fled to Vienna, where in 1923 he wrote *History and Class Consciousness*, a work which was to inspire many Western New Left radicals over four decades later. A dispute over strategy in 1929 in the Comintern led Lukács to withdraw into purely theoretical work. He moved to Moscow in 1933 and stayed in the Soviet Union until the end of the Second World War. Devoting himself primarily to aesthetics, he managed to escape the purges to which many of his Hungarian colleagues in Moscow fell victim.

Returning to Budapest in 1945 he took up a university post and actively supported the new Hungary. In 1949 he was strongly criticised in a campaign centred around cultural dogmatism. According to the new line, the problem with Lukács, although recognised as a staunch Party member, revolved around his view of realism in literature, which included the idea that some politically reactionary writers of classical European literature had nevertheless produced works which, in view of their style, insight and content, could be considered progressive. He once again withdrew into theoretical work. Lukács reappeared on the political scene during the 1956 Uprising, becoming minister of culture in Imre Nagy's short-lived government. Although he spent time with Nagy under house arrest in Romania after the uprising was crushed, he was allowed to return to Hungary in April 1957. He spent the rest of his life studying and writing about aesthetics, philosophy and politics.

Lukács is one of the few east European Marxists to have gained a degree of respect in the West, both in academic and political circles. Yet he always retained an orthodox attachment to the Party and often displayed elements of dogmatic simplicity, declaring in 1967, for example, that even the worst socialism was better than the best capitalism. Overall, perhaps the most surprising aspect about Lukács is that this maverick Hungarian Marxist managed to survive all the twists and turns of the international Communist movement and die a natural death in his own country at the age of 86.

In 1985 a statue of Lukács, commissioned by the municipal council and executed by the noted sculptor Imre Varga, was placed in Budapest's Szent István park, marking the centenary of his birth. It remained standing in the spot where it was unveiled for many years. Then in early 2017 the municipal council voted in favour of its removal.

Sándor Márai (1900–1989) wrote several articles during the period of the Commune and, as noted in the early part of Chapter 9, some were quite enthusiastic. He left Hungary for Germany in autumn 1919. After spending a number of years there and later in Paris, he returned to Budapest in the late 1920s. A prolific author, he would become noted for his rather conservative stance, though that didn't prevent certain attacks on him in 1942, at a time when he was being proposed for membership of the Academy of Sciences, for his role in 1919. In 1948, by now a staunch anti-communist, he left Hungary for Switzerland and then Italy, and after a few years he eventually settled in the United States. For a long time he was associated with Radio Free Europe. Márai committed suicide in San Diego in 1989. Deemed an archetypical 'bourgeois' writer, his works were regarded as unsuitable for publication in post-war Hungary until the approach of the 1989–90 changes, following which he became almost a cult figure in posthumous literary publishing. In recent years he has been 'rediscovered' and highly praised outside Hungary, too.

Zsigmond Móricz (1879–1942) was very active, as a writer and organiser, during both the 1918–19 Károlyi regime and the 1919 Council Republic, though in the latter period he more or less withdrew from public life in the second half of May. Nevertheless, he was subject to certain pressures after the fall of the Commune. The Kisfaludy Literary Society very soon set up a committee to investigate the activities of a number of writers, including Móricz. Provincial gendarmes arrested him in August for his earlier involvement in the Writers' Directory, but he was released after several days without charge. Later accusations revolved around the fact that he had received sums of money from the authorities during the time of the Council Republic. He was expelled from the Kisfaludy Society. His plays were not performed at the National Theatre for some years and he was regarded with suspicion by many for a long time. Notwithstanding such difficulties, he did manage to get published, for example in *Nyugat*

(Occident), of which for a few years after 1929 he was an editor. Irrespective of his role in 1919, for some he was anyway disliked for his unambiguous sympathy for the underdog and his critical appraisal of authority figures and of the conservative, gentry-dominated Hungary of his day. In the post-1945 era, in contrast, although not a 'proletarian writer' dealing with the industrial working class, he was regarded with some favour. Today he is one of Hungary's most celebrated writers of the twentieth century. Móricz always maintained his feelings for the peasantry, whose interests he had hoped were being advanced in 1919. He remained a prolific writer of short stories and novels, many of which were eventually turned into films.

József Pogány (1886–1938). In the wake of Hungary's Chrysanthemum Revolution of 1918, Pogány formerly a teacher, journalist, war correspondent and Social Democrat, became president of the Budapest Soldiers' Soviet. After the formation of the Soviet Republic he was People's Commissar for Defence, though he was very soon obliged to resign and take up other posts. In early August 1919 he fled first to Vienna and then to Moscow, where he died in 1938, though not through natural causes. He got caught up in Stalin's purges and was executed along with many other leaders of Hungary's 1919 'Bolshevik experiment'. Between his arrival in Moscow and his death there, Pogány was, for most of the time, a Comintern agent, sent to different countries. Like Béla Kun, he was involved in the failed 'March Action' of 1921 in Germany. The following year he went to the USA where, now calling himself John Pepper, he was supposed to assist the fledgling American Communist Party, though many of its members saw him as a disruptive character. After reluctantly returning to the Soviet capital, it was clearly no benefit for him that he had been 'sponsored' by Comintern leaders such as Zinoviev and Bukharin, both of whom lost their lives during Stalin's Great Terror.

Bertalan Pór (1880–1964) was active in the Arts Directory in 1919 and was among the painters producing large-scale propaganda posters for the Council Republic, after the fall of which he left Hungary, settling for many years in the Slovak part of Czechoslovakia. He travelled to Paris in 1934 and two years later he spent several months in the Soviet Union. In 1938 he settled in Paris. Following the German occupation of France he was held under arrest. After his release he took part in the French resistance. Pór returned to Hungary in 1948, where he took up a teaching post and was active in public life. In Hungary he was the recipient of a number of official awards.

Béla Reinitz (1878–1943). A prominent figure in the world of theatre and music in 1919, Reinitz was arrested by the police on the night of 8–9 August 1919 and held in custody. Accused of robbery—meaning appropriation and use of others' property following nationalisation of the theatres—his trial began on 9 February 1920. Despite being supported by many artists, he was sentenced to ten months in prison and barred from any official position for five years. However, the prison sentence was suspended on health grounds. Reinitz fled by boat to Vienna and later moved to Berlin. He returned to Budapest in 1931, thereafter living a rather isolated life, made more difficult by ill health.

Rózsika Schwimmer (1877–1948). A feminist and member of the executive committee of the Hungarian National Council in 1918, she was appointed by Mihály Károlyi to be Hungarian ambassador to Switzerland, but recognition of her credentials was refused by the Swiss and she was recalled by Károlyi after a short while. As a 'bourgeois feminist', Schwimmer was out of favour during the period of the 1919 Council Republic, but as a Jew and suspected Bolshevik her life was in danger during the 'White Terror' of the subsequent counter-revolutionary regime. Smuggled out of Hungary, she eventually arrived in the United States in 1921, but was not particularly welcome there either, being shunned due to her earlier anti-war activities, and in 1929 was denied US citizenship, allegedly for her refusal to indicate she would be willing to take up arms for the country. In the 1930s she campaigned for world government. In 1948 she was nominated for a Nobel Peace Prize, but she passed away, aged 71, before the award could be made. She would have been Hungary's first and (to date) only female Nobel Laureate. She died in New York City.

Ervin Sinkó (1898–1967). In 1919, the 20-year-old communist Sinkó had several roles—as a Party activist in Újpest, a member of the Budapest Workers' Council, a Red Army soldier, the commander of Kecskemét and a defender of the Soviet House in Budapest. He was also a critical thinker in relation to the tactics and ethics of the Soviet Republic. After the fall of the Commune Sinkó lived in many places, including Vienna, Zurich, Paris and Moscow. In 1934 while in exile in Paris, Sinkó completed his novel about 1919, *Optimisták* (Optimists). He then experienced great difficulty in getting it published, even in the Soviet Union, where he lived from 1935 to 1937. His diary notes of that period were eventually published as *A regény regénye* (The Story of a Novel). The work not only described the monotonously repetitive and often farcical obstacles he encountered with the Soviet literary bureaucracy, which reflected a certain ambiguity on the Soviet part regarding Hungary's Commune, it was at the same time a revealing and informed account of life in Moscow on the eve of Stalin's purges. Sinkó was lucky not to become himself a victim of the Great Terror and was able to return to Paris. During World War II he was involved with the Yugoslav partisans. After the war he lived in Zagreb, where he was mainly based for the rest of his life, devoting his energies to literary studies and political writing. He became a university professor and corresponding member of the Croatian Academy of Sciences and Arts.

Tibor Szamuely (1890–1919). Often perceived as one of the leading 'hard men' of 1919, after the fall of the Council Republic Szamuely fled in a car towards Austria on 2 August, but was arrested by the Austrian authorities after making an illegal border crossing. Both the Austrian and Hungarian authorities soon announced that he had shot himself, but that official version regarding his death was doubted by many.

Béla Uitz (1887–1972). In 1919 the artist Béla Uitz led a free school called the Proletarian Fine Arts Apprentice Workshop. He was also prominent in the creation of large-scale visual propaganda works, for example for the May Day demonstrations. After the fall of the Soviet Republic, he was imprisoned for a while before emigrating. In exile, he lived and continued to work in Vienna, Moscow and Paris. In Vienna he initially collaborated, as he had earlier in Hungary, with Lajos Kassák in the continued publication of the *MA* journal, but disagreements led to a parting of their ways and he was one of the founders of *Egység* (Unity), which was closer to the Communist Party. Uitz eventually settled in the Soviet Union, where he was highly regarded and won awards. However, in the late 1930s show trial proceedings were initiated against him. He was arrested and imprisoned, but released after about 18 months. He continued to live and create in the Soviet Union. Uitz returned to Hungary in 1970, two years before his death.

Péter Veres (1897–1970). We met Veres in Chapter 10 as the young revolutionary in Balmazújváros, eastern Hungary, who eagerly welcomed the news that the Soviet Republic had been proclaimed. In May 1919 Veres was taken prisoner and then held in a Romanian camp. He returned to Hungary in 1920, but due to his activities during the Council Republic he was sentenced to one year in prison. He later worked as an agricultural labourer and railway employee. He was active in the national organisation of agricultural labourers and in political life. In the 1930s and beyond he often wrote for left-wing and progressive publications about peasant life and the land question, speaking up for the village poor and agricultural proletariat in articles as well as novels. Between 1945 and 1949 he was president of the National Peasant Party and was a leading figure in the post-war land reform. He was also Minister of Defence for a while in the coalition government of the time. Although a supporter of post-war Hungary, he had many criticisms and was not always in official favour. In 1954–6, Veres was president of the Writers' Union and in that capacity, with his familiar big features and prominent moustache, and wearing his characteristic peasant 'uniform' of black boots, white shirt and no tie, he addressed a crowd on 23 October 1956 in Budapest's Bem Square. It was the first large public demonstration of the Uprising.

Sources Used and Useful Sources

Newspapers and journals appearing in 1919

Az Ember (Man)
Az Est (Evening News)
Az Újság (The News)
Fáklya (Torch). Mouthpiece of the cultural commissariat.
MA (Today). Journal of the radical cultural activist Lajos Kassák and his circle.
Magyar Iparművészet (Hungarian Applied Arts)
Magyarország (Hungary)
Népszava (People's Voice). Long-established newspaper of the Social Democratic Party. With the declaration of the Council Republic and unity with the Communists, *Népszava* officially became the daily morning paper of the united party.
Nőmunkás (Woman Worker)
Pesti Futár (Pest Courier)
Pesti Hírlap (Pest News)
Pesti Napló (Pest Diary)
Színházi Élet (Theatre Life)
Világ (World). In the pre-Commune era, official publication of the cultural ministry.
Vörös Film (Red Film)
Vörös Lobogó (Red Flag)
Vörös Újság (Red Gazette). Newspaper of the Communist Party, established in December 1918. During the Council Republic, it was officially the afternoon paper of the united party.

Manuscripts

A number of footnotes refer to (mainly unpublished) manuscripts 'in the PTI Archives', meaning the archives of the Institute of Political History in Budapest.

Books, articles, studies and other publications[1]

Ady, Endre, *The Explosive Country. A Selection of Articles and Studies, 1898–1916*. Budapest, Corvina Press, 1977.
Agárdi, Péter, *Kunfi Zsigmond*. Budapest, Új Mandátum Könyvkiadó, 2001. Selected writings of Zsigmond Kunfi, leading Social Democrat and People's Commissar for Education and Culture throughout much of the Hungarian Soviet Republic.
Apor, Péter, *Fabricating Authenticity in Soviet Hungary. The Afterlife of the First Hungarian Soviet Republic in the Age of State Socialism*. London and New York, Anthem Press,

1. All the websites listed in this bibliography were checked for accessibility on 6 July 2017.

2014. A detailed survey of how official attitudes to 1919 changed and developed in post-1945 Hungary.
Aradi, Nóra, *A szocialista képzőművészet jelképei* (The Symbols of Socialist Fine Arts). Budapest, Kossuth Kiadó/Corvina, 1974.
Aradi, Nóra, 'A Tanácsköztársaság művészete' (The Arts of the Council Republic), in: Németh, Lajos (ed.), *Magyar művészet 1890–1919* (Hungarian Arts 1890–1919), Vol. I. Budapest, Akadémiai Kiadó, 1981, pp. 613–24.
Aradi, Nóra & Győffy, Sándor, *A Magyar Tanácsköztársaság művészete* (The Arts of the Hungarian Soviet Republic). Budapest, Képzőművészeti Alap Kiadóvállalata, 1979. Individual reproductions of 32 posters, with an introductory study by art historian Nóra Aradi.
Ardó, Mária, *A Tanácsköztársaság színházi élete a sajtó tükrében* (Theatre Life During the Soviet Republic as Reflected in the Press). Budapest, Színháztudományi és Filmtudományi Intézet, 1959. A listing of articles appearing in 1919.
Ashmead-Bartlett, Ellis, *The Tragedy of Central Europe*. London, Thornton Butterworth, 1923.
Babus, Antal, 'Fülep Lajos az 1918–1919-es forradalmakban' (Lajos Fülep in the Revolutions of 1918–1919), *Új Forrás*, 2002, No. 3, pp. 30-51. See also: epa.oszk.hu/00000/00016/00073/020309.htm
Bakos, Katalin, *10 x 10 év az utcán. A magyar plakátművészet története 1890–1990* (Ten Decades on the Street. The History of Hungarian Poster Art 1890–1990). Budapest, Corvina Kiadó, 2007.
Bart, Isván, *Budapest krónikája—a kezdektől napjainkig* (Chronicle of Budapest—From the Beginning to Today). Budapest, Corvina, 2007.
Bartók, Béla Jnr (ed.), *Bartók Béla családi levelei* (Béla Bartók: Family Letters). Budapest, Zeneműkiadó, 1981.
Bartók, Béla Jnr, *Apám életének krónikája* (Chronicle of My Father's Life). Budapest, Zeneműkiadó, 1981.
Benson, Timothy O., *Central European Avant-gardes: Exchange and Transformation, 1910–1930*. London and Cambridge, Massachusetts, MIT Press, 2002.
Benson, Timothy O. & Forgács, Éva (eds.), *Between Worlds: A Sourcebook of Central European Avant-gardes*. London and Cambridge, Massachusetts, MIT Press, 2002.
Bodri, Ferenc (ed.), *Kernstok Károly és vendégei, látogatói Nyergesújfalun* (Károly Kernstok, his Guests and Visitors in Nyergesújfalu). Tatabánya, Kernstok Károly Művészeti Alapítvány, 2000.
Böhm, Vilmos, *Két forradalom tüzében. Októberi forradalom—Proletárdiktatúra—Ellenforradalom* (In the Cross-Fire of Two Revolutions. October Revolution—Proletarian Dictatorship—Counter-Revolution). Vienna, Bécsi Magyar Kiadó, 1923. Memoirs of a Social Democrat who in 1919 was, among other posts, the Red Army's Commander-in-Chief and later People's Commissar for Defence. For an internet version, see: http://mtdaportal.extra.hu/books/bohm_vilmos_ket_forradalom_tuzeben.pdf
Bóka, László, *Arcképvázlatok és tanulmányok* (Portrait Sketches and Studies). Budapest, Akadémiai Kiadó, 1962.
Bölöni, György, 'Vörös lobogó' (Red Flag), in: Halasi (1959), pp. 35–45.
Bónis, Ferenc, Élet–Képek: Bartók Béla (Life–Pictures: Béla Bartók). Budapest, Balassi Kiadó, 2006.
Borbás, György, *A millennium szobrásza Zala György : 1858–1937* (The Millennium's Sculptor György Zala : 1858–1937). Budapest, Kossuth Könyvkiadó, 1999. The title

refers to Hungary's 1896 Millennium Celebrations and the planning of what is today called Heroes' Square in Budapest. Many of the latter's statues were created by Zala.

Borsányi, György, *Kun Béla. Politikai életrajz* (Béla Kun. A Political Biography). Budapest, Kossuth Könyvkiadó, 1979.

Borsányi, György, *Októbertől márciusig* (From October to March). Budapest, Kossuth Könyvkiadó, 1988. A brief history of the Károlyi era, 1918–1919.

Borsányi, György, *The Life of a Communist Revolutionary, Béla Kun.* Boulder, Social Science Monographs/Highland Lakes, Atlantic Research and Publications, 1993. A translation, with some alterations and additions, of Borsányi's 1979 biography.

Borus, Rózsa (ed.), *A század nagy tanúi* (Great Witnesses of the Century). Budapest, RTV—Minerva, 1978. A record of interviews with eight prominent personalities, including Valéria Dienes, Ilona Duczynska and György Lukács.

Brailsford, Henry Noel, *Across the Blockade. A Record of Travels in Enemy Europe.* London, George Allen & Unwin, 1919. Includes a chapter entitled 'In Communist Hungary'.

Congdon, Lee, *The Young Lukács.* Chapel Hill and London, University of North Carolina Press, 1983.

Csaplár, Ferenc (ed.), *Magam Törvénye szerint. Tanulmányok és dokumentumok Kassák Lajos születésének századik évfordulójára* (As I See It. Studies and Documents Published on the Centenary of Lajos Kassák's Birth). Budapest, Petőfi Irodalmi Múzeum and Múzsák Közművelődési Kiadó, 1987.

Cséve, Anna, *Móricz Zsigmond.* Budapest, Elektra Kiadóház, 2005.

Cunningham, John, *Hungarian Cinema: From Coffee House to Multiplex.* London, Wallflower, 2004.

Czine, Mihály, 'Móricz Zsigmond a forradalmakban' (Zsigmond Móricz in the Revolutions), *Irodalomtörténeti Közlemények* (Annals of Literary History), Vol. 63, No. 2, 1959, pp. 217–33. http://epa.oszk.hu/00000/00001/00209/pdf/itk_1959_2_217-233.pdf

Czine, Mihály, *Móricz Zsigmond útja a forradalmakig* (Zsigmond Móricz's Road to the Revolutions). Budapest, Magvető Könyvkiadó, 1960.

De Marchi, Bruno, 'The red news-reel of the Tanácsköztársaság: History, dream and cinema imagination', *Hungarian Studies* 3/1-2 (1987), pp. 207–26. Budapest, Akadémiai Kiadó. http://epa.oszk.hu/01400/01462/00005/pdf/207-226.pdf

Derkovits, Gyuláné, *Mi ketten* (The Two of Us). Budapest, Képzőművészet Alap, 1954. Reminiscences of the artist Gyula Derkovits, by his wife Viktória Dombai.

Eastman, Crystal, 'In Communist Hungary', *The Liberator*, Vol. 2, No. 8, August, 1919, pp. 5–10. The American Eastman was one of the few reporters from Britain or the US to spend some time in Hungary during the Soviet Republic. A Hungarian translation of her article (A kommunista Magyarországon) can be found in Lukács (1987), pp. 250–63. All quotations in this book are taken from the original, English-language text, published in the USA.

Eckelt, Frank, 'The Internal Policies of the Hungarian Soviet Republic', in: Völgyes (1971), pp. 61–88.

Ék, Sándor, *Mába érő tegnapok* (Yesterdays Affecting Today). Budapest, Kossuth Könyvkiadó, 1968.

Eősze, László, *Kodály Zoltán—Élete és munkássága* (Kodály Zoltán—His Life and Work). Budapest, Zeneműkiadó Vállalat, 1956.

Escher, Károly & Vajda, Miklós, *Bajor Gizi.* Budapest, Magvető Könyvkiadó, 1958.

Fekete, Éva & Karádi, Éva, *György Lukács. His Life in Pictures and Documents.* Budapest, Corvina Kiadó, 1981.

Flórián, László & Vajda, János, *Reinitz Béla*. Budapest, Zeneműkiadó, 1978.

Forgács, Éva, 'In the Vacuum of Exile: The Hungarian Activists in Vienna, 1919–1926', in: Neubauer & Török (2009), pp. 109–21.

Gábor, Imréné (ed.), *A Magyar Tanácsköztársaság plakátjai* (Posters of the Hungarian Soviet Republic). Budapest, Kossuth Könyvkiadó, 1959. Reproductions of 48 posters with an introduction by Bertalan Pór.

Gál, Imre, *A polgár a viharban* (A Bourgeois in the Storm). Budapest, Duna, 1937. Day-by-day diary notes.

Garai, Erzsi (ed.), *A magyar film a Tanácsköztársaság idején* (Hungarian Cinema during the Soviet Republic). Budapest, Magyar Filmtudományi Intézet és Filmarchívum, 1969.

Gárdos, Mariska, *Kukoricán térdepelve* (Punished for Misbehaviour). Budapest, Szépiroldalmi Kiadó, 1964. Memoirs of a labour movement and socialist women's movement activist who was on the staff of *Vörös Újság* in 1919.

Gellért, Oszkár (ed.), *A diadalmas forradalom könyve* (Book of the Victorious Revolution). Budapest, Légrády, 1918. Testimony of members of the government, participants in the Chrysanthemum Revolution and 75 Hungarian writers.

Gerencsér, Miklós, *Vörös könyv 1919* (Red Book 1919). Lakitelek, Antológia Kiadó, 1993. Documents, decrees, press extracts and other material presented in a day-by-day chronology. www.valtozast.hu/web/

Gergely, Jenő, *A Magyarországi forradalmak 1918–1919* (Hungary's Revolutions 1918–1919). Budapest, IKVA, 1991. A pocket-book presentation for those sitting end-of-school or university entrance exams.

Göndör, Ferenc, *Vallomások könyve* (A Book of Testimonies), Vienna, published by the author, 1922. Memoirs of a prominent left-wing, but critical journalist and publisher.

Gratz, Gusztáv (ed.), *A bolsevizmus Magyarországon* (Bolshevism in Hungary). Budapest, Franklin-Társulat, 1921. A large volume containing critical studies by different authors. Includes chapters on the theatre, literature, fine arts and the press.

Gratz, Gusztáv, *A forradalmak kora. Magyarország története 1918–1920* (The Era of Revolutions. History of Hungary 1918–1920). Budapest, Magyar Szemle Társaság, 1935. Offers a negative interpretation of the Soviet Republic.

Hajdu, Tibor, *Az 1918-as magyarországi polgári demokratikus forradalom* (Hungary's Bourgeois Democratic Revolution of 1918). Budapest, Kossuth Könyvkiadó, 1968.

Hajdu, Tibor, *The Hungarian Soviet Republic*. Budapest, Akadémiai Kiadó, 1979a. Includes a chapter on the cultural politics of the 1919 Soviet Republic.

Hajdu, Tibor, *Március huszonegyedike* (21 March). Budapest, Kossuth Könyvkiadó, 1979b. A slim volume focussing on the events and developments culminating in the formation of the Hungarian Soviet Republic on 21 March 1919.

Halasi, Andor, *Pirkadása a magyar égnek : írók emlékezései a magyar Tanácsköztársaságról* (Dawn is Breaking over the Hungarian Sky: Writers Remember the Hungarian Soviet Republic). Budapest, Szépirodalmi Könyvkiadó, 1959.

Hay, Julius (Gyula Háy), *Born 1900*. London, Hutchinson, 1974. Originally published in German. A Hungarian translation was published in 1990 by Interart Stúdio with the title *Született 1900-ban*.

Imre, Magda & Szűcs, László (eds.), *A forradalmi kormányzótanács jegyzőkönyvei, 1919* (Minutes of the Revolutionary Governing Council's Meetings, 1919). Budapest, Akadémiai Könyvkiadó, 1986.

Janos, Andrew C. & Slottman, William B. (eds.), *Revolution in Perspective: Essays on the Hungarian Soviet Republic*. Berkeley/Los Angeles/London, University of California Press, 1971.

Jászi, Oscar (Oszkár), *Revolution and Counter-Revolution in Hungary*. London, P.S. King & Son, 1924. An analytical account of the events of 1918–19 by a prominent radical liberal/socialist and sociologist who was minister for nationalities in Mihály Károlyi's government following the Chrysanthemum Revolution.

József, Farkas (ed.), *'Mindenki újakra készül ...': Az 1918/19-es forradalmak irodalma. III. Kötet: A Tanácsköztársaság szépirodalma* ('Everyone is Preparing for New Things': The Literature of the 1918–1919 Revolutions. Volume 3: The Creative Literature of the Council Republic). Budapest, Institute of Literary History of the Hungarian Academy of Sciences, 1960. A collection of short stories, poems and other works.

József, Farkas (ed.), *'Mindenki újakra készül ...': Az 1918/19-es forradalmak irodalma. IV. Kötet: A Tanácsköztársaság publicisztikája és irodalmi élete* ('Everyone is Preparing for New Things ...': The Literature of the 1918–1919 Revolutions. Volume 4: The Journalism and Literary Life of the Council Republic). Budapest, Institute of Literary History of the Hungarian Academy of Sciences, 1967. A massive, 1221-page collection of documents.

József, Farkas, *A Magyar Tanácsköztársaság sajtója* (The Press of the Hungarian Soviet Republic). Budapest, Tankönyvkiadó, 1969.

József, Farkas, *Értelmiség és forradalom. Kultúra, sajtó és irodalom a Magyar Tanácsköztársaságban* (Intelligentsia and Revolution. Culture, press and literature in the Hungarian Soviet Republic). Budapest, Kossuth Kiadó, 1984.

Kakuszi, Péter B. (ed.), *Március* (March). Szeged, Lazi Könyvkiadó, 2006. A collection of early writings by Sándor Márai.

Kakuszi, Péter B., *Márai Sándor—a forradalmártól az értékőrzőig* (Sándor Márai—From Revolutionary to Keeper of Values). Szeged, Lazi Könyvkiadó, 2007.

Károlyi, Catherine, *A Life Together*. London, George Allen & Unwin, 1966. Memoirs of Katinka Andrássy, longtime wife of Mihály Károlyi and a character in her own right.

Károlyi, Mihály, *Memoirs of Michael Karolyi: Faith Without Illusion*. London, Jonathan Cape, 1956. In Hungarian as: *Hit, illúziók nélkül*. Budapest, Magvető Könyvkiadó, 1977. Károlyi was the prime minister and later head of state in the period between the 1918 Chrysanthemum Revolution and the proclamation of the Soviet Republic on 21 March the following year.

Kassák, Lajos, *Egy ember élete. Második kötet* (One Man's Life, Vol. II). Budapest, Magvető Kiadó, 1983. This edition contains the part entitled 'Kommün' (Commune) about the 1919 Soviet Republic, as well as the previous part covering the preceding months of 1918–19, both of which were omitted from some other post-1945 editions of Kassák's autobiographical work.

Katona, Béla, 'Krúdy és a Tanácsköztársaság' (Krúdy and the Soviet Republic), *Borsodi Szemle*, 1959, no. 2, pp. 105–8. www.krudy.hu/Szakirod/KatonaBela/KBBorSz59_2.html

Katona, Béla, 'Krúdy és az 1918-19-es forradalmak, II. rész' (Krúdy and the Revolutions of 1918-19. Part 2), *Szabolcs Szatmári Szemle*, 1969, no. 1, pp. 99–107. www.krudy.hu/Szakirod/KatonaBela/KBSzSzSz69_1.html

Kelen, Jolán, *Eliramlik az élet ...* (Life Rushes By). Budapest, Kossuth Könyvkiadó, 1976.

Kende, János & Sipos, Péter (eds.), *Visszaemlékezések 1919-ről* (Recollections of 1919). Budapest, Gondolat Könyvkiadó, 1989. A collection of participants' recollections.

Kenez, Peter, 'Coalition Politics in the Hungarian Soviet Republic', in: Janos & Slottman (1971), pp. 61–84.

Kettler, David, 'Culture and Revolution: Lukács in the Hungarian Revolutions of 1918–19', *Telos*, No. 10, Winter 1971, pp. 35–92.

Kisfaludi Strobl, Zsigmond, *Emberek és Szobrok* (People and Statues). Budapest, Képzőművészeti Alap Kiadóvállalata, 1969.

Koestler, Arthur, *Arrow in the Blue*. New York, The Macmillan Co., 1952. Contains a section recalling his experiences of 1919 in Hungary.

Kőháti, Zsolt, *Tovamozduló ember tovamozduló világban. A magyar némafilm 1896–1931 között* (Moving on in a Moving World. Hungarian Silent Films 1896–1931). Budapest, Magyar Filmintézet, 1996.

Koltai, András (ed.), *A magyar piaristák és a Tanácsköztársaság* (The Hungarian Piarists and the Council Republic). Budapest, Piarista Rend Magyar Tartománya, 2013.

Konok, Péter, 'Két terror Magyarországon, 1919–1920' (Two Waves of Terror in Hungary, 1919–1920), *Rubicon*, vol. 22, no. 213, December 2011, pp. 42–55.

Korácsony, András, 'Egy dilemma 1918–19-ben: Lukács György és Sinkó Ervin' (A Dilemma in 1918-19: György Lukács and Ervin Sinkó), *Medvetánc*, 1981, no. 1, pp. 41–53.

Korda, Michael, *Charmed Lives*. New York, Random House, 1979. The Korda family story by the nephew of Alexander Korda.

Kosztolányi, Dezsőné, *Kosztolányi Dezső*. Budapest, Holnap Kiadó, 1990. A 'biographical novel' about the poet and writer Dezső Kosztolányi, written by his wife.

Köves, Rózsa & Erényi, Tibor, *Kunfi Zsimond életútja* (Zsigmond Kunfi—A Life). Budapest, Kossuth Kiadó, 1974. A biography and selected works of the Social Democratic politician who was People's Commissar for Education and Culture in 1919.

Kun, Béláné, *Kun Béla*. Budapest, Magvető, 1969. Reminiscences of Irén Gál, the wife of Béla Kun.

Lampert, Vera (ed.), *Bartók Breviárium. Levelek-Írások-Dokumentumok* (Bartók Breviary. Letters, Writings, Documents). Budapest, Zeneműkiadó, 1974.

Lendvai, Paul, *The Hungarians: 1000 Years of Victory in Defeat*. London, Hurst & Co., 2003.

Lennig, Arthur, *The Immortal Count. The Life and Films of Bela Lugosi*. Lexington, University Press of Kentucky, 2003.

Levinger, Esther, 'Lajos Kassák, *MA* and the New Artist, 1916–1925', *The Structurist*, 25/26, (1985/1986), pp. 78–86.

Lukács, György, 'A bolshevizmus mint erkölcsi probléma' (Bolshevism as a Moral Problem), *Szabadgondolat* (Free Thought), December, 1918, pp. 228–32. For an English translation by Judith Marcus Tar see: *Social Research*, Vol. 44, No. 3, autumn 1977, pp. 416–24; www.jstor.org/stable/40970293 *Szabadgondolat*, edited by Károly (Karl) Polányi, was the journal of the Galileo Circle, a group of young radical intellectuals established in 1908, of which Polányi was the first president. The December 1918 issue was a special one devoted to Bolshevism.

Lukács, Georg, *Record of a Life. An Autobiographical Sketch*, edited by István Eörsi. London, Verso Editions, 1983. A series of interviews, in which Lukács's comments are much more readable and understandable than is generally the case with his works.

Lukács, György, *Forradalomban. Cikkek, tanulmányok, 1918–1919* (In Revolution. Articles and Studies, 1918–1919), edited by Miklós Mesterházi. Budapest, Magvető Kiadó, 1987.

Magyar, Bálint, *A magyar némafilm története, 1918–1931* (The History of Hungarian Silent Film, 1918–1931). Budapest, Magyar Filmtudományi Intézet és Filmarchívum, 1967.

Magyar, Bálint, *A Nemzeti Színház története a két világháború között* (The History of the National Theatre between the Two World Wars). Budapest, Szépirodalmi Könyvkiadó, 1977.

Mansbach, S.A. et al., *Standing in the Tempest. Painters of the Hungarian Avant-garde 1908–1930*. Santa Barbara, Museum of Art, 1991. On the Hungarian contribution to early 20th-century modernist aesthetics. Includes the role of artists during the 1919 revolutionary upheaval.

Mathé, Pál & Simor, András, *Új szavakat hallasz!* (You are Hearing New Words!). Budapest, Kozmosz Könyvek, 1979. Press snippets, cartoons, jokes and other material giving an insight into everyday life in 1918–1919.

McRobbie, Kenneth, 'Ilona Duczynska meets Ervin Szabó: The making of a revolutionary personality—from theory to terrorism, April-May 1917', *Hungarian Studies Review*, Vol. XXXIII, Nos. 1-2, (2006), pp. 39–92. http://epa.oszk.hu/00000/00010/00040/pdf/HSR_2006_1-2_039-092.pdf

Mitchell, David, *1919: Red Mirage*. London, Jonathan Cape, 1970. A fascinating overview of the many radical and revolutionary upheavals which broke out across the world in the aftermath of the First World War. Includes a fair amount about Hungary.

Molnos, Péter, *Derkovits: szemben a villággal* (Derkovits: Against the World). Budapest, Népszabadság/Kieselbach Galéria, 2008.

Móricz, Virág, *Apám regénye* (My Father's Story). Budapest, Szépirodalmi Könyvkiadó, 1954. By the daughter of the noted writer Zsigmond Móricz.

Munkácsi, Piroska (ed.), *A Magyar Tanácsköztársaság plakátjai az Országos Széchényi Könyvtárban* (Posters of the Hungarian Soviet Republic in the National Széchényi Library). Budapest, National Széchényi Library, 1959.

Nádass, József, 'Történelmünk írtuk' (We Wrote our History), in: Halasi (1959), pp. 189–210.

Nagy, Zsuzsa L., 'The Mission of General Smuts to Budapest, April, 1919', *Acta Historica Academiae Scientiarum Hungaricae*, Vol. 11, No. 1/4 (1965), pp. 163–85. www.jstor.org/stable/42554765?&seq=1#page_scan_tab_contents

Nemeskürty, István, *Word and Image. History of the Hungarian Cinema*. Budapest, Corvina Press, 1974.

Németh, Luca Anna, 'Az irodalmi modernség egy szervezeti kísérlete—A Vörösmarty Akadémia története és szerepe a 20. Század elejének irodalmi életében' (An organisational experiment of literary modernity—the history and role of the Vörösmarty Academy in the early 20th century), *Filológia.hu*, online journal of the Hungarian Academy of Sciences' Modern Philology Society, 2012, no. 2., pp. 48–79. www.filologia.hu/images/media/Onallo_cikkek_pdfben/Filologia_2012-2_48-79_NemethLucaAnna.pdf

Neubauer, John & Török, Borbála Zsuzsanna (eds.), *The Exile and Return of Writers from East-Central Europe: A Compendium*. New York and Berlin, Walter de Gruyter, 2009.

Nicolson, Harold, *Peacemaking 1919*. London, Methuen, 1964.

Ormos, Mária, *Világháború és forradalmak 1914-1919* (World War and Revolutions, 1914–1919). Budapest, Kossuth Kiadó, 2009. Part of a series on the history of Hungary. Brief, but informative and simply presented with lots of striking illustrations and contemporary photographs.

Osváth, Béla, 'A Tanácsköztársaság színházpolitikája' (Theatre Policy of the Soviet Republic), in: Szabolcsi, Miklós & Illés, László (eds.), *Tanulmányok a magyar szocialista irodalom történetéből* (Studies in the History of Hungarian Socialist Literature). Budapest, Akadémiai Kiadó, 1962.

Pastor, Peter, *Hungary between Wilson and Lenin: The Hungarian Revolution of 1918–1919 and the Big Three*. Boulder, East European Quarterly, 1976.

Pastor, Peter (ed.), *Revolutions and Interventions in Hungary and its Neighbor States, 1918–1919*. Boulder, Social Science Monographs/Highland Lakes, Atlantic Studies on Society and Change, 1988. Three dozen studies by a variety of scholars.

Péter, László, *Juhász Gyula a forradalmakban* (Gyula Juhász in the Revolutions). Budapest, Akadémiai Kiadó, 1965.

Petrák, Katalin & Milei, György (eds.), *A Magyar Tanácsköztársaság művelődéspolitikája: Válogatott rendeletek, dokumentumok, cikkek* (The Cultural Policies of the Hungarian Soviet Republic: Selected decrees, documents and articles). Budapest, Gondolat Kiadó, 1959. A wide-ranging collection of source materials.

Petrák, Katalin (ed.), *Tanúságtevők: viszaemlékezések a magyarországi munkásmozgalom történetéből. 3/b. kötet. Viszaemlékezések a magyarországi 1918–1919-es forradalmak résztvevőiről* (Witnesses: Recollections about the History of Hungary's Labour Movement. Vol. 3b. Recollections of Participants in the 1918–1919 Revolutions in Hungary). Budapest, Kossuth Kiadó, 1978.

Pongrácz, Erzsébet, *The Cinemas of Budapest*. Budapest, City Hall, 1998.

Pongrácz, Jenő (ed.), *Tanácsköztársaság törvénytár I. A Forradalmi Kormányzótanács és a népbiztosságok rendeletei, 1919 március 21—április 9*. (Council Republic Statute Book vol. I, Decrees of the Revolutionary Governing Council and Commissariats, 21 March—9 April, 1919). Budapest, Socialist Party of Hungary, 1919.

Remete, László (ed.), *Irodalom Forradalom, 1917–1919* (Literature—Revolution, 1917–1919). Budapest, Magvető Könyvkiadó, 1956. A collection of contemporary literary and other documents about the revolutionary events in both Russia and Hungary.

Riggs Hunt, Alice, *Facts About Communist Hungary*. London, Workers' Socialist Federation, 1919.

Romsics, Ignác, *Magyarország története a XX. században* (A History of Hungary in the 20th Century). Budapest, Osiris, 1999a.

Romsics, Ignác, *Hungary in the Twentieth Century*. Budapest, Corvina, 1999b. A translation of the previously listed work.

Rónay, László, *Márai Sándor*. Budapest, Magvető Könyvkiadó, 1990.

Sakmyster, Thomas, *A Communist Odyssey. The Life of József Pogány / John Pepper*. Budapest/New York, Central European University Press, 2012.

Serf, András, 'Tollfosztás. Irók meghurcolása a Tanácsköztársaság után' (Plucking of Quills. Vilification of Writers after the Council Republic), *HVG*, 25 July 2009, pp. 37–8. On the fate of Zsigmond Móricz, Mihály Babits and other writers following the fall of the Soviet Republic.

Serge, Victor, *Memoirs of a Revolutionary*, New York, New York Review Books, 2012.

Siklós, András, *Revolution in Hungary and the Dissolution of the Multinational State, 1918*. Budapest, Akadémiai Kiadó, 1988.

Sinkó, Ervin, *Optimisták. Történelmi regény 1918/19-ből* (Optimists. A Historical Novel about 1918–19). Budapest, Magvető Kiadó, 1979.

Sinkó, Ervin, *Egy regény regénye. Moszkvai naplójegyzetek, 1935–1937* (The Story of a Novel. Moscow Diary Notes, 1935–37). Budapest, Magvető Kiadó, 1988. Tells the intriguing tale of the difficulties experienced by Sinkó in getting his work about the 1919 events, *Optimisták*, published in the Soviet Union.

Sinkó, Ervin, *Az út. Naplók 1916–1939* (The Journey. Diaries 1916–1939). Budapest, Akadémiai Kiadó, 1990. Includes a large section recalling Sinkó's experiences in 1919.

Sipos, András & Donáth, Péter (eds.), *'Kelet Párizsától' a 'Bűnös Városig'. Szöveggyűjtemény Budapest történetének tanulmányozásához. I. kötet 1870–1930* (From the 'Paris of the East' to the 'Sinful City'. A collection of texts for the study of Budapest's history. Volume I, 1870–1930). Budapest, Municipal Archive/Budapest Teachers' Training College, 1999.

Staud, Géza, *A Tanácsköztársaság színház műsora* (Theatre Programmes During the Soviet Republic). Budapest, Színháztudományi és Filmtudományi Intézet, 1959. A listing of theatre productions.

Staud, Géza (ed.), *A budapesti operaház 100 éve* (One Hundred Years of the Budapest Opera House). Budapest, Zeneműi Kiadó, 1984.

Stróbl, Mihály, *Strobl Alajos*. Budapest, Holnap Kiadó, 2003. Biographical record and memoir of the noted Hungarian sculptor by his son.

Suchoff, Benjamin (ed.), *Béla Bartók Essays*. Lincoln and London, University of Nebraska Press, 1992.

Sugar, Peter F., Hanák, Péter & Frank, Tibor (eds.), *A History of Hungary*. Bloomington and Indianapolis, Indiana University Press, 1994. A collection of scholarly essays.

Szíj, Béla, 'Berény Róbert életútja gyermekéveitől a berlini emigrációig' (The Life of Róbert Berény from Childhood to Exile in Berlin), in: *Magyar Nemzeti Galéria Közleményei*, No. 4 (1963), pp. 113–23.

Szilágyi, Jolán, *Emlékeim* (Memoirs). Budapest, Zrínyi Katonai Kiadó, 1966. Recollections of Tibor Szamuely's widow.

Tabori, Paul, *Alexander Korda*. London, Oldbourne, 1959.

Tallián, Tibor, *Béla Bartók—The Man and His Work*. Budapest, Corvina, 1981.

Tóbiás, Áron, *Korda Sándor* (Alexander Korda). Budapest, A Magyar Filmtudományi Intézet és Filmarchivum/A Népművelési Propaganda Iroda, 1980.

Tőkés, Rudolf L., *Béla Kun and the Hungarian Soviet Republic: The Origins and Role of the Communist Party of Hungary in the Revolutions of 1918–1919*. New York, Praeger, 1967.

Tormay, Cecile, *An Outlaw's Diary (Part 2): The Commune*. London, Philip Allan & Co., 1923. Observations of a noted opponent of the Soviet Republic. For an internet version, see: http://mek.oszk.hu/07200/07270/pdf/outlaw2.pdf

Ujfalussy, József (ed.), *Dokumentumok a Magyar Tanácsköztársaság zenei életéből* (Documents Relating to the Musical Life of the Hungarian Soviet Republic). Budapest, Akadémiai Kiadó, 1973.

Ujfalussy, József, *Bartók Béla*. Budapest, Gondolat, 1976.

Ungvári, Tamás, 'Adalékok Babits Mihály pályaképéhez—1918–1919' (Contributions to the career of Mihály Babits—1918–1919), *Irodalomtörténeti Közlemények* (Annals of Literary History), Vol. 63, No. 2, 1959, pp. 235–50. http://epa.oszk.hu/00000/00001/00209/pdf/itk_1959_2_235-250.pdf

Veres, Péter, '1919. március 22-én' (On 22 March, 1919), in: Halasi (1959), pp. 251–9.

Vermes, Gábor, 'The October Revolution in Hungary: from Károlyi to Kun', in: Völgyes (1971), pp. 31–60.

Vincze, Edit S., Barna, Zoltán & Vértes, Róbert (eds.), *Új erők születése. A magyarországi munkásmozgalom történetének kronológiája a dualizmus és a két forradalom időszakában,*

1868–1919. augusztus 1. (The Birth of New Powers. A Chronology of the History of the Workers' Movement in Hungary during the period of the Dual Monarchy and the Two Revolutions, 1868 to 1 August 1919). Budapest, Akadémiai Kiadó, 1979.

Völgyes, Iván (ed.), *Hungary in Revolution, 1918–1919. Nine Essays.* Lincoln, University of Nebraska Press, 1971.

Vörös, Boldizsár, 'Árpád helyett Marx, József főherceg helyett Lenin. Történelmi személyiségek elutasítása és méltatása a Magyarországi Tanácsköztársaság hivatalos jellegű anyagaiban' (Marx instead of Árpád, Lenin instead of Archduke Joseph. The rejection and appreciation of historical figures in official materials of the Hungarian Soviet Republic), *Történelmi Szemle*, 3–4 (1999), pp. 403–10. www.epa.hu/00600/00617/00004/tsz99_3_4_voros_boldizsar.htm

Weltner, Jakab, *Forradalom, Bolsevizmus, Emigráció* (Revolution, Bolshevism, Exile). Budapest, published by the author, 1929. Recollections of a journalist and prominent member of the Social Democratic Party.

Willett, John, et al., *The Hungarian Avant Garde. The Eight and the Activists.* London, Arts Council of Great Britain, 1980. Catalogue and studies published in connection with an exhibition staged at the Hayward Gallery, 27 February to 7 April 1980.

Young, Percy M., *Zoltán Kodály: A Hungarian Musician.* London, Ernest Benn, 1964.

Zsuffa, Joseph, *Béla Balázs, The Man and the Artist.* Berkeley/Los Angeles/London, University of California Press, 1986.

Index

Descriptions of people in brackets give an indication of their role(s) in 1919 as referred to in this book.

Ady, Endre (poet and polemicist), 165, 166
  funeral of, 167
agricultural policy, 52, 180
alcohol, prohibition of, 40, 53, 84
Andrássy Avenue, 21
  and May Day activities, 21, 22, 23–4, 39
Andrássy, Gyula (former statesman), 61 n16
  statue covered, 34
anti-Semitism, ix, 40, 187
Arts Directory, 27, 48, 54, 61
Ashmead-Bartlett, Ellis (British writer), 155
Astoria Hotel, 10
attempted anti-regime putsch, 176–7

Babits, Mihály (writer), 97, 146–7, 166
  subsequent fate, 201
Bajor, Gizi (actress), 27
Balázs, Béla (cultural politician), 130, 136
  and fairly tales, 111–12
  as member of theatre socialisation committee, 98, 99
  subsequent fate, 201
Bartók, Béla (musician, musicologist, member of the Music Directory), 116–21
  lifestyle, 118
  expresses optimism, 118–19
  Miraculous Mandarin, The, 121
  on the Music Directory, 120, 163
  reflections on the Soviet Republic, 193
  on reform of music teaching, 119
  subsequent fate, 201–2
Battle of the Chain Bridge, 9
Bavarian Soviet Republic, 174
Bédy-Schwimmer, Róza (Rózsika Schwimmer, feminist activist), 10
  pre-Soviet Republic activity, 10 n9, 13 n12
  subsequent fate, 213
Benedek, Marcell (literary historian), 161
Berény, Róbert (artist), 42, 44, 54, 168
  subsequent fate, 202–3
  To Arms! To Arms! poster, 44, 44 n6
Bíró, Mihály (artist), 31, 42, 55, 168
  Man with Hammer poster, 50, 50 n9
  subsequent fate, 203
Blaha, Lujza (actress), 109
Böhm, Vilmos (prominent Social Democrat), 155, 183, 196
Bölöni, György (writer), 192–3
Bosnian National Council, 11
Brailsford, H. N. (British journalist), ix, 3
Bródy, Sándor (writer), 142
Budapest Council of Workers' and Soldiers' Deputies, 86, 159–60, 179
Budapest Workers' Council, 11, 15, 18, 47, 155, 174, 190, 194, 196

censorship, 8, 54, 136–7, 187–91
Charles IV, King 12
children, 94, 145–6, 162
  and cinemas, 86–7
  May Day activities, 38–9
  and theatre, 110–12
Chrysanthemum Revolution, 9–10, 165
  definition, xiii
cinema and the film industry, 81–95
  nationalisation process, 81–2
  Proletarian Academy, 85
  Vörös Riport Film (Red Newsreel), 93–5
City Park, 21, 27, 29
class and party, issues of, 41, 194–7
  Machajski, Jan Waclaw, 197

Clemenceau, Georges (president of Paris Peace Conference), 175, 176, 177
Communist Manifesto, The, 26, 28, 50, 91
Communist Party of Hungary, 11, 14–15, 17, 158–9, 160
  prominent members as victims of the Great Terror, 198
corruption, 181
Cserny, József (terror group leader), 183
Czech National Council, 9

Dankó, Ödön (poster artist), 46–7
Derkovits, Gyula (artist), 58, 59
Dienes, Valéria (dance teacher), 148–9
Directory for Arts and Museums, 56
Dohnányi, Ernő (musician, director of the Academy of Music), 115, 121, 123, 124
  subsequent fate, 203
Dombai, Viktória (art student)
  on the Nyergesújfalu free school, 58, 60
Duczynska, Ilona (student leader), 7, 36

Eastman, Crystal (American reporter), ix, 77, 136
  impressed by political posters, 43
economic situation, 178–81
education policy, 161–2
Ék, Sándor (art student), 62
  subsequent fate, 62 n20
'exhibition of the century', 63–8

Fedák, Sári (actress), 27, 113
  subsequent fate, 203–4
Ferenczi, Sándor (psychiatrist), 161
fine arts policy, 56
First World War, 6, 13
Franchet d'Espèry, General, 12

Gál, Imre (critical observer), 109–10, 189
Gál, Irén (wife of Béla Kun, working with Béla Reinitz), 125–6
Galileo Circle, 6
Garbai, Sándor (Social Democrat, president of the Revolutionary Governing Council), 155
Gárdos, Mariska (political activist and journalist), 23, 29, 39
  feels let down by Party leadership, 197
  subsequent fate, 204
Gellért Hill, 38
Gellért Hotel, 88–9
Gellért, Oszkár (poet), 165
Göndör, Ferenc (journalist), 74, 189–90
Goszthonyi, Mária (art student), 59
  on Károly Kernstok, 58
Götz, Irén (professor of chemistry), 160

Halasi, Andor (writer), 127, 129, 164
Hauser, Arnold (art historian), 161
Háy, Gyula (young enthusiast, future playwright), 19, 107, 142–3, 163, 180
Herczeg, Ferenc (writer), 132–3
Heroes' Square, 25
  and May Day activities, 21, 26
Hevesi, György (chemist), 161
Horthy, Miklós (Regent of Hungary in the post-Soviet Republic era), viii, 89, 89 n18
Horváth, Jenő (gypsy violinist), 113

Internationale, The, x, 19, 22, 23, 60, 94, 109, 116, 123 n33, 149
  and Zoltán Kodály, 122, 123

Jászai, Mari (actress), 106, 108
Jászi, Oszkár (radical liberal), 7, 12, 150–1, 155, 156, 163–4, 187–8, 192
  subsequent fate, 204
Joseph, Archduke, 9, 11
journalists' trade union, 191
Juhász, Gyula (writer and poet), 140–1
  subsequent fate, 204–5

Karinthy, Frigyes (writer), 97, 146
Károlyi, Mihály (prime minister then president of Hungary following the Chrysanthemum Revolution), 6, 7, 10, 12, 16, 17, 18, 174, 187
  subsequent fate, 205
Károlyi regime
  definition, xiii
Kassa (today Košice, Slovakia), 15, 175, 177

Kassák, Lajos (radical cultural activist and polemicist)
on Activism, 72
on the Communist Party, 72–3
dispute and differences with Lukács, 76, 77, 77 n22
on the funeral of Ervin Szabó, 7
on József Pogány and his play *Napóleon*, 103
Letter to Béla Kun in the Name of Art and its impact, 77–80
as member of the theatre socialisation committee, 98, 99–101
on music in the streets, 113–14
and the role of the *MA* journal, 73–4, 101–2
as poster censor, 54–5
on posters, 42
pre-Soviet Republic activity, 69
'Proclamation for Art!', 70–1
on the Proletarian Fine Arts Apprentice Workshop, 62
reflections on May Day, 40–1
on the Social Democratic Party, 71, 73
and the Socialist Literary, Artistic and Scholarly Society, 135
subsequent fate, 205–6
and the writers' registry, 130
Kelen, Jolán (former teacher and art enthusiast), 66, 67
Kenczler, Hugó (art historian), 67–8
Kéri, Pál (writer), 74
Kernstok, Károly (artist)
and the Nyergesújfalu free school, 57, 58, 59
pre-Soviet Republic activity, 56–7, 168
subsequent fate, 206–7
Kertész, Mihály (Michael Curtiz) (film-maker), 89–93
Jön az öcsém (My Brother is Coming), 90–2
subsequent fate, 92, 207
Kisfaludi Strobl, Zsigmond (sculptor), 26, 34–5
Kisfaludy Literary Society, 135
Kodály, Zoltán (composer, musicologist, member of Music Directory), 121–4
on the Music Directory, 122
subsequent fate, 207–8
'trial' of, 122–4
Koestler, Arthur (a schoolboy in 1919), x
Korda, Sándor (Alexander) (film-maker), 87–9, 168–9
subsequent fate, 88–9, 208
Kosztolányi, Dezső (writer), 97, 144–6, 166, 192
subsequent fate, 208
Krúdy, Gyula (writer), 143–4, 166
subsequent fate, 208–9
Kun, Béla (acknowledged political leader of the Soviet Republic), ix, 67, 77, 88, 158, 158 n21, 172, 174, 178, 184, 188
arrested and beaten in prison, 16, 17
blames the proletariat for downfall of Soviet Republic, 196
on censorship, 136–7
criticises war veterans' association, 195–6
and literature, 157, 157 n20
pre-Soviet Republic activity, 11 n11
subsequent fate, 209
Kunfi, Zsigmond (People's Commissar for Education and Culture), 101, 133, 156–7
on dictatorship, 185–6
on fanaticism, 195
on music culture, 116
pre-Soviet Republic activity, 54 n12
subsequent fate, 209–10

Landler, Jenő (Social Democrat), 28, 29
Lenin Boys, the, 95, 182–3, 189, 190
Liebknecht, Karl (German socialist), 22, 152
Lugosi, Béla (actor), 105–7, 170
subsequent fate, 210
Lukács, György (People's Commissar for Education and Culture – initially the deputy commissar)
on art policy, 67
'Bolshevism as a Moral Problem', 157
on censorship, 188
on the Communist Party, 160
dispute and differences with Kassák, 76, 77, 77 n22

and the 'exhibition of the century', 65, 67
on the Music Directory and Béla Bartók's role, 119
on politics and literature, 75
pre-Soviet Republic activity, 66 n27
on the Red Army, 156, 184–5
subsequent fate, 210–11
Luxemburg, Rosa (Polish-German socialist), 22, 152

Magyar, Lajos (writer), 137
Man with Hammer image, 35, 50
Mannheim, Karl (sociologist), 161
Márai, Sándor (writer), 128–9, 131
subsequent fate, 211
Márffy, Ödön (artist), 31
Margaret Island, 62
and May Day activities, 38–9
Marseillaise, La x, 22, 23, 96, 116
Marx, Karl
statue of, 26
Marx, Roger (French art critic)
on posters, 43
Masaryk, Tomáš (president of Czechoslovakia), 12
May Day events in Budapest, 19–41
Medgyessy, Ferenc (sculptor), 61
military intervention against the Soviet Republic, 171–8
Molnár, Ferenc (writer), 97, 143, 166
Móra, Ferenc (writer), 141–2
Móricz, Zsigmond (writer), 139–40, 166, 185, 192
impressed by visit to National Theatre, 108–9
subsequent fate, 211–12
on the writers' trade union, 133–4
music, 113–26, 169
Music Directory, 117, 124–5, *see also* separate entries for Bartók and Kodály
official policy regarding, 114–15
and recruiting, 113
soldiers' concerts, 116
workers' concerts, 115

Nádass, József (young poet), 149
Nagy Lajos (writer), 131, 170
National Council (of 1918), 7–9, 10–11, 12, 16
National Council for Intellectual Production, 130, 134
Nemes Lampérth, József (artist), 42, 48, 61
Nicolson, Harold (young diplomat), 172–3
Nyergesújfalu free school for the arts, 57–60

Pallos, Sándor (assistant cameraman, subsequently murdered), 85
Parliament Square (today Kossuth Lajos Square)
and May Day activities, 32–4
Paulik, Béla (film industry commissar), 82–3
People's Commissariat for Education and Culture, xii, 130, 159
People's Commissariat for Military Affairs, 23
People's Commissariat for Social Production, 32
Pogány, József (Social Democrat politician), 102–4
in the cultural commissariat, 80, 104, 186
as a playwright, 102–3
subsequent fate, 212
political posters, 42–55, 168
for recruiting purposes, 43–8
Pór, Bertalan (artist), 27, 31, 42, 48, 148
subsequent fate, 212
Workers of the World Unite! poster, 50
post-First World War radicalism worldwide, 151–4
post-Soviet Republic emigration
general experiences of, 198–201
Proletarian Fine Arts Apprentice Workshop, 61–3

Radical Party, 7, 10
Rákosi, Jenő (writer, conservative polemicist), 132, 133
Red Army, The (Hungarian), 173, 174, 176, 178 n16
film workers' battalion, 82–3

Reinitz, Béla (cultural politician)
as chair of theatre socialisation committee, 98, 99, 107
as head of Music Directory, 117, 123, 125
subsequent fate, 213
religion and the churches, 186–7
Révai, József (communist writer and editor), 74
revolutionary Christianity, 140 n37
Revolutionary Governing Council, xii, 83, 97
banning alcohol, 53
death sentence for rebellion, robbery and looting, 182
film industry nationalisation, 81
formation of, 18
on May Day activities, 32
on theatres, 3
Riggs Hunt, Alice (American reporter), ix
Rippl-Rónai, Ödön (art collector), 66
Romanian National Assembly, 15
Romanian National Council, 12
Russian Revolution
effects of, 154–5

Schwimmer, Rózsika (see Bédy-Schwimmer)
Serbian National Council, 15
Sinkó, Ervin (political activist), 140 n37, 156, 184
subsequent fate, 213–14
Slovak National Council, 9, 10
Smuts mission to Budapest, 172–3
Social Democratic Party (SDP), 7, 10, 11, 13–14, 16, 17–18, 158–9
Socialist Literary, Artistic and Scholarly Society, 130, 134–5
Soldiers' Council, 8, 10, 12, 18, 170, 194
Somogy county, 18
Zsigmond Móricz visits, 139
Soviet House (Hungária Hotel), 140 n37, 174, 176
State Opera House, 96
Stróbl, Alajos (sculptor), 26, 27
Szabados, Sándor (head of National Council for Intellectual Production), 134, 134 n19
Szabó, Ervin (prominent radical thinker). 7, 36, 187–8
funeral of, 7
Szamuely, Tibor (prominent hard-line communist), 31, 66
condemns strikes as counter-revolutionary, 195
and the May Day events, 30
pre-Soviet Republic activity, 30 n21
subsequent fate, 214
and terror tactics, 182–3
visits to Nyergesújfalu free school, 59, 60
Szeged, 15, 140, 141, 142
Szélpál, Árpád (cultural polemicist)
'Revolutionary Art or Party Art?', 71–2
Szép, Ernő (writer), 138, 166
Szilágyi, Jolán (artist), 30, 31, 47, 66

terror and violence, 182–6
theatre life, 96–112
actors and May Day, 107
actors' status, 104
actors' strike, 104–5
nationalisation, 3, 97
Napóleon, by József Pogány, 102–3
theatre policy, 98
theatre socialisation committee, 98–102
ticket prices, 97–8
Tisza, Count István (former prime minister), 5, 5 n2
Tormay, Cécile (writer)
strongly critical views about May Day 40
Tóth, Árpád (poet), 139
Trotsky, Leon
quoted on May Day, 28–9

universal suffrage, 14
Uitz, Béla (artist), 26
pre-Soviet Republic activity, 60
and the Proletarian Fine Arts Apprentice Workshop, 61, 62, 63
Red Soldiers, Forward! poster, 45–6
subsequent fate, 214
'We Need a Dictatorship!', 60–1

Varga, Jenő (economist), 180–1
Várnai, Zseni (poet), 20–1, 107
Veres, Péter (socialist activist), 149–50
  subsequent fate, 214–15
Vérmező (Field of Blood), 37
Vértes, Marcell (artist), 42, 48–9, 168
Vix, Lieutenant-Colonel Fernand, 17
Vix note, the, 17, 18, 171, 173

Weltner, Jakab (Social Democrat, journalist), 189, 191
writers, 127–47 (for individual writers, see separate entries)
  Marx Translation Committee, 137
  policy regarding writers and literature, 135–8
  registration committee, 132
  revolutionary presentations in theatres, 99
  Translators' Bureau, 138
  Vörösmarty Academy, 166–7
  Writers' Council, 127–8, 129
  Writers' Directory, 130, 134
  writers' registry, 130
  writers' trade union, 133–4

Zala, György (sculptor), 26
Zöldi, Sándor (film technician), 85